GREGORY O'BRIEN was born in Matamata in 1961. Since the early 1980s he has exhibited paintings, illustrated books and published numerous collections of poetry, non-fiction and a novel. As well as co-editing three anthologies of New Zealand poetry, O'Brien has co-edited (with Te Miringa Hohaia and Lara Strongman) *Parihaka; the Art of Passive Resistance* (VUP) which was co-winner of the Biography and History Prize, Montana New Zealand Book Awards, 2001. Since 1997 he has worked as a curator at City Gallery Wellington, presented an occasional poetry programme with Kim Hill on National Radio, and run a poetry workshop at the International Institute of Modern Letters at Victoria University.

Victoria University Press

ESSAYS & INTERVIEWS

Flight of the Phoenix: Critical Notes on New Zealand Writers
James Bertram (1985)

Disputed Ground: Robin Hyde, Journalist
Gillian Boddy & Jacqueline Matthews (eds) (1991)

How to Be Nowhere: Essays and Texts 1971–1994
Ian Wedde (1995)

Doubtful Sounds: Essays and Interviews
Bill Manhire (2000)

A Dissolving Ghost: Essays and More
Margaret Mahy (2000)

After Bathing at Baxter's: Essays and Notebooks
Gregory O'Brien (2002)

In preparation:

Keri Hulme
Elizabeth Knox
Vincent O'Sullivan

AFTER BATHING AT BAXTER'S

ESSAYS AND NOTEBOOKS

GREGORY O'BRIEN

VICTORIA UNIVERSITY PRESS

FOR DENNIS McELDOWNEY

VICTORIA UNIVERSITY PRESS
Victoria University of Wellington
PO Box 600 Wellington

ISBN 0 86473 418 2

First published 2002

Victoria University Press would like to thank the publishers and editors of the works in which these essays have previously appeared

Cover: *Untitled* (2001), collage by Brendan O'Brien.
The section-header illustrations are by Ralph Hotere and Mary McFarlane, *Ruaumoko* (1999) (photographed by Julia Brooke-White, courtesy of Janne Land Gallery), p15;
Brendan O'Brien, *Untitled* (2001), p99;
Noel McKenna, *Fringe Dwellers* (1999), p177.

Published with the assistance of a grant from

Printed by PrintLink, Wellington

Contents

7 Black square dance—an introduction
14 Acknowledgements

I AN ALPHABET WITHOUT EDGES

17 After bathing at Baxter's
46 Southern Woman—Ruth Dallas
53 An alphabet without edges—from a Janet Frame notebook
62 Imagine the imagination—Margaret Mahy's *Dissolving Ghost*
66 A journey around Kendrick Smithyman's *Atua Wera*
81 High cultural life—Eric McCormick's *An Absurd Ambition*
84 Widening horizons and worlds regained
—a conversation with Dennis McEldowney

II THE SHAPE OF LIVING

101 *Morning Glory in Springtime* in autumn—self-portrait
103 An attempt at the first page of an autobiography
105 The shape of living children I
109 Lost and living children
111 Aspects of his face
114 East born
120 Wild horses
123 The exact size of the world
126 The dark plane leaves at evening
145 North Piha bach with typewriter

148 The second Ada
152 Radio Birdman
158 A long sentence in Czech ending in English
159 The shape of living children II
163 The man who wrote the book about the weather
166 Electricities

III FRINGE DWELLERS

179 Blue Monk, Black Light—Ralph Hotere and Thelonious Monk, a notebook
195 No road to follow—Eric Lee-Johnson
199 *These May Mornings* in October—Rosalie Gascoigne
202 Big tree transmission—Colin McCahon's tau cross
209 Breaking open the luggage—Denis O'Connor's 'concrete poetry'
213 First on the left past the art supermarket, the magic theatre—Martin Edmond's *The Resurrection of Philip Clairmont*
217 I am a shepherd
218 Chunk of landscape, chunk of memory—the paintings of Euan Macleod
225 Changing the light—Noel McKenna in Taranaki
229 The outsider within
239 Somebody say something—Colin McCahon's *Storm Warning*

260 The public interest—an annotated bibliography

283 Index

Black square dance
an introduction

This is the only art worth bothering with. Not art that adorns and softens life but art which is at once a benediction and a judgement . . .
(John Wheelwright)

The excursions and inquiries that make up this book present a detailed, if not quite comprehensive, account of how I spent my thirties. The most recent writing here dates from mid-2001, around the time I turned forty. James K. Baxter is, to some degree, the starting point of all these essays. After bathing, as a young man, in the Whanganui River of Baxter's poetry, much of my subsequent reading and writing, painting and thinking was shaped by his dreams of self, society and artistic creation.

After Bathing at Baxter's begins in the realm of the literary with explorations of Baxter, Janet Frame, Ruth Dallas, Kendrick Smithyman and others. I often find myself returning to the work of the generation of artists and writers born between 1910 and 1930, as their productions reflect so compellingly the rigours, excitements and idealism of an era when being an artist really was going against the grain. The first section of *After Bathing at Baxter's* concludes with a conversation with another notable member of that generation, Dennis McEldowney. I've long been intrigued by a statement Joyce makes, by way of his mouthpiece Dedalus, in *Ulysses*: 'The supreme question of a work of art is: Out of how deep a life does it spring?' The work of the aforementioned writers (and the visual artists dealt with later in this book) suggests such an unfashionable proposition might contain a surprising amount of truth.

The second section of the book, 'The Shape of Living', is a series of autobiographical peregrinations, exploring the way images and experiences are processed in life just as they are in art. Many of these pieces, dating from around 1994, began as meditations on pieces of music.

The third section, 'Fringe Dwellers', is devoted to the visual arts, particularly as they interface with language (as in the work of Ralph Hotere, Colin McCahon, Rosalie Gascoigne and Denis O'Connor), although in the piece that begins this section, 'Blue Monk, Black Light', the music/visual art interface is the prevailing one. Given that it has always been against my nature to partition off the different art forms, I can happily assert there is much traffic across the three zones of this book. As Horace wrote, 'ut pictura poesis'—as in painting, so it is in poetry—the various art forms offer potent ways of experiencing one another. They are metaphors for one another.

The collection concludes with a miscellany of critical writings masquerading as a bibliography. While practitioners of the 1910–30 generation make up most of the subjects of the essays in the book proper, the miscellany, titled 'The public interest', observes more recent writers and artists.

*

Unintentionally, *After Bathing at Baxter's* emerges from the river of its creation as a book much preoccupied with childhood. Virtually all the pieces in the second section are based on boyhood experience—and I'm further intrigued to note the tumultuous appearance and re-appearance of children elsewhere in this jungle gym of a book. Children often appear here as harbingers of wisdom, insight and not a little sustaining madness. On that score, I might mention a recent conversation one evening, long after bedtime, when my small son came running into the living room. He clamped himself to my leg and told me he was scared. Moments earlier he had been lying quietly abed when, out of nowhere, he had been 'menaced by a Black Square'.

'No, not a thing,' he said, 'but not nothing either.'

He made the shape of a square with his fingers in the air.

'A Black Square.'

After coaxing him back to his room and dispelling any other Black Squares from the darkness, I pondered his complaint, eventually drawing the conclusion that, like many people working in the visual arts, I too have been menaced by a black square: Malevich's *Black Square* of 1915, to be precise. That endlessly, marvellously problematic canvas is, at once, the consummate embodiment of both the material

Dick Frizzell, *Little Rotter,* 1996, oil on canvas.

and immaterial potentialities in modern art. Malevich's painting figures, in some respects, as a full stop in Western Art—but it is also a question mark, an exclamation mark and a deletion. And so it will remain.

Scores of artists have been challenged, provoked, baffled and, indeed, menaced by this painting—among them Dick Frizzell who, in *Little Rotter* (1996), inserted a compost bin inside its sacrosanct interior, bringing it back into the realm of informal, vernacular art. Painters John Drawbridge and Stephen Bambury have spent years of their working lives exploring it. (Visiting New Zealand in 1998, the director of the Stedelijk Museum in Amsterdam, Rudi Fuchs, admitted he was himself haunted by Malevich's *Black Square*—although it was the absence of the Russian-owned work from the almost-definitive collection of Malevichs in his institution which got on his wick.) Ralph Hotere has not only made a friend of the ominous black square but he has used it to depict an actual friend: Hone Tuwhare, as he appears in the frontispiece to the recent poetry collection, *Piggyback Moon*. In this case Hotere configures the poet as a black square, rendered in charcoal with the inscription, E HOA—*hey, friend*—stencilled above.

If children have a habit of ducking in and out of many of the essays in this book, I would hope that the pieces of writing themselves have retained something of a childlike capacity for wonder and delight. I would far rather that writing about art and literature resembled a verandah than an airless room, a lookout post instead of a bunker. In these essays I would like to think I have located myself firmly on the balcony, gazing towards whatever horizons are offered me. Reading back through these essays, I find myself recurrently drawn to art in which form and content, surface and depth, abstract concerns and those pertaining to representation are in a state of realignment; work which both *means* something and *is* something—a symbiosis exemplified for me by the work of McCahon and Frame respectively. As is the case with Malevich's *Black Square*, I want art not only to somehow contain the world but also to be detached from and free of it.

*

Sifting through over a decade of writing, the question arises: what was I up to when I wrote the pieces gathered here? Like Ian Wedde, standing on the threshold of the continent of prose which became *How to Be Nowhere* (Victoria University Press, 1995), I find myself asking what it was that motivated these pieces. In my case it was a simple desire to explore, on my own terms, some things I felt passionately interested in. This unruly conglomeration of documents—accounts of seeing, listening, thinking and imagining—arose out of curiosity and, most often, enthusiasm. Bearing in mind the words of John Wheelwright, the writing tends more towards benediction than judgement. I don't have the inclination to deal with literature or art that doesn't engage me, that fails to alter my world in some way. To put it another way, as far as I am concerned criticism is an act of conviction rather than willpower. Life's too short, art can go on far too long.

As I mention in the essay 'Electricities', a year or two working in the television industry early in the 1990s galvanised the impulse to start writing *about* poetry and painting when, in the commercial environment of television at that time, engaging intelligently with those topics was tantamount to insubordination. I doubt I would have headed off in the direction I did if it had not been for my sojourn as an arts advisor for the short-lived programme *The Edge* (1993–94)—so I find myself looking back gratefully on that experience.

I have never drawn any particular distinction between creative writing and non-fiction. For me, they come from the same source; they are fuelled by the same energies and aim, ultimately, at similar ends. The pieces that follow are continuous with my work as a poet (an overlap manifest in 'Electricities'). Like poems, I think of these essays and notebooks as orchestrations of phenomena, a sifting and balancing of particulars to suggest some outward shape or inner essence.

If this book is in part, then, a kind of intellectual autobiography, a tracking of various enthusiasms, it is not an exhaustive one. I deliberately chose not to include essays about art and spirituality (of which I have produced quite a few). I had just read James Hall's extraordinary book, *The World as Sculpture*, which has a passage about the at-times cramped relationship between religion and painting. Hall describes the title page of a seventeenth-century devotional manual which depicts 'Christ carrying the cross on a hill surrounded by *nine* painters seated at their easels. These sons-of-St-Luke are some of the first *plein air* painters, and some of the first paparazzi . . . Christians are called upon to "imitate Christ in the lives" with the unerring accuracy of "famous and outstanding painters".' Enough, I thought. For the present book I would keep in mind Pablo Neruda's plea that the creative artist should remain earthbound and close to the material world.

*

For some years now a clipping from the *Evening Post* has followed me around. It is one of a small number of documents which I am forever losing, then finding, then losing again. Every time I come across this article I re-read it. After some years of being hounded by this press clipping I photocopied it and discarded the original, in the process losing its exact date. The article is called 'Long overdue farewell to mystic provincialism' and was written by Ian Wedde during his stint as the *Evening Post*'s arts reviewer—a time looked back on by many as the Golden Age of arts journalism in Wellington. The article is a wrap-up of the creative activity in the Capital during 1983—Wedde sings out the old year and calls in the new, hailing along the way the National Art Gallery's Rita Angus retrospective exhibition as a 'farewell to a necessary but also mystic provincialism'. Strangely enough, the sub-editor responsible for the headline added 'long overdue' and removed the 'necessary but', imbuing the piece with an overriding sense that at last we have dispelled something nasty from the room: 'mystic provincialism'.

Richard Killeen, *Fishcase* (from *'Seals, shields, signs, stacks, strips'*), 2001.

During the years that Wedde's article has fallen apart, been reborn as a photocopy, then resumed its disintegration—in cupboards, drawers, trouser pockets or scrunched into unlabelled manilla folders—I have pondered what exactly 'mystic provincialism' might be. Perhaps the term suggests the paradoxical nature of the best art: a sense of being earthbound and local yet also capable of flight. I also found myself returning to the question: if we have indeed bade farewell to mystic provincialism, what have we replaced it with? And if it is gone, haven't we every right to expect it to be replaced with something at least as good if not better? It's an apposite question to ask of the artworks of the present epoch: do they really hold their own alongside the 'mystic provincialism' of Angus or early McCahon or Janet Frame, of Ralph Hotere's Aramoana works or Rosalie Gascoigne's dialogue with her adopted home, the landscape outside Canberra? The works of those artists certainly haven't gone away—which leads me to think that perhaps we haven't farewelled mystic provincialism as comprehensively as the *Post*'s sub-editor thought we should. And, if you look carefully around the more interesting contemporary artists, there are signs of mystic provincialism's reinvention and rebirth. Just as it was a cornerstone of Brasch's *Landfall*—and counterbalance to a necessarily secular spirit—it is an essential ingredient in the work of Laurence Aberhart, Bill Hammond and quite a few other mystics in the church of the world. I imagine, walking across the parched expanse of the present era, Richard Killeen carrying suitcases and lunch-containers full of cut-outs; a gamelan orchestra, directed by Jack Body, is accompanying the choir at St Mary of the Angels, Wellington; Dinah Hawken is adjusting the trees, leaves and stones in her poetic landscape. 'Mystic provincialism' is also to be found in the sound-sculpture of Phil Dadson, the photographs of Megan Jenkinson and Anne Noble, in the best songs of Martin Phillipps and The Chills, in Wedde's 'commonplace odes' and in the best paintings of John Walsh, Johanna Pegler, Saskia Leek, Michael Harrison and Shane Cotton. This is going to be a very long goodbye indeed.

Gregory O'Brien
November 2001

Acknowledgements

I'm grateful to Victoria University for appointing me as 1995 Writer-in-Residence, during the tenure of which I completed most of the pieces in 'The Shape of Living'. Since that time my involvement in the English Department and, more recently, the International Institute of Modern Letters at Victoria has been immensely productive. I'm grateful to all the students that have completed the poetry workshop and to the staff, in particular Bill Manhire. I also thank Lara Strongman, Rebecca Wilson, Neil Semple, Mary-Jane Duffy, Michele Taylor, Tommy Honey, Kate Darrow, Mark Amery, Paula Savage and everyone at the City Gallery Wellington. Many thanks to the following for their encouragement at various times: Robin Dudding, Ralph Hotere, Mari Mahr, Justin Paton, Karl Stead, Janet Frame, Jonathan Williams, Brendan O'Brien, Chris Price, Iain Sharp, Laurie Duggan, Andrew Johnston, Ken Bolton, August Kleinzahler, Kim Hill, Meredith Monk, Pare Tito, Te Miringa Hohaia, Marti Friedlander, Jacquie Baxter, Robert Cross, Kathlene Fogarty, James Brown, Robyn Marsack, Ian Wedde, Damien Wilkins, William Dart, Michael King, Sue Brown, Paul Millar, Jenny Neligan, Victor Meertens, Mark Williams and Jane Stafford. Thanks to all the artists who gave permission for their works to be reproduced here; to the family of Rosalie Gascoigne; and to the Colin McCahon Research and Publication Trust. I appreciate Fergus Barrowman's enthusiasm, Andrew Mason's skilful copy-editing, and the commitment of Victoria University Press to 'the book that would not end'. And my love and gratitude to Jen, Jack-Marcel, Felix and Carlo for putting up with long nights and days of this.

I

AN ALPHABET WITHOUT EDGES

After bathing at Baxter's

Liner notes for an album

> 'You were a bird and you lived very high
> rode on the wind when a breeze blew by
> said to the wind as it blew you away
> that's where I wanted to go today . . .
> and I didn't know that I need to have you around . . .'
> ('The Ballad of You and Me and Pooneil', Jefferson Airplane,
> *After Bathing at Baxter's*, RCA, 1967)

In the photograph I am seventeen and have recently moved north to Dargaville. I am riding the Railways bus from Auckland on a hot Sunday afternoon after two days' reprieve from the small town. Falling asleep, face pressed up against the warm glass of the window, the pink Price Milburn edition of *Jerusalem Sonnets* rests in my lap. I have just read 'Poem for Colin 22', we are nearing Wellsford and I am thinking how Baxter has left no room for anyone else to write poetry in this country.

*

A few years later I am on a bus from Sydney to Melbourne, passing through Goulburn. It is 1982 and the *Collected Poems*, Baxter's, follows me around. A travelling doorstop. Just outside the town of Goulburn, I notice a dilapidated billboard with the following slogan writ large:

> STAMP OUT BARE FEET
>
> BAXTER'S SHOES

This essay first appeared in *Sport* 11, Spring 1993, at a time when Baxter's reputation seemed to be in a trough. With the *Collected Poems* out of print and Baxter twenty years dead, no one was saying much. Since then, Baxter has re-emerged in an extraordinary variety of ways—in print, on stage, television and CD and he was even the subject of a modern dance epic, Michael Parmenter's *Jerusalem*.

Multiple Baxters I—Nigel Brown, *Driveway Painting*, 1974, oil on board, collection of Ralph Hotere.

Multiple Baxters II—*The Two Baxters*, Millwood Press, 1979, cover design incorporating drawing by Margaret Lawlor Bartlett.

Whenever making the Sydney/Melbourne road journey during the early 1980s, I always found this sign an occasion to reflect on the writer who certainly put bare feet on the map of New Zealand literature. When visiting Australia in 1987, I discovered the billboard had disappeared—as, I suspect, had the small-town shoe factory.

*

In the early 1980s, the painters Nigel Brown and Philip Clairmont wrote an irate letter to the *New Zealand Listener* complaining about the imposition of an admission fee by the family on whose front lawn Baxter is buried. The walk up to Baxter's grave at Jerusalem will still cost you a couple of dollars if you're not Catholic and well connected. If you happen to be a member of the Catholic clergy you'll get to visit the grave for nothing and probably be invited in for dinner as well—a pot full of boiled sausages, a plate of glowing white bread (like the glowing white gravestone, inscribed HEMI, beyond the dusty green lawn which is regularly mown by a fastidious electric weed-eater).

Baxter, in the afterlife, continues the same paradoxical, compromised existence he suffered, bemoaned and celebrated up until his death in 1972. Baxter's Romanticism, in all its permutations, is probably one of the reasons he isn't such a useful cog in the wheel of current literary discourse and as a result has fallen from critical favour—just as that aspect in e.e. cummings's work led to years of neglect. (On the subject of Romanticism, it's worth noting that Thomas Merton, in a 1936 essay, recorded 11,394 definitions of the term 'Romantic'.)

'Turning brown and torn in two'[1]

Something that strikes me, reading Baxter, is a curious lack of any real mysticism. Oddly, for someone who wrote and talked extensively about the reflective life, Baxter never achieved anything like the meditative or monastic state. Stillness, detachment, profound silence are all qualities hard to associate with any phase of Baxter's life. Interestingly, of the Nine Permanent Emotions of Indian mystical thought—

the heroic
the mirthful
the wondrous
the erotic

tranquillity

sorrow
fear
anger
the odious

—tranquillity is the only one Baxter never quite embodied. While the poems hanker after a coherent and convincing spirituality, they seldom attain it. Perhaps because Baxter was too immersed in this world, or else obsessively opposed to it. Militancy and monasticism are tricky weights to balance.

He was also obsessed with the externalisation of his beliefs and perceptions—he couldn't internalise them—and, as a result, the process they enacted tended to be a public rather than a private one. Critic Alan Riach points to 'Baxter's erratic but easily identifiable procedure as a "maximalist" poet: the social vision he implies in his poetry is one he wished to extend in material terms to the organisation and functioning of society itself'.

In hindsight, the poet's legendary barefoot walks up the River Road to Jerusalem appear more like masochism or showmanship than a convincing display of self-control and transcendence. You could easily think it was a kind of vanity that kept Baxter so bedraggled and ill-kempt. In removing himself from the bounds of society's expectations and propriety, he was—unconsciously perhaps—raising himself above that society. And, from there, he could sit in judgement on it.

*

Following in the great New Zealand tradition of the jack-of-all-trades, Baxter set himself up as an amateur theologian. His 'religious' books—*The Flowering Cross, Thoughts about the Holy Spirit, The Six Faces of Love*—have energy and conviction, but suffer on account of their erratic learning and hurried composition. Neither entirely works of theology nor of mysticism, his writings don't ascribe to either of the two strands or modes of religious thought. Without a deep understanding of theology as a system and without the truly revelatory insights of a mystic, Baxter's religious writings are marooned somewhere in the middle, on their own peculiar ground. They remain most interesting for what they reveal of their author and the fruity 1960s. They also throw a curious albeit sometimes unflattering light on the poetry, emphasising, as they do, the weaknesses instead of the strengths.

The right substance

As a child—c.1970—the Woodstock music festival and Baxter's Jerusalem commune were indistinguishable in my mind. I recall seeing in the *Listener* and daily newspapers the identical muddy rivers, the pale, distantly naked bodies. And, in hindsight, I recall the same soundtrack—it is Jefferson Airplane's *After Bathing at Baxter's*.

After Bathing at Baxter's, Jefferson Airplane, album jacket, RCA Records, 1967.

*

While Baxter embraced the counterculture, its values and vocabulary, with a wholehearted commitment and sincerity, from the 1990s the epoch appears a brief, self-defeating cultural moment, no longer particularly relevant or illuminating. It was an excessive and, in all sorts of ways, a makeshift era. Baxter's poems occasionally suffer the same muddle and self-delusion that befell Jefferson Airplane's epoch-defining album *After Bathing at Baxter's* (released in December 1967). Perhaps it was the breadth of Baxter's genius that he could incorporate the language, world view, mannerisms and even clichés of an era within poems like 'Autumn Testament', yet the poetry is undiminished—at best, it is given a new life, the 'poetic' and the 'non-poetic' entering into a counterpoint, the end result of which is integrated and wholly poetic.

Jerusalem-period Baxter does ask you to swallow quite a lot of the author's personal beliefs and views. The reader has to grapple with a kind of hippie Catholicism, an extreme anti-materialism (but one that's not entirely convincing—Baxter went on about giving up, as well as physical possessions, 'mental possessions' including poems. But, if anything, his writing only accelerated right up until the time of his death).

By the late 1960s, Baxter had filtered out of his poetry much that was baroque or dressed up, ornamental or purely 'literary'.[2] His poetry had shed a great many skins by the time he began his last poems: the late sonnets, a few religious songs and some diatribes against the police, the state, the folks at home. While the late poetry constantly risks being heavy-handed and overblown, for Baxter that was a far lesser sin than being effete or ineffectual. Baxter was, after all, a man with a mission.

Far out

While late Baxter could often be accused of grandstanding and sermonising, at least he hardly ever indulged in that other great 60s pursuit, *weirdness* (the out-of-it instrumentation, the exoticism[3]). Elements in Baxter's late vocabulary have dated rather badly (the *alternative lifestyle* terminology where police are 'fuzz', women 'chicks', drug addicts 'junkies', and people are addressed as 'Man'), but compared with the members of Jefferson Airplane he now appears a very conservative, responsible hippie indeed. Perhaps the drugs weren't as good down here.

How Baxter would align himself, twenty years after his death, now that the so-called counterculture and the dominant culture are so thoroughly interwoven, is anybody's guess.

Poster for Newman Hall poetry reading, 1984, Nigel Brown.

An era, an institution

> 'It's a wild tyme . . .'
> ('Wild Tyme (h)', Jefferson Airplane, *After Bathing at Baxter's*)

Essentially, Baxter wasn't trying to kick-start a ground-breaking new experiment at Jerusalem, he was trying to reactivate and reinterpret a form of tribal life that was there before—on the Whanganui River in the form of Maori life. He was also invoking the spirit of Eric Gill's Ditchling or Capel Y Ffin (like Gill, Baxter retreated further and further from the 'corrupt' city but, paradoxically, was always drawn back there). His communal ideals fell somewhere between the Utopian socialists and the spirit of late 1960s communes in North America.

It was an era of simplifications and wishful thoughts—of imaginative flying machines winging their way above the corrupt and unbeautiful cities.[4] Like Grace Slick and Jefferson Airplane, Baxter at Jerusalem believed that filling an old house with down-at-heel people could be a kind of *restoration* of what was meaningful and responsible in human society. Unfortunately, while the Utopian, idealistic establishment can exist happily as a high-flying idea, it has a tendency, whenever it touches ground, to undo itself—just like Gill's Ditchling. Baxter's community of people would never be able to match his community of words.

For the love of

> 'You've got the whole world in your hands . . .'
> (Mastercard Visa ad campaign, 1993)

Ezra Pound muttered across a dinner table or in print that the two great topics of poetry are God and Money—two items seldom lacking from the Baxterian agenda, but two topics (one he believed in, one he heaped scorn upon) not really given much space in current discussion of poetry.

A man with a mission

> 'It is not the worldly eclecticism of multiple knowledge that enriches but perseverance in a favourable furrow and the loving silent effort of a whole life.' (Georges Rouault)

For the twelfth anniversary of Baxter's death, Father Eugene O'Sullivan, of the Catholic chaplaincy at Auckland University, organised a memorial poetry reading and exhibition. The reading itself was a memorable, slightly incongruous affair involving perhaps sixty people—nuns, elderly flower children, academics, potters, poets and painters. I recall the American writer Bill Millett arriving with poet/critic Iain Sharp, both wearing white shirts, black trousers, jackets and shoes, looking every bit like the Blues Brothers.[5] At one point during the Newman Hall reading, Bill Millett stood up and recounted how Baxter, in his last days, had worked at Millett's Psychedelic Poster Shop in Mt Eden Road. Millett remembered Baxter as 'a hopeless worker with useless hands . . . he couldn't do anything with them'. As the story goes, the job didn't last long and the poet's life only a little longer.

*

Like the Newman Hall reading, these notes might themselves be a kind of 'wake', an attempt to see who, twenty years after Baxter's death, would turn up for such a function.

Millett's offsider at the Newman Hall function, Iain Sharp, published three books of verse in the early to mid-1980s. Sharp's poems, like those of Bill Manhire, provide an interesting, off-key counterpoint to Baxter's, a mischievous gloss. Both Sharp and Manhire usually incorporate a central talking/feeling/seeing poet-persona within the work—only theirs is a Pierrot-like clown mutation of the Poet with a capital P. They set out to sabotage the reader's expectations instead of confronting them head on. They play the Disappearing or Invisible Man to Baxter's Omnipresent Man. Of all the conversations with Baxter's shade at this imaginary wake, Manhire's and Sharp's are the most oblique and the most amusing.

> How to relax in this world,
> that's the real question . . .
> ('The Real Question', Iain Sharp, 1985)

'James K. Baxter memorial paperweight'

Bill Manhire comes back from a South Island holiday with a car boot containing selected stones from the Matukituki Valley. These he bestows on various friends, mentioning their origin and the origin of Baxter's 'Poem in the Matukituki Valley'. 'E, Brother,' he says, hinting at one factor curiously absent in James K. Baxter—a sense of self-irony.

The stone is smooth and always cold: a fragment of riverbed lost to its river. It occurs to me that self-irony can coexist with the deepest meaning and sincerity.

Suburban maze

An image recurs of the young, reluctant schoolteacher Baxter at Epuni Primary School in Lower Hutt. He is horizontal atop the school's jungle gym. The sky above is turbulent, the skyline interrupted only by trees and the roofs of surrounding houses. Scarves of smoke flap from the chimneys. Baxter is wrestling with the jungle gym as if it were a diabolical monster—a mechanical mutation of something invented by Fuseli. Baxter is riding the back of the beast. The air above the surrounding field shifts ever so slightly. The grass twitches. But he is going nowhere.

*

It's worth noting that the suburban/family life so slagged off in Baxter's poems—*the suburban malaise*, as he thought of it—has reappeared in recent poetry in quite a different guise. Jenny Bornholdt, Andrew Johnston and Damien Wilkins are three youngish poets brought up in Lower Hutt who feel that their origins are worth a serious, affectionate yet often ironic look. This supposed battle zone between Calvinism or Capitalism and the Individual can be glimpsed in the work of these poets as a curious, paradoxical place bathed in golden evening light—hardly a Celtic twilight, more like a Robin Morrison photograph—acknowledging the possibility that people growing up and living in such settings can have rich inner lives. And the suburban ground can, after all, yield meaningful images and symbols. It's a site as valid as Hiruharama or the Matukituki Valley (but without the inbuilt, auto-pilot Romanticism of the wilderness).

In the current batch of poets, there's a glee, a Dadaist indulgence in word and image—a mobility or levity—reflecting the fact that, for much of post-Baby Boom New Zealand, the most important formative reading experience wasn't necessarily the Bible (or, for that matter, the *New Zealand Tablet*), but was just as likely to have been *The Reader's Digest*, *Best Bets* and quite possibly the surf magazine *Tracks*.

The newer generation is more accepting of the surface chaos of life, without resorting to radical political or spiritual remedies. Their poems imply that the view from a speeding bicycle is at least as valid as the view from an ivory tower or pulpit.

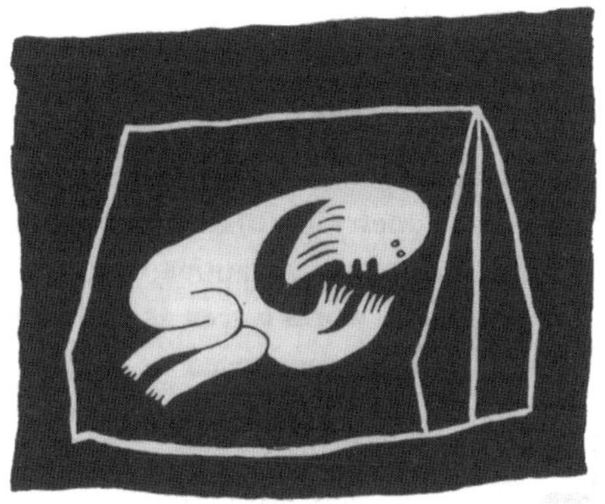

Drawing, 1984, by the author.

> Pedal at first, then let the road take you down
> into the dark as black as underground
> broken by circles of yellow lowered by the street lights . . .
> ('Instructions for how to get ahead of yourself while the light still shines', from *Moving House*, Jenny Bornholdt, Victoria University Press, 1989)

You can also track a general movement away from symbolism, towards imagism in poetry like that quoted above. Here light and darkness don't rely on theological connotations to attain many layers of meaning—the world is multilayered and profound enough just as it is. And, as life is experienced as a series of disorderly, often inexplicable fragments, a viable method of 'writing it' is as a series of poetic fragments. Particularly in the work of Bornholdt and Johnston, there is no searching for blueprints or master plans, just an acceptance that life is, essentially, as it is *experienced*—i.e. all over the place (reflecting an authorial stance and 'momentary' focus you could indeed source to *The Reader's Digest*'s 'Life's Like That' column).

Muddy river

It looks almost beautiful from a distance, especially with the sky reflected in it. But would you *get in it*?

Only occasionally blue, the Whanganui River is Baxter's 'slow, brown god'; repository of history and spirituality, but also courier for the sewage and waste of the town of Taumarunui and for all the chemicals and slop from thousands of acres of farmland.

Like the Whanganui River, New Zealand poetry is an impure stream, with numerous tributaries, offshoots, and debris floating downriver. The larger-than-life, yet somehow elusive, figure of James K. Baxter, instead of helping to clarify or define this river, has served only to muddy it further. Baxter could be thought of, conveniently, as a marker buoy or beacon—run-down, largely ignored, obscured by Time and its various tides, but still standing and issuing noisy instructions.

*

It's difficult to gauge the extent of Baxter's influence over younger New Zealand poets because different people have taken different things—no school or convenient grouping has been forthcoming. However, while there are no obvious angles, there are vistas of refracted light and echoes or resonances.

Because Baxter was such a singular prophet-like figure, towering in his brilliance, his idiosyncrasy, his rightness and his wrongness, no one was going to directly inherit the role or step into his shoes. He served to atomise New Zealand poetry, leaving a chaos or variousness in his wake. I suspect few younger poets would be comfortable with having the label BAXTER or BAXTERIAN stamped on any of their luggage, let alone on their person. But I'm left with a curious image after reading poetry by the younger writers of the 1980s.

I imagine a formation of young poets walking into the distance. Unbeknown to them, there are mirrors on their backs. And in these mirrors Baxter is reflected, sometimes distorted and dishevelled, at other times appearing transcendental, saintly. The poets themselves are confidently walking into the future, instead of dwelling on this or any other past. But they still bear the image of Baxter on their backs.

*

By the time he reached Jerusalem, Baxter was advocating 'free expression' in both art and life. The fact that he was able to be himself and be brilliant at the same time sets him apart from the majority of writers who have followed. Even when discarding 'art's cloak', his work is still permeated with a sense of that 'art', its tradition. What weaknesses and excesses the poet allows emerge as—to use Clement Greenberg's phrase—'the necessary awkwardness and faux pas of original creation'. When Baxter is 'bad' he is choosing to be, unlike some of his contemporaries or successors.

On the other hand, few poets in the 1990s could be accused of the excesses Baxter manifested in both art and life—perhaps now that the staple crop of the counterculture is the bean sprout, not the marijuana plant, everyone has become less self-centred and ultimately more responsible.

*

Since the 70s there has been a widespread—but little discussed—tendency for the poem to be treated less as a crafted or 'made' artwork and more as the direct and urgent vehicle through which the poet vents his or her spleen.

That was the note Baxter went out on—witness his last dated poem, 'Ode to Auckland'. The conviction and overtly stated political intent in Baxter's ode aren't very far removed from the 'protest' poetry of recent years, usually penned by women or Maori poets—Roma Potiki, Janet Charman, Heather McPherson, Apirana Taylor, to name a few.[6] These poets have a far greater allegiance to Baxter than, say, to Curnow. Like the later Baxter, theirs is a poetry with a purpose—it is a stick with which to beat the narrow-minded and the power-wielders. It can be a cry from the heart, a primal scream even. Such 'message' poetry is aimed at a broader audience than the usual poetry crowd. Its relationship to its constituency is usually simple and direct—a broadcast on behalf of, as well as to, those of like heart and mind.

Baxter also anticipated the 'paua shell goddess' alternative spirituality embraced by many artists and writers since the 1970s. His Catholicism often wandered off in the direction of pantheism, his work incorporating this, as well as a poetically useful animism and a few errant strains of Zen Buddhism. For a lighter-hearted manifestation of these now widespread spiritual fixations, you could turn to the anarchic, cranky poetry of Iain Sharp:

> In their most religious moments
> the zen masters look like bandits . . .
> Oh I love them. I love them.
> I want to be one of their number.
> I want to throw off my cardigan,
> my socks, my shirt, my trousers,
> don a tattered old kimono,
> pick up my swag in a handkerchief
> on the end of a bamboo pole,
> and go where the reeds sway softly,
> and the heron slices bare sky.
> ('Zen Art for Meditation', Iain Sharp, *She is trying to kidnap the blind person*, Hard Echo Press, 1985)

Keri Hulme's poems manifest a localised spirituality, not exactly inherited from Baxter, but similarly sourced in an awareness of Maoritanga, a mystification of place, and a belief in the prophetic and oracular role of the poet. Hulme also indulges in a certain self-mythologisation which is very much in the Baxter mould—the poet as sounding board for the cosmos, as the stage on which various theological and ideological battles are fought.

*

Baxter's integration of poetry and prose in books like *Jerusalem Daybook* foreshadows the emergence of the prose-poem as a viable form in local writing. His 'Elegy for Boyle Crescent' consisted of a series of prose fragments and appeared in *Islands 1* (Spring, 1972), where it was listed in the journal's contents as 'Verse', a radical redefinition for its time. Since then, the prose-poem has been a minor but noteworthy stream in New Zealand poetry. Writers including Murray Edmond, Jenny Bornholdt, Michael Harlow, Dinah Hawken, Michael Morrissey and Miro Bilbrough, to name a few, have pursued it.

Another late-Baxter form, the journal or diary shuffling between 'poetry' and 'prose'—ultimately avoiding any distinction—has been developed by writers including Hulme, Bornholdt, Anne Kennedy and Cilla McQueen. Rob Allan has also picked up the extended poem sequence in his *Karitane Postcards* (1991). Here Baxter's series of 'letters' is given a more contemporary permutation by way of a series of 'postcards'. And, as is the case with postcards, the writing can be as cryptic and fragmented as it chooses to be. The communication can be as impressionistic or relaxed as the postcard format suggests.

A sequence of sonnets

> 'I'd really like to see if he thinks in sonnets . . . '
> (Michael O'Leary, *Out of It*, Earl of Seacliff Art Workshop, 1987)

Since the *Jerusalem Sonnets*, the locally produced sonnet sequence has been constantly revived and reinvented. A history of the post-1972 New Zealand sonnet sequence would have to include—for a start—C. K. Stead, Ian Wedde, Dinah Hawken, Leigh Davis, Robert Sullivan and Michele Leggott.

Ian Wedde was one of the first to pick up the long-winded sonnet sequence. He made it even hipper and smarter than Baxter managed, dropping the Catholic mysticism and replacing it with a humanism and animism derived from Pablo Neruda, among others. In *Earthly*, Wedde's sonnets are faster moving than Baxter's, more convoluted and riddled with literary allusions and echoes. They play an internationalist tune against Baxter's predominantly nationalist one and reflect to some degree modernism's replacement with a local version of postmodernism which has swayed, if not dominated, New Zealand poetry in recent years.

Wedde also drops the poet-persona fair and square in the centre of the poem, which is where Baxter liked him to be. Although Wedde, like Graham Lindsay, clouds that persona in irony and complexity—we read 'him' as a literary construct as well as a version of the poet himself. Poet and poem undercut each other. There's a slippage which Baxter would never have allowed, content as he was to play Jeremiah, to secure himself a seat and to sit on it.

River with eels

Graham Lindsay, particularly in his first book, *Thousand Eyed Eel*, picked up and processed a lot of Baxter—the barefoot on the ground realist, the commingling of the commonplace and the spiritual, of life in the suburbs and life breaking out of those suburbs.

Lindsay is still walking the same floor as Baxter, only more self-consciously so. Whereas Baxter used the Self as an anchor or poetic cornerstone, seeing and experiencing everything in relation to it, Lindsay acknowledges language itself as an unstable and unpredictable force within the poem, capable of relegating the 'poetic self' to the back seat. In contrast, Baxter always handled language as though it was the surest, truest thing the poet had at his disposal (an unfashionable view in these postmodern times). Lindsay's approach weakens or fragments the authorial voice, giving the work a more objective and ambiguous quality. The poem becomes a craggy and idiosyncratic mechanism but—and this is much to Lindsay's credit—remains grounded in a common, or shared, reality. The reader is rarely left behind or lost in the slipstream.

Graham Lindsay comes closer to being the 'the postmodern

Baxter' than anyone. His allegiance with Baxter has decreased over the years, but back in 1980 he was even prepared to send a few lines down into the ground where Baxter lies buried:

> Can you hear me down there
> Baxter?
> There're no lights on in the tophouse
> now you know that the windows got broken?
> Nga tamariki have grown up & left you old man
> alone in that hole.
> Oh I cd get you out
> with a spade & a jemmy. I'd make that special trip.
> Tho I guess yr hair is grey
> and the flesh has dropt away
> after four years what would be left
> but bone & sack.
> Still I would embrace you . . .
> (from 'The Embrace', *Public*, Ridge Pole, 1980)

A path up the river

Jacques Maritain's definition of poetry as a 'divination of the spiritual in the realm of the senses, to be expressed in the same realm' is useful here.

Contemporary writers walking a loosely related 'spiritual' floor to Baxter include poets like Bernadette Hall, Joanna Margaret Paul and, in a veiled and private way, Elizabeth Smither. They share a reflective Catholicism, Zen-like in its concentration on using the 'concrete' to reveal the 'spiritual'—a catholic, in the sense of *universal*, notion of accepting the world, contradictions and all, yet still managing to see beyond the limitations of contemporary society, its politics and ugliness. A more accommodating approach, then, than that of Baxter, who often got no further than staring down the barrel of his poetry at the society he so tirelessly rejected.

The sensitivity and pared-down language of Hall and Paul is a long way from the badgering tone and prolific noise of Baxter. Their delicacy of touch, their cultivation of stillness, is ultimately more akin to both Eastern and Western meditative traditions.

for ming

All the best things
start in small rooms
where a few gather
& talk & eat & laugh
& kindle & spill like
candles in paper cups.
(Bernadette Hall, *Of Elephants Etc*, Untold Books, 1990)

Although her recent writing has become denser and more elaborate, Bernadette Hall's poetry—and the spirituality it encapsulates which is by no means a conventional Catholicism—is a poetry in which:

All the windows
are open. Ivory tides wash out, wash in
& you sing the mysteries: that love
is a gift; that nothing is ever lost;
that death is the centre of a long life.
(Bernadette Hall, 'Amica', *Heartwood*, Caxton, 1989)

A note on reduction

Language, in Joanna Margaret Paul's poetry, is frequently drawn back to monosyllables, the plain words of common prayer. In her writing and visual art work, she culls all superficial or superfluous elements, removing everything that is not intrinsic.

though grass may die
its roots remain
and shoot again
at the year's prime,
not so my pain
its root is green
its shooting time
needs no spring rain
(from '2 Versions of a Chinese Poem', Joanna Paul, *A Chronology*,
Sarjeant Gallery, Wanganui , 1989)

Joanna Paul is concerned more with the *cultivation* of space than with the using up or domination of that space. The poems have an objective feel—a sense of pictorial space, the careful placement of object/image within the poem, and a sense of composition (the harmonic blending of sounds and materials into a coherent, yet strangely 'open', picture).

There's a receptiveness to the unordered natural world which contrasts with Baxter's constant need to read natural phenomena as part of his autobiography or inner journey.

Baxter was after a kind of reduction to essentials, if not always in his poetry (which sometimes tended towards the verbose) then at least on a personal level, as he sought to enact a 'primitive' Catholicism which shunned materialism, the cluttering of one's life with money, possessions, worldly aspirations. In a social sense, Baxter's Jerusalem community was striving for this kind of reductionism, renouncing the trappings and trivialities which not only dominate but define modern life.

Poets like Joanna Paul and Bernadette Hall succeed in attaining a purity of intention and form in their work. What is possible within their *private* worlds proved impossible for Baxter as he continually grappled with the world at large, characteristically overstepping the mark of what was humanly, individually achievable to embrace Utopian, communal ideals.

The tragedy of Baxter is that, while he was aware of the individual's need for spiritual and mental 'realisation' (and acknowledged this as a prerequisite for social life), only his poetry proved capable of such realisation—in both his public and private lives it eluded him.

Like Hall and Paul, Michele Leggott manifests a minimalism or elementalism—her poems are mindscapes across which images and forms (of language, of speech) drift. But for all their floatingness they present a worked-over, intellectualised universe. The poems offer a secular take on territory similar to that of Joanna Paul, invoking, as they go, the lineage of Objectivism, from William Carlos Williams to Louis Zukofsky to Lorine Niedecker. In having a secular base as opposed to a transcendental one, Leggott's relationship to poets like Paul and Hall can be seen as a refreshing, warm-spirited variation on—or revision of—the Baxter/C. K. Stead stand-off of the 1960s.

New Zealand in black and white

> The more perfect the artist, the more completely separate in him will be the man who suffers and the mind which creates. (Goethe)

> Though Mr Baxter's works cover a wide field, he writes always and primarily as a New Zealander; and for this reason his comments on the photographic sequence *New Zealand in Colour* are of special value. (Flyleaf, *New Zealand in Colour*, Reed, 1961)

Baxter's world had clearly defined borders—it was enclosed within a world view, a personalised frame through which he looked. It is not a floating world like, say, that of Bernadette Hall or Joanna Paul. Whereas they are inclined towards a broader and less morally assertive position, Baxter always wanted to manipulate his material to attain a pre-determined end. He was concerned with creating a coherent universe—one ordered by humankind and the Deity, one with a specific meaning and morality.

It's ironic that Baxter, the moralist whose universe was divided into black and white, in 1961 wrote the text for a picture book called *New Zealand in Colour*.

Not surprisingly, in this as in other instances, Baxter isn't content to do as the book's introduction states and 'let the photographs tell their own story'. On the first page he's already coming on like an antipodean William Blake: 'A City of a kind has been made. The hydro-electric dams at Roxburgh or Mangakino, the productive farms in place of endless tussock or bush, the tidy townships, the suburbs that climb hill-slopes towards the sun, and the honeycomb of factory and office buildings where each man has his appointed job under the eye of the clock—these are the works of the City, finite, exact and reasonable, designed for the fulfilment of limited aims . . .'

The moralist and social critic in Baxter never rest. Even when describing the rustic world of the farmer, he hastens to add that 'the farmer may own a new Zephyr and his wife may attend adult education classes in the nearest town'.

Of 'the recurring colours of sky and water', he chips in, 'they stand perhaps for what can only be known through silence and patience—a lucidity which man stands outside, an order greater than the human one'. In fact, Baxter usurps the benign intention of the scenic picture book by saying: 'In a sense our sequence [of photographs] is made to direct your attention to this world in which we live but to which we so rarely belong.' The harshness of the poet's inner landscape might have been able to coexist with the tourist vistas of the scenic wonderland, but only temporarily and in a somewhat strained fashion.

Stories leading to more stories

The contemporary poet with a comparable social programme to Baxter's is Dinah Hawken, whose poems, without losing any of their focus on individual experience, do comment on and question existing power structures. In *Small Stories of Devotion* she transcends the private/public demarcation by use of dream-like narrative and some Jungian excavation of selves within the self.

Hawken, who is a feminist, is also (and this is something she shares with Baxter) a moralist, although the moral content in her work is to be found deep within the swim of things that is the poem. As well as being a progression forward from Baxter's poetic method and purpose, Hawken's poetry demands also to be seen as a reaction against Baxter's. Many of the things Baxter was prepared to accept Hawken takes to task, particularly concerning sexual politics and the Catholic belief system. Hawken offers a very thorough and thought-provoking revision of the Baxterian agenda and method.

Her first book, *It has no sound and is blue*, includes a sonnet sequence in which fifteen of the sixteen poems use the same schema as Baxter's late sonnets. In their spoken/written quality, they echo the *Jerusalem Sonnets*, although in their mood and voice they come across as more sophisticated—less earthy but every bit as heartfelt. Like Baxter, Hawken has a few ideas about how the world could be improved:

> If we could all get together—just once—like a sea
> of winter trees flicking into leaf, then choosing
> the right swami, the right economic theory, the right diet
> wouldn't matter, since any particular one
> would be wedged against the nature of things
> and it's the nature of things I'm opting for . . .
> (from 'Traces of Hope', *It has no sound and is blue*, Victoria University Press, 1987)

One conversation, many monologues

There's a story a one-time bureaucrat tells of how, as a young civil servant, he had to accompany a visiting Japanese diplomat around the South Island. The visitor was interested in English literature and the bureaucrat had been advised by the programme organiser in Wellington that Baxter had invited them to dinner on the night of their Dunedin visit—it was 1967 or 68, while the poet was Burns Fellow.

He and his guest arrived and sat drinking for a while. Janet Frame turned up. And the evening wore on. Dinner was not served. Eventually the nervous twenty-five-year-old started worrying that perhaps there had been a misunderstanding and there *might not be any dinner*. At an opportune moment, he ducked into the kitchen to discover nothing, in fact, was in the oven.

He then contrived to manoeuvre the Baxters, Janet Frame and the Japanese guest out the door, into the waiting Government car, and off to a Turkish restaurant. Drinking under-the-counter red wine, the civil servant spent the rest of the evening talking to the two women while Baxter, at the other end of the table, soliloquised to the Japanese visitor. It sounded like one of his *New Zealand Tablet* sermons—only longer, and punctuated every few minutes by an 'Ah so' from the attentive audience.

*

Two young poets grappling with the Baxterian mode are John Newton and Robert Sullivan. Newton picks up on the rural, moralistic, death-obsessed, early Baxter (but permeating it with layers of irony and an almost postmodern detachment). Sullivan's 'Tai Tokerau poems' manage a reconciliation between the urban and rural environments (something Baxter's could never facilitate). Like David Eggleton, Sullivan embodies the Poet come down from the Holy Mountain, his ethics and ideals somehow still intact. There's a youthful optimism in Sullivan, contrasting with Baxter's bleakness, his sense of a man winding down to his own death—and seeing society, at large, mirroring this personal decline.

Central margins

It is April 1986. A surprisingly large crowd has gathered in a church at the top of Ponsonby Road. Fr Eugene O'Sullivan is to read Baxter's *Jerusalem Sonnets*. The church interior is virtually blacked out, except for a reading lamp on a small table at the front. Eugene is sitting in a wheelchair beside the table, his nervous hands holding a first edition of the *Sonnets*.

Eugene starts reading to the invisible audience, his voice breathy and straining, his frail legs twisted uncomfortably beneath him. He reads the sonnets. And as the reading progresses, his wheelchair begins to move slowly towards the audience—Eugene is slipping away from the light of the lamp and into the blackness. As he moves forward, he is reduced to a silhouette—but the poems continue unabated, despite the fact the book has vanished into the shadow of his torso. And the pages, in darkness, continue to turn—every two sonnets. By the time the sequence is brought to a close, Eugene's knees are almost touching the knees of someone in the front row of the audience.

*

The Holy Life and Death of Concrete Grady, James K. Baxter, cover design by Colin McCahon, Oxford University Press, 1976.

If, in recent years, Baxter's poetry has been seen as irrelevant or marginal, it's also worth noting that the progress of New Zealand society in the 1970s and, more dramatically, the 1980s has undermined (and, for that matter, mocked) much of what the poet argued for: the socialist state, the truly catholic church, the need to acknowledge, as Pakeha, that the Maori is 'our spiritual elder brother'.

Within the poems themselves, much now appears outmoded—Despair, the Void, the Soul, all the Gods and Goddesses have become clichéd and largely discredited (although poets including Hulme, Hawken, Roma Potiki and Heather McPherson still tread this Christian/post-Christian turf, albeit in a self-confident revisionist manner).

Lines of influence, other than those mentioned here, could be traced back to Baxter. One equally valid line would include Hone Tuwhare, Peter Olds, Sam Hunt, David Mitchell, David Eggleton, Apirana Taylor, Roma Potiki . . . And that's without introducing such complicated and relevant figures as C. K. Stead and Leigh Davis into the picture.

*

Baxter's idea of the poet as the conscience of the people doesn't hold much water these days. It's a naïve notion anyway—Ian Wedde's belief in the poet as 'sceptic', located just outside the mainstream of society, is a better and more humble model for the 1990s. The poet no longer has to manifest the 'illness of the tribe' like the measel or leper in the early church. He or she no longer has to suffer on everyone's behalf.

The Poet, as embodied by Baxter, was responsible to his Ideals, but—in his case—was also paradoxically irresponsible. He behaved badly, was capable of the extraordinary inconsistencies and contradictions which were to prove creatively fertile but personally disastrous. At the same time as he espoused the poet as a 'cell of good living', he was a great misbehaver, like Dylan Thomas 'a lover of the human race, especially of women'.

Yet, somehow, James K. Baxter's poetry maintains its gravity, its conviction and its profundity. During Eugene O'Sullivan's reading of the *Jerusalem Sonnets*, these qualities were staggering and undeniable. It also struck me how the poems could maintain their grip on a theologian like Eugene who, during Baxter's life, constantly questioned and challenged him, who never accepted for a moment Baxter's personal, artistic and ideological excesses. But Eugene would have been the first to acknowledge the power of the poetry. Arising, as it did, so deeply out of the experience of one person it was capable of becoming the experience of many.

Two houses

There's certainly a book sitting around waiting to be written about New Zealand poetry in the 1970s, the atomisation that took place—a frenetic movement between and beyond the imposing figures of James K. Baxter and Allen Curnow.

The noisy collision between the writer and his universe as enacted by Baxter is in marked contrast to Allen Curnow, whose work centres on an orderly relationship between the personal and the public worlds—something he achieved (and is still achieving) through a poetic distancing, filtration of experience, a high-mindedness or good taste, an impeccable order. A far cry from Baxter's unruly house! The breakneck energy that drove Baxter's poetry was what Curnow, arguably, sought to remove from his writing. Relying on an intellectual and temperamental equilibrium, Curnow was engaging a different sort of motor—in the end a longer-running, more maintainable mode of poetic travel. One that wouldn't derail him by the age of forty-six.

After bathing at Baxter's

> 'No man is an island, he's a
> peninsula.'
> (Jefferson Airplane)

It's possible the psychedelic, late-60s Baxter has come back into fashion, if the cover of the 1992 paperback edition of Frank McKay's biography of Baxter is anything to go by. The OUP cover design features two Warhol-like multiple images of the young Baxter bathed in fluorescent light, with unnatural greens and yellows. It's strongly reminiscent of the film of the 1967 Monterey Rock Festival. It looks as though James K. Baxter has accidentally found his way on stage during Jefferson Airplane's set, his face bathed in hallucinogenic, saturated colour. The dry ice has just parted, like a Red Sea, and the light show is about to start.

Nigel Brown, *Driveway Painting*, 1974, oil on board.

Jim afloat

> '..... James K. Baxter ..... Baxter ..... the Baxter of the *Jerusalem Sonnets* ..... Baxter ..... the late Baxter ..... Baxter ..... the "dour ghost" ..... Baxter ..... a series of tacks across the wake of James K. Baxter ..... Baxter ..... Baxter ..... Baxter ..... recontextualising Baxter within these deconstructive ..... James K. Baxter ..... James K. Baxter .....'
> (Mark Williams, introduction to *The Caxton Anthology of New Zealand Poetry 1972–1986*, Caxton, 1987)

Perhaps Baxter is still widely read for his 'wisdom', for the intense world view his poetry reflects, which remains, twenty years down the track, still as intriguing and accessible as ever. Riddled with interesting and relatable paradoxes (the ongoing love/hate relationship between the poet and his world), his poems enact various personal dramas, inner and outer conflicts. The species of 'wisdom' they purvey is also appealing, not because the poet necessarily was 'wise', but because he comes on so wise yet his life was, well, such a self-induced muddle. There's something inherently *human* and relatable in that.

If not acknowledged as a formative influence on the present generation, Baxter pre-empted them in a number of formal and imaginative ways. This might be recognised more except that Baxter, the person, still leaves most writers embarrassed or uncomfortable—an undesirable, or at least questionable, member of the family tree. It's still hard to embrace the poetry without bear-hugging the Great Man himself. So he's still being skirted around; people cross to the far footpath.

It's ironic that the 'personality cult'/guru aspect which made Baxter such a public presence during his life now provides a barrier that needs to be negotiated to get at the work itself.

*

From time to time James K. Baxter comes back into sight. His physiognomy and assorted lines still pop up in the paintings and prints of Nigel Brown. Peter Olds published a poem in 1992 entitled 'Oh, Baxter Is Everywhere' (although the poet *appears* not to appear anywhere in the piece). Baxter features in Michael O'Leary's 1987 novel *Out Of It* as the twelfth man in an imaginary cricket squad, alongside such teammates as Janis Joplin and a veritable squad of Jimmies: James Joyce, Jimi Hendrix and Jim Morrison. On *New Zealand Geographic* magazine's pictorial map of the Whanganui River, there he is, head and shoulders nudged in between the river and the beaming countenance of Mother Mary Joseph Aubert.[7]

He gets a mention in even more surprising contexts. Some of his poetry titles are included in a bibliography of hundreds of books by anyone called Baxter at the back of the English artist Glen Baxter's hilarious tome *Glen Baxter, His Life* (Thames & Hudson, 1983). Closer to home and to the topic: in *AND 1*, Alan Loney, being interviewed by Leigh Davis, stressed what a fine and overlooked *critic* Baxter was and, at the launching of *AND 4* in 1985, one of the magazine's contributors said that he imagined if Baxter was still alive he would be working in the field of ethnopoetics *à la Jerome Rothenberg*.

*

There have been more profound thinkers, social critics, theologians—but when the dust has settled, Baxter will stand the test of time, his poems remaining uncommonly certain of themselves, yet still swaggering with the weight of the Great Man upon them.

If there is one quality the poems embody more than anything else it is what the Chinese refer to as *genius*—'the rhythmical vitality of life'. That's exactly what can be found throughout Baxter's work, his collected poems reading like an enormously alive and alert autobiography.

Thinking of Baxter, the view from 1993, I'm left with two impressions. The first is of Baxter as the central motif in Elizabeth Nannestad's poem 'stone figure':

> Some medieval
> simple soul in stone
> holds the church roof . . .
> the blackbirds of panic seize upon you
> year after year
> and build their rickety
> shit-streaked nests in your hair.
> You're gripped by their scrag.
> You stay there.
> (from *Jump*, Auckland University Press, 1986)

When embarking on this account, I decided not to refer to—or reread—any of Baxter's writings (with the exception of two books I happened upon in second-hand bookshops while engaged on the project—the tiny tract 'A walking stick for an old man' and the picture book *New Zealand in Colour*). I wanted to excavate the residue of 'Baxter' inside myself, to find out exactly what was still there and how persuasive it was.

Without defining Baxter or his influence, these notes might at least have registered some traces, certain avenues down which more systematic and rigorous investigations could proceed.

Again I recall the bus approaching Wellsford and my wondering at the time—nearly a decade after the poet's death—how anyone in New Zealand could write poetry without first dislodging the great weight of Baxter's achievement from them—what then seemed to me an impossible task. My memory continues back another decade to an encounter which is the final impression I am left with: that Baxter hangs around New Zealand poetry today much the same way he used to hang around Auckland's Vulcan Lane—cross-legged on the footpath, a girl not far off. Which was how I first saw him, c.1971, as a young boy heading for Whitcombe and Tombs to buy a magazine called something like *The World At War*.

Change of Rules (above) and *Out of it* (*Sport* 11 cover and back cover), woodcuts by Nigel Brown, 1993.

Notes

1 Heading from the title of a song by Chris Knox.

2 An interesting correlative to this shift is the evolution of the poet's books from the exquisitely printed hardbound Caxton publications of the 1940s, by way of some plain Oxford editions, to the ascetic design of the first edition of *Jerusalem Sonnets* and the dayglo Price Milburn covers of the late 'Jerusalem' books. From the late 1960s until his death, Baxter resorted to all manner of mimeographed publication—'A walking stick for an old man' is little more than a few scraps of paper. These late 'publications' came thick and fast on stapled foolscap (little-known works like his *Handbook for the Christian Militant*), reflecting a disaffection with the book as object and the channels through which it had to move.

3 *After Bathing at Baxter's* included such memorably weird song titles as 'A Small Package of Value Will Come to You, Shortly', 'The Last Wall of the Castle', 'Shizoforest Love Suite', 'Two Heads' and 'Won't You Try Saturday Afternoon'. Jefferson Airplane released a record earlier in 1967, *Surrealistic Pillow*, and two equally 'far out' albums the following year: *Crown of Creation* and *Bless Its Pointed Little Head*.

4 Perhaps the 1960s aren't that easily dismissed. The British jazz journal *The Wire* devoted its May 1993 issue to 'May 1968'. And, coincidentally, in that issue, music critic Biba Kopf wrote: 'Of the music bonding the age's broken pieces, Jefferson Airplane's binds best . . . *After Bathing at Baxter's* is JA's most musically, if not politically, ambitious record. Awry raga rhythms funnel a concussive polyphony of voices, ringing guitar distortions, feedbacking and spliced tape/song chatter . . .'

5 Since then Iain Sharp has gone on to become the Blues Brother—singular—of New Zealand literature—smarter and harder-hitting than everyone else, and, arguably, better dressed. (Baxter was certainly the worst-dressed person in the history of New Zealand letters, apart from his brief, fashionable forays into wrong-way-round coat wearing during his Otago University days. While he dressed badly, he certainly dressed the part—particularly in his counterculture, sagelike later years. The clothing became part of that myth. Baxter's sheer audacity and extremism, in this instance and elsewhere, bring us around to Aristotle's assertion that 'poetry implies a happy gift of nature or a strain of madness'.)

6 The interesting post-Baxter anthology, from this vantage point, is *The New Poets* (ed. Murray Edmond and Mary Paul, Allen & Unwin, 1987).

7 While making these notes, I revisited Jerusalem on the Whanganui River. While I was there, to my surprise, Mother Aubert, foundress of the Home of Compassion order, seemed a far more apparent ghost than Baxter. The poet seemed relegated to a few newspaper clippings pinned to a wall in the old convent and a stern, framed photograph inside the church. I didn't visit the gravesite above the settlement this time—it didn't seem worth bothering the family again—and my aunt Rita, who is a Sister in the Jerusalem convent, was eager to take me on a tour of the old church buildings. She spoke fondly of various visitors to the settlement in recent months, including Iain Sharp, Jenny Bornholdt, Alan Brunton, Sally Rodwell, Joanna Paul (whose colour photocopy montages grace the old convent walls) and the painter Pauline Thompson. 'The middle of nowhere' must be on the way to or from somewhere to attract such traffic.

Southern Woman

Ruth Dallas

South of Timaru, the Southern Man remains a prevalent myth, constantly being revived on billboards and in media ads, often clutching a can of Speight's beer in one hand—a lone figure, although sometimes accompanied by other men temporarily on leave from their primordial lone state. These no-nonsense figures are usually covered in spume from waves, droplets of sweat clinging to each tanned, wind-blasted brow, or caked in mud fresh from the playing field or wilderness. Billboard-sized versions dot the highways to and from Dunedin, where they are particularly thick on the ground around Carisbrook. With the demise of cigarette advertising, the Marlboro Man appears to have been well and truly rehabilitated by southern regionalism.

Alongside this prevalent mythology of 'southern' maleness, it's worth considering a parallel strand of femaleness, as manifest by Ruth Dallas's recently published, updated *Collected Poems* (Otago University Press, 2000). The South has certainly nurtured a wealth of uncompromising, staunchly independent women artists—witness, besides Dallas, Frances Hodgkins, Doris Lusk, Janet Frame, Marilyn Webb and Cilla McQueen, for a start. All manifest an intense inwardness which is resolute yet neither hardened nor inflexible. Rather, it is their responsiveness and capacity for empathy which strike the viewer or reader, whether confronting Hodgkins's early portraits or Frame's complex narrators.

The painting by Kathryn Madill (another Southern Woman) on the cover of Ruth Dallas's new book is an archetypal, rural scene with two sheep, a girl and a woman and a small child. The composition could have been lifted from any number of Dallas's poems in which the menfolk are definitely 'elsewhere'. The pictorial space is curiously flat, the figures isolated by grim tracts of pasture—an appropriate image, I guess, for the under-populated provinces of Southland (where she was born in 1919) and Otago, where she has lived much of her adult life.

Ruth Dallas certainly seems to have walked the hard yards away from the 'southern men', both archetypal and actual. 'Disappointed in love', as she describes herself after an early romantic entanglement, she has gone on to claim her own independent space, from where she has written about parental love, friendship and family, with a few retrospective glances in the direction of failed romantic love. 'Song', 'A Girl's Song' and 'On Reading Love Poems' are probably the most brilliantly gloomy love poems produced in this country. However, like traditional English folksongs or the melodies of John Dowland, they temper loss, sadness and unease with an almost unaccountable sweetness.

As the blurb-writer for Dallas's 1991 autobiography *Curved Horizon* asked: 'At a time when Brasch, Fairburn, Glover and others spoke bitterly of the lack of support given to New Zealand artists, how did a single woman from Southland live and work as a writer, establishing herself as a poet and author of international regard?' How, indeed? A simple, almost ascetic life, for a start. In her autobiography, she generously acknowledges the early help granted her by Monte Holcroft and Charles Brasch, with whom she worked on *Landfall* for some years.

The quality of the work in Dallas's *Collected Poems* begs the question why she isn't as well known as, say, Lauris Edmond. Geography explains this to some extent. Southland is our Siberia—as Damien Wilkins suggests, it 'occupies a space in the New Zealand psyche which all nations reserve for their extremities'.

There's also the matter of temperament. Like Ralph Hotere painting away in the 'favourable furrow' of Port Chalmers, under a succession of broad-brimmed hats, so too Ruth Dallas has kept her head down, remaining true to an inner compulsion rather than to the demands of a public career.

There is a tendency for literary historians to seek out crucial moments, turning points, instances where things are either revealed or renounced: Curnow's 'Landfall in Unknown Seas', his 1960 anthology, the death of James K. Baxter in 1972, the arrival of a wave of 'Feminist' poets in the mid-1970s, the Wedde/McQueen Penguin anthology of 1985 are all cases in point. The problem with this approach is it can't really cope with the long, persistent span of a poet like Dallas (art history has similar problems trying to place seventy prolific years of painting by Toss Woollaston).

Like that of Woollaston, Dallas's work offers a meditation on land

and habitation, on solitude and various permutations of community. Both cool and warm winds blow across the paddock of these poems. While there is certainly a darkness indwelling here, it is not the Frame-esque darkness of the individual at odds with society—it is more melancholy than that, particularly when the poet is meditating on time and progress. Dallas is a 'nature poet' in the best sense of the term and accordingly posits humankind on a canvas of which it is but one, unexceptional part.

In contrast to Hone Tuwhare's 'Rain', which acknowledges nature's redemptive and purifying powers, Dallas's 'Night Rain' presents that same motif as a harbinger of death, of annihilation:

> Under the drumbeat of the rain
> Bone by bone
> Lies down;
>
> Some to rest and some to toss
> Listening
> To the rain,
>
> The rain that thumps
> Its nails on a copper skull
> And pocks a face of stone,
>
> Rain that will wash will wash
> The hand that writes
> Will wash the ear, the eye away.

'Night Rain' is a bleak but not a despairing poem. The incessant monosyllables create a patter that is incantatory, almost magical in its plainness—a plainchant, if the Scottish settlers of Southland ever sang one. Elsewhere Dallas's reflections on nature are more ambivalent and echo both earlier poets—like Mary Ursula Bethell—and those who have followed: Dinah Hawken, Michele Leggott and Cilla McQueen. There's a directness and ease in the relation to nature (take note, Southern Men):

> A broom-tree, bearing a thousand seed-pods,
> And every pod supplied with ten seeds,
> Took up its station on the boundary,

I addressed it politely
Excuse me, but one of us must go.
For answer it cracked a seed-pod.
The dry seeds fell like smallshot.
Truly, it fired the first round.

This locates itself somewhere between Ursula Bethell's 'Detail' and Emily Dickinson, with a nod towards Lorine Niedecker's minute dramatic monologue:

My friend tree
I sawed you down
but I must attend
an older friend
the sun

While Dallas's poems are steeped in 'a sense of place' (to use a tired expression), they certainly aren't peppered with place names or specific references. If they describe landscape exactly and evocatively, 'place' is left to reverberate in the reader's mind rather than on a map somewhere.

Like the 'moment' of black in a Matisse canvas or Niedecker's use of the occasional 'rogue' rhyme, it is the well-rendered detail that counts in Dallas's poetry. Also a sense of vernacular, of the human-made which provides an emotional scale enabling the work to transcend both the impersonal and the sublime—the two pitfalls of nature poetry in general.

A cabbage tree is not an interesting tree.
Its single trunk resembles a telegraph pole.

Elsewhere Dallas complains that 'a telegraph pole disfigures / even the moon' and again: 'Insulators, power-poles, / Scribble out the view'. So humankind's clumsier interventions into the natural world do not go unreprimanded. Perhaps this, too, is part of the 'southern woman' character: practical, quick of mind, full of good, if at times stroppy, advice. 'Poem for a cabbage tree' was, in fact, written for the tree which still stands in front of Brasch's beach house (or, in the local lingo, 'crib') at Broad Bay on Otago Harbour. Dallas's vocabulary and syntax are close to that of a botany textbook, but subtly turned and tuned elsewhere. Her cabbage tree is a radio receiver, drawing tremors from further afield. In this instance, and in many others besides, the poem has something of Brasch's meditative manner.

Alongside a sense of remoteness, there is an intensity to this poetry which Dallas herself sources to two events in early adolescence. Recalling a quintessentially Joycean epiphany, she wrote in a 1965 *Landfall* essay of 'a poetic vision of the acres of flowering lupins that I had seen covering a waste of sand-hills on a remote coastal farm; and, with the vision, the sense of wonder they had aroused, and a desire to express in a poem what I felt about them.'

The visual register in the poems has something of this vivid, almost hallucinogenic intensity—an intensity which was further heightened by the deprivation she endured when as a sixteen-year-old, having lost the sight in one eye, she faced the very real prospect of having to live out the duration of her life in total darkness:

> In hospital at first both my eyes were bandaged for complete rest, and I had to lie flat on my back and not move a muscle, not even to sit up and eat, but be fed by a nurse. It was an eerie experience to leave the outside world and lie motionless in darkness . . . It was to feel like a root under the ground, with all leaves and branches gone; all the senses seemed closed; only sound and smell penetrated . . .

Ruth Dallas went on to recover a workable proportion of her sight, and the poems chronicle her returning to—and regaining of—the physical world. At times the visual register is so acute you could easily think of Dallas as an Imagist poet—particularly in the pared-down, Zen-inflected work of the early 1960s. Consider, also, the opening couplet of her classic 'Milking before Dawn' from the 1953 volume *Country Road*:

> In the drifting rain the cows in the yard are as black
> And wet and shiny as rocks in an ebbing tide . . .

How close that comes to Pound's evocation of passengers in the Metro like 'petals on a wet black bough'. There is a complete absence of rhetoric—sound and sense are unhurried, pristine and accurate.

Janet Frame asked in a 1965 *Landfall* essay: 'Are there "pockets" of poetry in the world as there are "pockets" of depression and wealth, areas breeding poetry like a rare plant which the nation eats to satisfy an extra appetite, enjoying the pleasant taste without thinking too much of the dangers of the "insane root".'

The south of the South would seem to be such a pocket—perhaps a holed pocket would be an even better image, with all manner of losses and surprise finds, disappearances and discoveries.

As a motif for the southern imaginative spirit which Ruth Dallas's *Collected Poems* so magnificently embodies, I find myself thinking of an arts festival I attended somewhere south-west of Timaru. After an expedition to some Maori cave paintings in a nearby valley, we returned to the lawn behind the homestead where lunch was being served. Our host was a Southern Man of a different cloth—not your archetypal Speight's Man, but not quite Charles Brasch either. Shortly after lunch, he excused himself, then, only minutes later, came roaring through the air above us in a yellow World War I biplane, barely clearing the treetops.

The image that lingers, however, came a short while later when a huge black front arrived, wheeling in from the direction of the Southern Alps. Rather than flee such a thundering wall of weather, our host continued his acrobatics, looping then flying vertically up the edge of the blackness as though he could somehow land there. Like an insect, he zoomed up and down the face of the oncoming storm.

Maybe that will do as a motif for Ruth Dallas's 'southern' creative enterprise. There's a cranky colonial character to it, certainly, but also a willingness to front up to this land and its conditions. Similarly, Dallas remains committed to an older technology—that of the poem—and is willing to confront Darkness in its various guises. As she writes:

> Some poets like singing in the mountains.
> Others lift up their voices in the tub.
> I like singing in a storm.

The poet, then, is like the bright yellow biplane, flying up the face of the heaviest weather—like a gull riding 'over the bright wave and dark wave', climbing up to its 'high and windy place'. That is what this book and its author manifest: a manner of seeing that transcends sight and a resolute flying in the face of it all.

Noel McKenna, *Woman Writing,* 1999, watercolour, courtesy of Niagara Galleries, Melbourne.

An alphabet without edges

from a Janet Frame notebook 1988–2000

Late one night in 1994, I returned home from a movie to find a message from Janet Frame on my answerphone. The voice on the machine sounded distressed and—despite the fact it was after 11 pm—I felt compelled to immediately return her call.

*

A few years earlier I had shared a pot of tea with Janet Frame at the Sargeson Residence in Auckland. I have a photograph of the two of us clasping mugs of tea which, like satellites, appear to be orbiting the teapot which sits brewing away at the centre of the table. As I recall, Janet confessed that she disliked tea. She pretended to drink it socially. (No matter how many times she sipped, the level in her mug remained the same.) Alone, it was always coffee. She recalled being a keen tea-drinker until, aged five, *something happened*. The taste became 'tainted' and had stayed that way ever since.

*

At the time of the late-night telephone call I was working on a documentary about Frame's writing for television. She had provisionally approved the proposition and I had sent her a letter with a rough outline of the programme which would include some interview footage with her. We had already filmed her reading at the International Festival of the Arts in Wellington the previous month. So we had marvellous footage of her reciting the short poem 'The Wyndham Pond', a story from *The Lagoon* ('My cousins who eat cooked turnip'), an extract from *Daughter Buffalo* (which she said she had chosen to read to prove that she could write proper sentences!), and a second poem to finish.

*

She picked up the telephone almost at once, then ducked away to turn down the volume on her television. She sounded surprisingly relaxed and apologised for being a bit sharp on the answerphone. That was just her answerphone manner, she said. However, she had been taken aback by my letter.

*

For Janet Frame, every day is two days, every week two weeks. April 1988: she is working on *The Carpathians*, writing in the morning, sleeping midday, then another day's writing every evening. Every month is two months. Every year two years. Every lifetime . . .

*

I stressed that our proposed documentary would tell the story of her books, her art, rather than her life *per se*. To this she replied that the books reflected crisis points, times of great difficulty and unrest in her life. So, if we were to follow the books—which leant so heavily on people and places she knew—we would basically be covering the exact same ground as her life.

*

Her early aspiration was to become a poet, and she still admits her desire to write 'a good poem'. It is the highest form of writing, she says tentatively. She does not refer to any of her works as 'novels' or to any of her poems as 'poetry'. They are all explorations. One day I hope to write *a novel*. One day I would like to write *a poem* . . .

*

One morning there is a workman up a ladder outside the Sargeson Residence in Albert Park. The man is drilling into the side of the building, attempting to fasten a series of letters to the cement. The letters are scattered on the ground, facing the sky (like the alphabet that comes raining down in *The Carpathians*) The words appear reluctant to cling to the rough surface and eventually the man abandons the project, collects his letters and comes back a week later with another, more resilient drill.

*

In *The Adaptable Man*, she says she made up a place called 'Tyd' and also a place called 'Eye'. All the place names in the book were to do with water. She had been living in Devon—although she wrote the book upon her return to New Zealand. 'Eye' is the old word for Ireland. She went quite deeply into the Old English and Danish sources of those names. Why? Because, she says, it adds meaning, enriches the books . . . the use of particular things, materials and so on.

*

Seeing both sides of things is the novelist's business, she says on the telephone, and seeing more sides if there are more than that. Things have to be spun or turned slowly around so all the angles become apparent. In this respect, her approach is closer to that of a sculptor than a painter, a constant altering of angles, of movement through time and space and around a given object or situation.

So I imagine all the objects of the world rotating slowly and Janet Frame as the only unmoving thing—unmoving, that is, apart from the flurry of activity which is her writing hand.

*

She is reading Samuel Johnson's *Lives of the English Poets*, and adds, mischievously, she likes watching *Days of Our Lives* on daytime television. Another life, that of Sir Walter Scott, is not too far off. Janet Frame says she prefers to read poetry and non-fiction. She reads 'to find things out'—'a typically New Zealand trait'.

*

When she was staying in Santa Barbara, a university professor and his wife took her to the gardens. As they looked at the flowers, her hosts said how much Erlene (a character in *Scented Gardens for the Blind*) would have liked them. There was a sense that the character was considered by them to be a real person. And there was also a sense that they thought Janet Frame was that person, that she was Erlene.

She says she is interested in gardens but she is no gardener. If you are a writer, she continues, then everything is of interest. You have to empty yourself and then you fill up with the things and characters. And you become them and you imagine what they feel and what ideas they have. But people always seem to assume the ideas are yours . . .

*

We have been talking on the telephone for over an hour. Janet asks me what sort of things we would want to talk to her about in the documentary. I say that if we had been able to film our present telephone conversation that would have been more than enough for the film.

When I visited her at the Sargeson Residence in 1987 I joked about what a good idea it would have been if I had secreted a tape recorder away in my backpack and that afternoon's conversation could remain as a few hundred metres of magnetic tape.

This worries Janet and she inquires, only half joking, if I am in fact recording our present conversation—which, of course, I am not—although, afterwards, I sit for hours replaying it in my mind, writing down fragments.

*

There is a woman in *The Carpathians* who loves making beautiful lists. Frame is herself a maker of such lists, of 'farmers farming / sun sunning / rain raining / gunners gunning / pain paining . . .'

Moving into the Sargeson Residence some months after she has moved out, I found myself looking for traces of her around the rooms. In a small notebook, I found the following inventory—another 'beautiful list'—carefully written by hand:

New Collins Concise English Dictionary
1 electric fan
2 (nondescript) pillowcases
3 face-cloths in varying stages
2 tea-towels
Happy writing from Janet Frame!

Another of Janet Frame's 'beautiful lists' appears on page 2 of *The Carpathians*. The list trickles down the page, beginning with *The Lagoon*, *Owls do Cry*, *Faces in the Water* . . .

*

Sam Hunt once related how he had first encountered Janet Frame, over twenty years earlier. At the time an unknown young writer, he was staying alone at a motor camp near Mokau on the west coast of the North Island. The iron sand and surreal driftwood must have seemed, at that time, a suitable backdrop for the dreams and aspirations of a young poet. Sam Hunt was leaving the cooking room at the motor camp when, as he went out the door, a frizzy-haired woman scuttled in.

A few minutes later, he thought to himself, that must have been Janet Frame. And then he thought nothing more of it.

Nearly two decades later, when Sam Hunt eventually came to meet Janet Frame at a writers' festival, she said oh yes they had met before—she remembered him from the Mokau camping ground way back then.

*

When she mentioned her reluctance to go in front of the camera, I told her how there were now cameras so small they could fit on the tip of a ballpoint pen (and the very same lenses were used these days inside cricket wickets—and cost $2000 to replace every time a fast ball scored a direct hit). This was the wrong thing to say. Janet Frame thought such a device sounded diabolical. It was not the camera itself she was intimidated by—it was the words and images that would be flowing into the camera lens, eventually to re-emerge on television screens around the country.

*

Janet Frame, when confronted with the prospect of being in a book of photographic and written portraits of writers, said it sounded like the kind of thing she could send off to aunts at Christmas and they would say: 'Goodness, I never realised she wrote books!'

*

Another reason not to appear on television

The writer, she says, is at one end of the novel and the reader is at the other and they are totally different. What can she say that will be of use to the reader?

*

Janet has a 'collection' of poems in her drawer. It has been there for some years, unmoving although occasionally thought of. I suggest she dust it off and send it out into the world—but the poems don't seem quite prepared for such a journey. There is so much ice and coldness in them, she says. So much North America. As, I suppose, there is so much Dunedin in *The Pocket Mirror*. So much Levin in *The Carpathians*. And so much of the world in all of them.

*

> Every authentic poem contributes to the labour of poetry. And the task of this unceasing labour is to bring together what life has separated or violence has torn apart . . . Poetry can repair no loss but it defies the space that separates. And it does this by its continual labour of reassembling what has been scattered.
>
> *John Berger*

*

When writing *The Carpathians*, she is aware (as writers must always be) that the novel demands, intermittently, that she go upstairs and have a sleep. Then, in due course, she can come back down and resume writing. Only, with the novel in question, she is worried it is the characters in the book, instead, who are disappearing upstairs from time to time, leaving her downstairs at her work. So the book finds itself carrying on being written without the characters in attendance. And this is not as it should be.

*

May 1994. Janet Frame is still shaken from her encounter with the Inland Revenue Department a couple of years earlier. We discuss word processors—a conversation we began at the Writers and Readers Week—and she mentions the 'TRASH' mechanism, where files or tracts of writing can be dumped, can be removed from her existence. She says she has yet to master that function on her computer. She wants to dump all the dealings she has ever had in her life with the Inland Revenue Department there, but doesn't know how, yet.

*

Karl Stead and Janet Frame are talking about 'dead wood' in novels and how you have to somehow get someone from A to B and that can't always be the most interesting thing. Karl, from time to time, switches the television on to check on the cricket test. It is a warm, late-summer afternoon governed by cicadas, the players moving about their play. Janet Frame says the beauty of poetry is that it doesn't require 'dead wood'. Her comments are punctuated by the thock of a wooden bat and the wooden sound of the ball. Janet Frame is a 'poet'—there is no dead wood to be found anywhere, only curiously living wood. Her work, a gloriously living tree.

*

> A certain provincialism of feeling is invaluable. It is the essence of individuality and is largely made up of that crude enthusiasm without which no great thoughts are thought, no great deeds done.
> *Thomas Hardy*

*

The painter Michael Stevenson was living in Palmerston North at the time and asked me where Janet Frame lived—a question I didn't feel I could answer. He said it was just as well people didn't know because in this bogan town, there were certain protocols for honouring esteemed citizens. One involved, he said, the driving of loud, smoking cars up and down the street of the fêted person at all hours of the day and night. And her letterbox . . . Michael went on . . . if she was really *someone* then her letterbox wouldn't last five minutes. Around here, if you're really someone your letterbox gets stolen. And when you replace it, it gets stolen again . . .

*

Arrangements are made to visit Janet Frame a few days later, this time with a photographer. Nine in the morning is suggested but I am worried this might be too early for her. But no, she would rather we came earlier . . . eight . . . seven o'clock is decided upon. Janet Frame is worried her day will be ruined and points out that the arrival of mail is often enough to unsettle her from a day's work. She would rather the photos were taken, the job done and complete and out of the way.

The photographer, Robert Cross, and I do everything we can not to cheat the novelist of her day. We laugh and drink another pot of tea. And Janet seems to enjoy having her photograph taken—but is unwavering in her refusal to be photographed in front of a window or looking through one.

She disappears into the bedroom for recostuming (a friend has just given her a top and she thinks it prudent that she be photographed wearing it). When the time comes to depart, Robert and I feel proud that we have not wrecked the novelist's day. But, as we leave, Janet says she too will be going out soon. No work to be done here now, her day in ruins.

*

Janet Frame said the documentary sounded like the kind of thing that should be made when she was dead. You know someone is wanting to write a biography but I won't let that happen either, she said. That would be even worse than a documentary. If we were to make the programme she would have no living part in it. She would render herself an absence, noting in a subsequent letter that absence, for her, is the first necessity of presence.

*

I bumped into Janet Frame, Jacquie Baxter and Peter Alcock at the Hocken Library in February 1999. I hadn't spoken with Janet since our two late-night telephone conversations and had always felt guilty that somehow I had made a nuisance of myself—a feeling aggravated by the fact I had, on that occasion, been an emissary for a medium and industry I had little faith in. Maybe she had detected this at the time—the fact that, ultimately, the appearance of a new collection of Frame's poetry (that volume with all the ice in it) would have meant infinitely more to me than a television programme.

Much to my relief, at the Hocken she didn't mention the documentary but went at once into considerable detail about our morning with the photographer at the Sargeson Residence in 1987, and the vexed question of a blouse a friend had given her.

*

Mary-Jane Duffy, a friend who lives on the Kapiti Coast, announced yesterday that Janet Frame had been sighted on the weekend, bobbing in the waves off Paekakariki, between the rocky foreshore and Kapiti Island. Floating there like a beacon or marker.

Maybe that image sums up Janet Frame: a floating, swimming figure, looking back at a mainland where—as she noted in *A State of Siege*—'few eyes looked further than their own front lawn and their motor mower, and those who gazed out to sea kept to the three-mile-limit . . . and did not recognise the signs of the new migration, did not observe the waves crowded with fleets of hungry minds'.

Or maybe Janet Frame is, herself, looking out to sea. Either way, she figures as both a visionary and, increasingly, an essential part of the 'view', of life as it is being lived in this country, now.

Imagine the imagination
Margaret Mahy's Dissolving Ghost

Some years back, photographer Robert Cross and I corralled together twenty-one contemporary New Zealand writers for a book aimed at interested or perplexed grown-ups and bright teenagers. First up in *Moments of Invention*, which appeared in 1988, was Margaret Mahy; the book concluded with Janet Frame. At the time I imagined these two figures as being like bookends—pillars of both the craft and the imagination; both of them fitting and substantial enough presences to hold in place the nineteen writers who filled the space between them.

Robert and I travelled around the country. We visited Frame at the Sargeson Residence in Auckland, then, some months later, Mahy at her Church Bay home. As well as being comparably substantial artists, these two bipolar (in our book plan) figures were remarkably different as writers yet also, as became increasingly apparent, interestingly similar.

If Mahy was the writer of light, of buoyancy and liberation, Frame struck a darker, more restrained note. If Mahy wrote for the child in all of us, then Frame wrote for the adult that exists inside every child. Or so it might appear at first, but—of course—once you dug a little deeper, vistas of redemptive space opened up in Frame. And something darker and more foreboding emerged in the most clearly, brightly voiced of Mahy's tales. In both of them a constant interplay of gravity and levity, light and shade, brilliance and something which is at times heartbreakingly ordinary. This paradoxical quality, I suspect, is at the heart of creative genius.

If Frame tends to present life as a juggernaut we must handle with stealth in order to survive, Mahy sees the world more as a great machine that we can and should tamper with. And while the results might occasionally be disastrous for the individual, such an approach contains the possibility of success and elation. For Frame, language is healing; for Mahy it is more a preventative medicine or, more exactly, a vitamin supplement ensuring, at least, the possibility of health.

While Frame is commonly thought of as a doyen of the inner life,

Margaret Mahy is the public speaker, a performer in person as well as on the page. During the 1980s Mahy was often photographed—and existed in the public imagination—wearing a multicoloured wig which she would don, to the delight of all assembled, at readings in libraries and elsewhere (you could almost think of this get-up as a fluorescent revision of the Frame hairdo). This 'persona' drew attention to some of the qualities you find in Mahy's writing: the sense of adventure and risk, and the need for unabashed brilliance up front, a dash of imaginative magic to jump-start commonplace reality.

My favourite photograph of Mahy, however, runs counter to this public version. It was taken during Robert's and my afternoon at Church Bay, and has the writer standing in her garden. It is a conventional double portrait, sort of: Mahy is on the left while, to the right, there is a tree in which a cat is perched. Her hand is scratching the preferred zone behind the feline's ear. It is, at once, a photograph of two 'human' presences and also of two arboreal forms. Just as the cat and tree have a figural presence, Mahy's body becomes the tree trunk—a branch extends diagonally from her side. Behind and above the two figures, blossoms explode in the brilliant black and white of Robert's photograph.

Photograph of Margaret Mahy at Church Bay, Robert Cross, 1987.

And so we arrive at *A Dissolving Ghost* (Victoria University Press, 2000), a book in which Mahy's intelligence explodes in the brilliant black and white of her prose. It's a book full of wisdom, as just about any paragraph taken at random would prove:

> We build ourselves as we grow. Our physical structure is the basis around which we extend a mental and spiritual structure, of which imagination is a vital part. Structure is the key word here, for suppose that imagination, so far from being the shapeless, vague and dreamy cloud we often feel it to be, has a potentially beautiful, intricate and possibly unknowable structure of its own.

While Mahy goes on to imagine the imagination as a crystal, I also find myself thinking of it as a woman-tree, its arm-branch extending out to stroke a cat-tree, against a backdrop of chaotic blooms. *A Dissolving Ghost* hints at art's paradoxical nature as something inherently structural yet also, by necessity, shapeless and free-form.

Mahy's tone and manner in the book are, generally, speculative. Most of these pieces began as public lectures so they have the quality of—to use the author's description—'a set of opinions and speculations launched from lip to ear through the unreliable air . . . I always think of them as sets of possibilities and guesses which other people can test and then accept or reject according to their own knowledge and convictions.'

Needless to say, Margaret Mahy is frequently, brilliantly funny and has an ever-vigilant eye and ear for the right word or phrase which, just once in a while, can open up elusive areas of experience like a magic key. She can be magnificently incisive and impassioned at the same time. In 'Touchstones' she parallels the writing of Lewis Carroll and physics, then goes on to explore the imagination as 'a synthesising agent'. She tackles with humility and aplomb such big themes as faith, loss, memory and truth. ('Pursuing truth in literature,' she writes, instructively, 'is like pursuing a chimera, a dissolving ghost . . .') Unfailingly, she avoids the essayist's trap of staring admiringly into their own mirror and the pitfall essay-writing novelists often fall into of sounding like they are grooming themselves for their imminent Booker Prize acceptance speech.

Mahy is certainly scholarly in the thoroughness of her attentions, but mercifully she doesn't conform to Anne Carson's definition of a scholar as 'someone who takes a position . . . who knows how to limit himself to the matter at hand'. Mahy is a thinker of the perambulatory, discursive kind. With the intelligence (as well as the personable nature and poise) of a cat in a tree, she leaps from branch to branch.

My only reservation is that I wanted the book to be bigger. As it is, it certainly doesn't feel like it has exhausted or defined the outer boundaries of Mahy's creative territory—in fact the book sticks pretty much to Mainstream Mahy: her unfailingly wise utterances about story, character, language and the imaginative life. The points she makes are crucial—but now that she has made them, she should be encouraged to range more freely in whatever direction she feels inclined.

At the conclusion of *A Dissolving Ghost*, I found myself making a list of essay topics I would like Mahy to get on with: pirates, the regional landscape, the body in children's literature, the use of trees, the art of librarianship, snow, Christchurch, the South Island, the mass media.

In fact, all of the above subjects do surface in the assembled essays. But maybe if the audience wasn't sitting so expectantly in front of her—as they were on the occasion of so many of the pieces in this book—then we would see Mahy stretching out more.

'We build ourselves as we grow': Margaret Mahy as a writer is still, happily, in a state of construction, building and growing a body of work of paramount importance to both children and adults. She is one of a line of New Zealand genuises that also includes Janet Frame, Rita Angus, Katherine Mansfield and Frances Hodgkins. She is a *makar*, in the truest sense. A person of vision. A gem.

A journey around Kendrick Smithyman's Atua Wera

1 State of the art

The wheel in front of me moves of its own accord as we steer a course away from the Dargaville foreshore. I am strapped inside one hull of a twin-hulled speedboat. Each hull bears a six-cylinder, two-hundred-and-something horsepower outboard motor. The brown waters of the Northern Wairoa River are drawn noisily up into the cooling systems of these engines, then discharged behind us, the trickle becoming a white veil of spray as we increase speed. (I have to strain my neck to observe this as my full-face helmet restricts peripheral vision.) The driver in the other hull spins his steering wheel—which is identical to the wheel in front of me—then presses the accelerator.

The vessel (which the driver told me earlier was a 'state of the art' racer) labours for a moment as it lifts up out of the water, the cavity between the two hulls becoming a tunnel of air on which we accelerate, turning southwards down the river.

Within minutes, a small town is passing to the right of us, with its school, a church or two, the white walls and gleaming roofs of a few streets' houses. At this moment, we are travelling at just under one hundred miles per hour and I am staring sideways past the profile of the other helmeted head, transfixed by the motionless township of Te Kopuru, where the poet Kendrick Smithyman was born in 1922 and where, during the Depression, he was brought up in a rest home run by his mother.

2 A view of the Northern Wairoa from Wellington

From my present vantage point—a winter afternoon in Wellington with volumes of Smithyman's poems arrayed around me on the floor—the roar of the two outboard motors is stirring up the Northern Wairoa River and the landscape which runs like two parallel rails on either side of the expanse of brown water. The noise is unsettling the town, interrupting the quiet upbringing of the poet . . .

Directly behind us, in the distance now, the wake of our boat has just touched both sides of the river. The surface of the Northern Wairoa, observed from a vessel travelling at this speed, is made of velvet: a buzzing, vibrating material, a warm glow emanating from its depths. Or it might be a light table on which transparent images are shone up into our eyes.

3 *A true story*

There was a story Kendrick Smithyman related on a number of occasions concerning his mother's retirement home in Te Kopuru. Two of the elderly residents had fought on opposing sides during the American Civil War and, whenever they passed in the corridor, each would attempt to strike the other with his walking stick.

4 *Arrival and departure*

I have two means at my disposal with which to begin thinking about the poetry of Kendrick Smithyman. The first is a powerboat slicing in half the Northern Wairoa River. The second we will come to.

Smithyman's last, greatest book was published by Auckland University Press early in 1997—two years after the death of its author. *Atua Wera* is a momentous, extraordinary book-length poem, rich in characters, details and the faintly modulated voices of history as filtered through the very particular sensibility of the poet.

Atua Wera (the fiery god) is the story of Papahurihia, a nineteenth-century Maori leader and tohunga, who lived in the Hokianga area, about seventy miles north of Smithyman's birthplace.

Smithyman knows the territory of the poem. More than that, he is *of* it. Since he was a child, he has felt the 'cold breeze over the gumfields / where trees bled, died, fell, became swamp', and the perambulations of colonial history. Beneath the swarm of historical details, we discern an obsessive attachment to, and curiosity about, the small twists and turns in the natural history and human affairs of the North:

> Makoare Taonui went to war,
> went with him his brother Te Huru
> who was killed, went with him his son
> Daniel and his son Abraham.
> "I have a maul and wedge," said
> Macquarrie, "that will split Heke"
> but his own were split first,
> Te Huru, then Abraham. They never took
> the bullet out of him . . .

Kendrick Smithyman *knows* the patterns small vessels leave behind them in the shallow water of a harbour, the puzzling movements of estuary tides; theirs is an enigmatic music or language not unlike the music/language of his poems. The poet's business is to deploy words so as to convey the mental, as well as natural, patterning of such phenomena; to invent a language that carries these associations in its very fabric.

Like the waters of the Kaipara or Hokianga harbours, Smithyman's poems have always been sites for all manner of indirection, anachronism, convolution and what at times appears to be awkwardness. In the end, however, they offer a coherent if perplexing experience, one true to both the order and the chaos of the natural world and its processes.

5 *Ending with clarity*

For the most part, the verse in *Atua Wera* is clearer and crisper than you might expect of Smithyman—the epic scale of the poem means the poet isn't trying to achieve his usual fanatical compression and constant turning around of phrases and meanings to realign or reconfigure them. (He still makes such manoeuvres but the relaxed, unfolding manner of the story being related, the characters being sketched in and the demands of *their* voices keep the poem from becoming too embroiled.)

While phrases from source materials—historical documents, oral histories, the Bible and so on—enter the poem relatively untouched, such pre-existent materials are positioned within the bulk of the poem to achieve a carefully manipulated linguistic surface. The 261-page poem is aligned with recent historical 'documentary' poems by Evan

S. Connell, Ernesto Cardenal and Laurie Duggan, although the closest poetic work I have read to *Atua Wera* is Thomas Merton's 1968 sequence *The Geography of Lograire*, which similarly blends ethnographic and historical sources to enter into the life of various ethnic communities, most pertinently a tribe from Papua New Guinea. Like Merton, Smithyman is able to inhabit the spaces of superstition, measuring the distance between cultures and tracing the links and disjunctions.

Also, like Merton's poem, *Atua Wera* tracks the progress of an assured voice entering unstable territory and attempting to inscribe some kind of order on that state of chaos (or, more correctly, that yet to be understood order). Both books arrive at similar conclusions: that the fabrications of history (which are supposedly fixed and factual) and religion/superstition (supposedly fluid and imagined) are of the same order.[1]

6 *A structure to fall apart in*

There's a paradoxical sense in Smithyman that the more structured the writing, the less clear the meaning. In *Atua Wera* he allows the structures to relax, to unwind, to flow and blend—hence, a greater clarity when compared with the rest of his oeuvre. The poetry is relaxed enough to become at times prosaic, but it also maintains a forward momentum Smithyman's short poems often lack (or, more correctly I suspect, don't want). Perhaps this stems from the origins of the poem in oral records and transcriptions—it is less *written*.[2]

This book casts a long illuminating shadow back over all of Kendrick Smithyman's work. Time will tell, but I suspect this complex, majestic poem will be a key to unlocking the historical, literary and ethnographic materials Smithyman's other poems carry within their apparently inscrutable bulk. Leaving behind a huge piece of work like *Atua Wera* will certainly come to be seen as a key event in the life of this poet. Smithyman knew exactly what he was doing.

7 *Northern Wairoa vista*

When I moved to Dargaville in late 1978, aged seventeen, I was aware that at least two New Zealand writers had been associated with that township nestled alongside the Northern Wairoa River. The first, Jane

Mander, had—or so I was told—been a reporter on the *Northland Times*, the newspaper on which I was about to become employed. The second was Kendrick Smithyman, whose birth in Te Kopuru was sufficient impetus to set me reading his poetry. Not surprisingly, I was soon experiencing difficulties with the verse which even my youthful enthusiasm couldn't alleviate. I was flummoxed by the dense surface of the poetry, its wide, often arcane sphere of reference, its unusual (to my ear) musicality, the profound (it would seem) murkiness of its thought and the unpredictable directions in which that thought was directed.

My experience of first reading Smithyman is indistinguishable from my experience of living in Dargaville and, as part of my reporting job, travelling to Te Kopuru, Glink's Gully and environs. It was a region that (in keeping with Smithyman's poetry) didn't offer up its meanings, pleasures or beauties all that readily.

Probably the closest poet to Smithyman I was aware of at the time was Dylan Thomas—although the Welsh poet's soaring intonation and mystical attachment to nature made Smithyman seem, by comparison, fettered and earthbound, or else lost somewhere in the library. While Smithyman offered washes of imagery mediated through an obsessive eye and an alluring intelligence, his poetic voice—as I then experienced it—was the crusty intonation of a man struggling with very difficult materials and insistent that we share in that struggle.

I spent over a year living in the vicinity of the Northern Wairoa River—known variously as the Upside-Down River or the Gravy River, on account of its slow-moving, heavily silted bulk—during which time I made little progress with Smithyman's verse. By 1980 I had decided to transplant back to the city and study art history and English at Auckland University, where, coincidentally, Kendrick Smithyman was a lecturer in the English Department.

8 Point of origin

Soon after leaving Dargaville I saw Francis Ford Coppola's film *Apocalypse Now*. That now-famous Conradesque gunboat journey up a Vietnamese river took me back to the experience of speeding down the Northern Wairoa River with which I began these reflections. If there is anything I hunt out in Kendrick Smithyman's poetry, it is those strange, dislocating instances when Northland touches the rest of the world, when the muddy Northern Wairoa River flows off across other territories, just as, in James Joyce's imagination, the River Liffey flowed beyond the borders of Ireland and through other countries.

It's not that Smithyman's poetry keeps returning to the 'point of origin'—to the Te Kopuru rest home and environs—rather that the location has somehow moulded or informed the writing.

It is a point from which the poet operates, is orientated.

His poetry carries within it the isolation of the Northern Wairoa district and the area's curious mingling of cultural elements—Maori, Pakeha, Dalmatian and other. Without detracting from the singularity of his approach, Smithyman has a kindred spirit in the abstract artist Milan Mrkusich (born 1926), who also hails from the Dargaville district and laid out a similarly personal set of creative objectives then devoted his life to their realisation. Like Smithyman, Mrkusich has been accused of being deliberately arcane and oblique. He too has been involved in a struggle to find or construct new kinds of sense, to evolve a language alert to the nuances and buried meanings of life in this country this century.[3]

9 *A short history / epistemology / cosmology*

> Papahurihia had taught that the missionaries would be burned in the fire of Satan, and his followers would enter an afterlife in a land of happiness. The Catholic missionary Louis Catherin Servant said that this would be a land in which there was neither cold, nor hunger or thirst: 'you enjoy unending light. Everything is found in plenty, flour, sugar, guns, ships; there too murder and sensual pleasure reign'. The afterlife became a world of earthly delights, much better than the Protestant heaven, which Papahurihia had described as little better than hell, because its inhabitants had 'nothing but books to eat'.
> (Judith Binney, in *The Dictionary of New Zealand Biography, Volume One*)

Imagine the entire contents of the Oxford dictionary, not to mention the King James Bible, tipped onto a Northland beach early in the nineteenth century and, from there, swiftly covering the province with a new layer of meanings and significances, disrupting, mutating and merging with the systems of belief and sign that already covered the landscape.

And what else does the language do when it arrives here? It immediately starts recording—in journals, sermons, letters, legal documents and newspapers. *Atua Wera* is a re-enactment—from both Maori and Pakeha perspectives—of this spread of written and spoken language, with its attendant matrix of knowledge and belief. The poem's widely flung verbal net captures details from daily life, material and verbal exchanges, military campaigns and violent altercations as well as moments of prayer, prophecy and judgement.

Besides the structures of belief and knowledge, the materials and objects of daily life at that time were also changing. Now there were books, documents and the 'flour, sugar, guns, ships' the Catholic missionary observed. As with the cargo cults of Melanesia, these objects became the new talismans. They complicated and changed the existing cosmology. The written (or painted) word attained considerable status, particularly in its capacity to record names and genealogies. Words were soon appearing on the hallowed walls of meeting houses, and the ability to read and write were, it follows, greatly valued.[4]

Smithyman's voluminous book contains much evidence of this spread of language. This is recounted through the voice of the geographer, the Old Testament preacher, the historian, the believer, the sceptic and, importantly, the poet in the late twentieth century. The poem is attuned to the movements in belief and knowledge—the 'shifting shapes'—and also the confusion that arose in a region that for a time juggled such varying and often conflicting belief systems. *Atua Wera* witnesses the already complex Maori culture becoming even more complex.

In imposing a purely poetic order on its materials, the poem skirts around the structures and demands of 'historical' writing, to include within its fabric all the inconclusiveness, half-finished arguments, enigmas and contradictions which history is uncomfortable dealing with. Smithyman recovers many telling fragments:

> 'As it was, matters were well managed,
> several were slightly wounded, and all were
> arrested, but none were killed
> and, after all, a little blood letting and hard labour
> does a Maori no harm.'
>
> *Colonel Gudgeon,* 1905

Besides such 'first-hand' accounts, there are fragments of children's songs, inventories of place names and trees, roll-calls of ancestors, and oracular utterances. Out of these disparate forms and their various voices, the poem's truth emerges:

> TRADITION
>
> 'He wanted to settle things—you know,
> like having things peaceful.
> He and Aperahama went down south to talk
> to Te Kooti. They took him an important gift.'
>
> What the gift was is not known/remembered.
> Only, it was precious, prestigious.
>
> This is fact. Fact credits believing.
> Believing authenticates fact.

In an age intent on examining the past to understand the present, *Atua Wera* establishes in both its form and its content the impenetrability and sheer mystery of much human history. While New Zealand's past contains much injustice and exploitation, the country was also shaped by accidents, superstition, erratic behaviour and both good and bad luck. In acknowledging these variables, and by delving into the mythical and fantastic as well as the 'real', *Atua Wera* could well be described as a 'magic realist' epic.

10 The trip down the Northern Wairoa continued

It was near the end of the Pouto Peninsula that one of the propellers of the speedboat on which I was travelling hit something. Fortunately, we had slowed considerably at the time. The driver later told me it was probably a sheep carcass, floating invisibly just beneath the surface of the river.

My assignment as a journalist was to write about how it felt to travel at nearly one hundred miles per hour up and down the brown river. Instead I found myself writing about the slow, choppy journey back up the Northern Wairoa, nursing one busted motor.

11 A great bag of them

Back at Te Kopuru, some movement in the town can now be discerned. A truck drives up the middle of one road, stopping adjacent to each letterbox; someone is polishing something; a bicycle skids across a lawn . . . Twenty minutes later we reach the southern end of Dargaville with its two steaming takeaway bars and ancient dairy factory. Waves lap against the rusted car bodies that form a breakwater on the river's edge. Somewhere a game of netball is in progress; a policeman delivers a bootful of confiscated toheroa to the town hospital, where the best seafood chowder in the world is served (but only to patients). Out of the very corner of my eye, a Maori man has driven a mile or two out of his way to deposit a hitch-hiker at his doorstep, then he offers him a sack of unusual-shaped kumara from the back of his utility.

The driver says that these most beautiful-tasting vegetables, on account of their unconventional form, are unsaleable. The young man, a journalist, is speechless with gratitude.

'They are yours,' the Maori man says, lumping a great bag of them onto the porch.

12 Root crop

The huge sack of kumara the farmer from Ruawai gave me stands, or more correctly leans, against the wall in the kitchen where, particularly in the evenings, it has the presence of a human being. Often in the late afternoons the entire house smells of the most excellent Ruawai soil. When I finally leave Dargaville, the sack of misshapen vegetables is still a quarter full.

That sack of kumara is a useful metaphor for Smithyman's poetry: a collection of unorthodox, dark, elusive shapes that probably won't ever be swallowed up or embraced by the marketplace. Yet these unorthodox, irregular poetic forms and constructions are, as *Atua Wera* attests, extremely well attuned to the oblique, enigmatic forms of human history.

In Smithyman's poetry, luminous details are extracted from the general darkness, but even in the broad light of day these details remain mysterious and elusive. As does the poet himself. Smithyman, like

Papahurihia, is 'a shifting shape in a fog. / He was, is, metaphor. And mystery.'

In *Atua Wera*, the poet offers us a dark, mysterious bag of kumara, an anthology of personages and events dug from difficult ground. These shapes and sounds are a gift, then. As the Maori farmer said to the young writer, 'They are yours.'

13 A notable Australian surrealist

A few years after my Dargaville adventure I was living in Sydney and acquainting myself with the journal *Angry Penguins*, which was published out of Melbourne during and after World War II. The magazine seemed to be the only convincing manifestation of Surrealism in the antipodes I had come across, apart from the work of Len Lye. (*Angry Penguins* became famous in 1944 for publishing the 'Ern Malley' poems, which precipitated a major international literary scandal.) It was in a 1945 issue of *Angry Penguins* that I came across three poems by Kendrick Smithyman.[5] What struck me reading these poems was that the voice which had eluded me a few years earlier now made at least some sense in the context of *Angry Penguins*. Lines of Smithyman's like, 'And the singular gull climbed / across channels drifting to lost islands . . .' sat comfortably in the context of a journal that had published the Ern Malley poems, with their memorably over-the-top imagery: '. . . I am still / The black swan of trespass on alien waters' and 'the swung torch scatters seeds / In the umbelliferous dark'.

Smithyman, as far as I was concerned, had become rather quickly a Notable Australian Surrealist—which made me think about the radical, highly strung metropolitan reality of the Australian literary avant-garde and the dour isolation of the west coast of Northland. It was out of these two diametrically opposed realities I began to discern in Smithyman a surprisingly potent mixture of internationalist and intensely regionalist concerns and sensibilities. His Northland experience was, I suspect, a defining one for him and one that, funnily enough, found a context out there in the wide world beyond New Zealand.

14 Point of contact

The point at which the propeller of the million-dollar speedboat hits the sheep carcass is the point which ignites the Smithyman poem—where the imported, sophisticated apparatus of Western culture stirs up the gravy-brown waters of the local, bumps into the particular.

The great works of art created in New Zealand this century embody to some extent this collision between the imported and the indigenous. (Often the regional element seems to have the last word and, as the speedboat of international modernism limps back to the boat ramp, the river flows, eddies and swirls onwards, exactly as usual.)

15 Content of a river

If the apparent murkiness and impenetrability of Smithyman's diction, ideas and allusions have built barriers between some readers and the meanings or experiences at the core of the poetry, I suspect the poet would counter by asserting that all experience is mediated—by language, history and memory. To look for simple answers in the poetry is as unrealistic as looking for them in past and present experience.

Like the Northern Wairoa River, the writing is necessarily murky and weighted down with details from the poet's life and the uncoverings of his inspired and far-ranging researches. (Importantly, Smithyman's oeuvre asserts that literature, music and history are as intrinsic to life as the supposedly less constructed experiences of the individual—they are not simply intermediaries or secondary sources.)

In *Atua Wera* the words are ruminative and at times even prayerful, respectful of the past and of that immense wealth that is cultural inheritance. In this, his last poem, Smithyman sifts through the stuff of history both intellectually and emotionally, creating a very individual map which, as well as locating some remarkable characters, also outlines the concerns that dominated his career as a poet: the primacy of language in all human thought and endeavour, the significance of geography, culture and knowledge, and the possibility of (and struggle towards) a state of equilibrium in human affairs.

At the book's conclusion, the last line of the 296th poem, what we are left with isn't so much silence as a sense that the voices of the preceding pages will continue talking. The arguments, oracular utterances, the tender and difficult voices will continue to play on this Northland landscape, this expanse of New Zealand literature, for all time.

16 The opposite of television

It would be hard to imagine anything more at odds with the mass market entertainment business than Kendrick Smithyman's poetry. Like the English critic Herbert Read, Smithyman must have abhorred the 'collectivist, cybernetic' mass culture which, to this day, seems intent on reducing artists to entertainers and art itself to simple-minded escapism. Read could see the position of the artist at risk as far back as the 1960s, when he wrote:

> It is not a cheerful prospect for the arts, though there will be more and more artists in the sense of the word used by the entertainment industry. It will be a gay world. There will be lights everywhere except in the mind of man and the fall of the last civilization will not be heard above the incessant din.

When *Auto/Biographies*, Smithyman's penultimate book, was shortlisted for the New Zealand Book Awards in 1993, I was working on a television 'arts' programme entitled *The Edge*. The day the collection arrived in the office, a member of the production team happened to ask me which New Zealand writers might make good, accessible fodder for our television audience. She picked up Smithyman's book and asked me what it was like.

The only reply I could think of was: *the opposite of television*.

17 A world or two

Between the disparate poles of mid-century, bohemian Melbourne, with its *Angry Penguins,* and the Northern Wairoa district with its floating sheep carcasses, I locate the figure of Kendrick Smithyman. The experience we are offered in *Atua Wera*—and in much of Smithyman's output elsewhere—is that of losing oneself amidst the co-ordinates of an exceptionally broad map and of being immersed in a complex choreography involving numerous characters moving into and out of a land- or city-scape. As Peter Simpson has observed:

'Through his exploration of place and locality in particular, Smithyman has become a kind of archaeologist of consciousness at local, national and global levels.' What we are given is a poetry with the breadth and generosity to embrace a number of times, a number of places, a number of worlds.

While Smithyman's poems are certainly capable of transcending the intense privacy in which they were fashioned, the writing never completely leaves that privacy behind. For all their richly experienced and evoked references to the natural world, they remain very much the property of the mind and ear of the poet. Accordingly, they offer much insight into Smithyman's personality. One section of *Atua Wera* could conveniently be read as a self-portrait of the poet:

MANOAO

Manoao is pakeha Barrier pine.
You don't see it except
north of Auckland.
Most pakeha wouldn't know
if they saw it,
not a common tree.
Kin are well known,
rimu much talked about.
Not manoao.
    There's always
got to be one, different,
a bit of a loner.
Even in company.

In both their vividness and obliqueness, the poems detail the inner life of an individual thinking and feeling his way through life, right up until the time of his death:

Darkness along crests of the ranges
not end of day darkening, a something which spread up
out of the sea all over early afternoon.
Lightnings played from ridge to ridge,
then thunder, more thunder.
Everyone knew, somebody important was going to die.

18 The business

Isn't this the purpose of real poetry: to perplex and bother whatever individual consciousness it encounters out there in the cybernetic, collectivist mass? To revive old, unresolved discussions and arguments? To present personal and social histories in their infinite complexity and inconclusiveness? To celebrate how the mind and the world work? By whatever means, and no matter how circumspectly, to lift the reader/listener out of the present moment and dislodge or at least challenge their presuppositions? Smithyman made no concessions when it came to the business of being a poet: these were the questions he asked, and then he would take to task the questions themselves and his own capacity to ask them.

19 Kendrick returns to the northern beaches

After all the geographical and cultural globetrotting of the earlier poetry, *Atua Wera* represents a homecoming of sorts, a slow return. It is also a resting-place, where the persona of the poet allows itself to fade into the general detail, where his characteristic voice blends with all the voices the poem and its sources have to offer. Smithyman explores the beliefs and actions of Papahurihia with the same attentiveness and exhaustiveness he usually devoted to his own. It's not hard to sense a feeling of kinship between the two polymaths: Smithyman's and Papahurihia's influences and purposes are each about as wide-ranging and mysterious as the other's. They are both interpreters of dreams and perceptions. Both are profoundly attached to the Far North. As with the Maori prophet, the meaning of Smithyman's life's work is bound to both reward and perturb people for many years to come.

20 Back to the river

While the murky waters of the Northern Wairoa might reflect both the opaque surface and the depths of Kendrick Smithyman's poetry—the slow-moving, ponderous bulk of it as well as the wealth contained there—at the same time, and perhaps even because of this murkiness, when the time of day is right, these waters are capable of reflecting the most majestic scene. As if the muddy river has become one with the indescribably beautiful sky.

Notes

1 Coincidentally, *The Geography of Lograire* and *Atua Wera* were both the last literary excursions of their respective authors, and both were published posthumously.

2 Like Allen Curnow in his Hokianga-based sequence, 'An Abominable Temper', Smithyman is able to introduce a twentieth-century sensibility into a poem that is immersed in the nineteenth century without disrupting its fabric of thoughts and words.

3 Another Northlander with similar objectives, Ralph Hotere (born at Mitimiti, 1931), might well enter the conversation at this point, as could photographer Peter Peryer (born 1941), who spent his childhood in the Far North, living for a time at Ohaeawai, the site of a major defeat for the British army during the Northland War and a location cited in Smithyman's long poem.

4 See Roger Neich's *Painted Histories: Early Maori Figurative Painting* (Auckland University Press, 1993). Jonathan Mané-Wheoki pointed out in a talk at the City Gallery, Wellington (1997) that levels of literacy among Maori in the nineteenth century may well have been higher than those among the settler population.

5 The same issue also included poems by Louis Johnson and short stories by Frank Sargeson and Greville Texidor.

The Northern Wairoa River from near Te Kopuru, with Tokatoka in the distance, photograph by the author shortly after his arrival in the district, December 1978.

High cultural life
Eric McCormick's An Absurd Ambition

I recall meeting up with art historian Eric McCormick at an exhibition opening at RKS Art, Auckland, in the late 1980s. I was accompanied by a friend of mine, a doctor recently returned from overseas, who was wearing a French sailor's hat. Eric had met my friend before but on this occasion he made a point of saying that, of the two of us, my friend (who must have resembled a character from a Jean Genet novel) was definitely *the poet*, not I. You only needed to look at the two of us he said, there was no question.

I mention this encounter because I think Eric McCormick's conception of creativity and his conception of sexuality—in his case, homosexuality—were inextricably interwoven. And while the title of his book, *An Absurd Ambition* (Auckland University Press, 1996), refers to a youthful yearning to be a writer, it also hints at a notion of idealistic, romantic love that McCormick was captive to.

Early in the book we witness a melding of sexual and intellectual energies in a passage concerning a brief visit to Taihape (McCormick's birthplace) by the dashing young English poet Rupert Brooke, just prior to the First World War. McCormick paints a vivid and highly ironic portrait of himself as a young man feverishly trying to ascertain whether in fact Brooke had slept a few nights in the town while he—McCormick—was a child living there. The very possibility of having been in such proximity to this 'young Apollo' he describes as 'electric'.

The author's sexuality is related with both restraint and frankness—he is neither hysterical nor evasive (that is, unless you take his characteristic understatement as a form of evasion). He relates with detachment and ironic self-regard how, while studying at Cambridge in the late 1920s, 'One hot afternoon a fellow boarder, a young English student, invited me to wrestle on his bed, which I did; but he was so weak and flabby that I overcame him in a few seconds, and went on with my reading . . . The girdle of chastity may on occasion have been dented but it was still unbreached . . .'

Editor Dennis McEldowney, who knitted the volume together from various published and unpublished sources, states in his introduction that 'on one point Eric was adamant from the beginning of our collaboration: his homosexuality, which he regarded as an integral part of his personality, must not be concealed . . .' The book achieves an exemplary balance, neither privileging McCormick's homosexuality above other identity-defining influences nor in any way downplaying it. A good many of McCormick's love affairs, McEldowney suggests in his introduction, amounted to nothing more than glances across a crowded room—heightened encounters not unlike the way McCormick would engage with, say, a Frances Hodgkins watercolour. An experience of profound yet detached communion.

Certainly the book captures McCormick's evolving sensibility and his discerning eye. He observes/recalls with sparkling clarity his small-town childhood and education at Wellington College. He then looks back at the changing fashions for visual arts among 'the small circle of intellectuals on whose outermost perimeter I now began to move', and notes how etchings were replaced at a certain time by anything oriental: 'Respectable virgins ransacked the Chinese shops of Wellington's red-light district for rice bowls and fish plates of approved design . . . Another spin of the whirligig, and lo! orientalism was relegated to second place or wholly discarded in favour of the colour reproduction. First Botticelli . . .'

If there was an aimlessness to the artistic inclinations of this group of wannabe aesthetes that indicated the state of New Zealand 'High Culture' generally, it would be Eric McCormick and a few others who would argue the case for, and eventually mould, something more coherent and longer lasting—a notion of art as an intrinsic part of the life of the country instead of a fashionable recent arrival at the import emporium.

An Absurd Ambition is rich in vignettes and surprising details from McCormick's daily life. There's even an account of an outing, while the author was still at school, to Eastbourne with the young Robin Hyde (Iris Wilkinson): '. . . on the return to Wellington, Iris insisted on smoking a cigarette, a gesture of defiance which, she proudly related, was reported by a prefect and nearly led to her expulsion . . .' McCormick himself was altogether a meeker being and, as McEldowney has observed, 'didn't so much flout accepted behaviour as show himself indifferent to it'.

By the time this account concludes, having taken us up to the mid-1950s, McCormick has emerged as a capable historian of his own inner life as well as a cultural historian, refusing to gloss over or ignore all the manifest wrong-headedness and naïvety you would expect of a young man growing up in the first half of this century (it beggars belief that, on release of this book, a *New Zealand Listener* reviewer could be wounded by a few daft, puerile remarks).

If the young McCormick feared anything it was the spectre of mediocrity: 'I see a long life in front of me, a life of mediocrity, of teaching year in and year out, losing ambition and becoming gradually more self-centred, more friendless, desiring friends, yet repelling offers of friendship.' That certainly was not how things turned out the 1993 publication of a book of essays honouring McCormick's achievement, *Writing a New Country*—edited by James Ross, Linda Gill and Stuart McRae—attested to the friendship and high regard McCormick achieved and maintained until the time of his death in 1995.

By writing important cultural history, especially in a country like New Zealand where such commentary wasn't exactly thick on the ground, a writer as good as McCormick was destined to become a part of that history himself. And so he did. We are immensely fortunate to have this book, and we were even more fortunate to have had Eric McCormick himself.

Widening horizons and worlds regained

a conversation with Dennis McEldowney

Gregory O'Brien: One of the first times we met, Dennis—in early 1984—I remember having a cup of tea with you and Elizabeth Smither in the old Auckland University Press office in Grafton Road, then the three of us crossed the road to use the photocopier in the German Department. I recall clearly feeling as though the three of us belonged to a particular kind of tribe—not the 'literary' tribe but one defined by a certain geographical point of origin. I'm sure we crossed the street in style—like the crooks in *Reservoir Dogs* or those New Zealand First MPs of three years ago. We had just been talking about our Taranaki connections—mine through my mother's family at Te Namu . . . Elizabeth's are pretty obvious. What was your connection with Taranaki?

Dennis McEldowney: Now you're asking. My mother was born at Warea, where her father was sole-charge teacher. My father had cousins farming at Puniho. He was staying with them when he met my mother in the Pungarehu post office, close to Parihaka. My grandfather later bought a farm in Te Namu Road—your uncle owns it now, I believe. We spent our summer holidays there. That lumpy landscape, dotted with mounds of volcanic shingle like tumuli, with boxthorn hedges, macrocarpas, muddy cowyard, garden overgrown with rampant nasturtiums, was my childhood paradise. Not lost—I can recall it at will—but quite different from the windswept, spray-scoured landscape I saw with adult eyes.

G: I guess I've spent quite a bit of the last couple of years rediscovering Taranaki while working on the 'Parihaka' exhibition and book—which

---

This 'conversation' was conducted via email during the new year period, 2000–2001.

has just gone off to the printers. Funnily, I was up at Parihaka recently, having afternoon tea with the Hohaia family (who, incidentally, I feel close to because they come right next to my mother's family—the Hickeys—in the Taranaki phonebook) . . . Anyhow we were talking about our various relationships with Taranaki and I actually surprised myself by saying that, when I died, Taranaki was the only place I could imagine being buried—the graveyard which adjoins the old Te Namu pa site, the landscape we crashed around as small children. Staying at Parihaka and working on the project has radically changed my relationship to the province—which had faded somewhat in recent years. My childhood devotion to the place has returned, although the place has dramatically reconfigured in some ways. Have you been there recently?

D: I haven't done any rediscovering of Taranaki for a quarter of a century, although a Chambers cousin still lives in Opunake and there

'The Taranaki Relations.' Dennis McEldowney's grandmother, Mrs Chambers, in the centre; Gregory O'Brien's grandmother, Mrs Hickey, behind her on left. Te Namu farm, 1940s. (Sr Rita Hickey—see p45—on extreme left.)

are more McEldowneys in the Taranaki telephone directory than there are now in the Irish one. My Opunake is still essentially the childhood summer holiday one—a generation earlier than yours. Your ancestors and mine didn't go to school together, because the Hickeys were taught by nuns and the Chambers kids weren't. But your grandfather and mine were both chairmen of the Opunake Co-operative Dairy Company, a generation apart. At the age of about ten I was taken to see Parihaka, on the same outing in the old Model T coupé (with a dicky seat in the boot) that took us to the lighthouse at Cape Egmont. I remember the Te Whiti memorial at Parihaka, but I don't remember any Maori around. Looking back, the striking thing about my memories of Opunake is the absence of Maori, except for the line of kuia in long black frocks sitting on the pavement, against the wall of the courthouse I think, smoking pipes. But that may simply have been a child's colour blindness, taking in only the exotic. I learned much later that the Chambers family had close Maori friends—the name Hohaia is familiar to me—and I remember my grandmother's excitement when Dick Scott's *The Parihaka Story* came out. At last the truth was told! Which is perhaps an unexpected reaction from an Opunake dairy farmer on former Maori land.

G: Parihaka certainly wasn't on my childhood map of Taranaki—although my mother's cousins, the Hurleys, had a farm adjoining the pa and we used to stop there every time we drove by. Funnily, a kaumatua at Parihaka remembers the elder Hurleys as a tall, large, incredibly pale Irish immigrant couple who spoke a mixture of Maori and Gaelic which was incomprehensible to everybody except their immediate family. My mother remembers going up to Parihaka in the 1930s. In fact she is godmother to one of the Tito children, who have very strong links with the place. The Taranaki of my childhood is mostly coastal with adjoining hay paddocks. Although we lived in Auckland, most of my childhood memories are of Taranaki, because that was where we spent all our school holidays and ninety per cent of the interesting things that happen to schoolchildren occur during holidays. I could make a list of things: the first time I had a bad asthma attack (and the moonlit drive to find a doctor), the wailing women wearing karaka leaves at my grandfather's burial, a huge washed-up whale on the coast by the Tito farm, a first encounter with snow . . . Despite living in Auckland for nearly forty years, my mother still refers to Opunake as 'Home', in much the same way colonials used 'Home' to denote England. I guess, to some extent, we're all continually involved in inventing a sense of belonging, a sense of place. What other locations do you carry around—the 'Warm South', the 'Cool North'?

D: Sorry, I was distracted by the cat bringing in a bird for me to admire. I swore at her. She purred. Do you know why in my youth houses never had cat-doors? Because there was always a window open. And I was in my thirties before I slept in a house where the doors were locked at night. Which is an oblique way of answering your question. One of my vivid childhood memories is of the cat of the time jumping in the window, early in the morning, and dragging over my mother's pillow a not-so-small malodorous fish it must have found stranded on Sumner beach. I don't think in my case it was true that ninety per cent of the interesting things happened in the holidays. If Opunake is 'Home', Sumner is perhaps even more 'Home'. But then so are Upper Hutt, Dunedin, the eastern suburbs of Auckland: so many 'Homes' can bring on nostalgia that I am almost homeless. But the place I spent longest in during my younger days, Papanui in Christchurch, is not 'Home'. Papanui is not a natural home, anyway, but also I spent much of the time there in bed, a condition and therefore

The author and Dennis McEldowney photographed by Marti Friedlander at the opening of *Hotere—out the black window*, Auckland Art Gallery, June 1998.

a place I wanted to escape from. And of course all these homes we invent are only in the mind. The Sumner vivid in my mind no longer exists. The beach I played on was long since swept away. My brother says this was because the Borough Council, which we had then, was preoccupied with sin. They didn't like what went on concealed in the undulations of the lupin-covered sand-hills, so they levelled the sand and built a promenade. Nature, personified by the sea, took its revenge.

G: Your mention of the relationship between coastline and sex sent me scuttling to the bookshelf to find *James K. Baxter as Critic*. There's an essay in there, 'Symbolism in New Zealand Poetry', where he confidently wraps up what various aspects of landscape symbolise in New Zealand poetry. Having dealt to the sea, mountains and bush, he reaches the coast and sums up its various poetic applications:

> THE BEACH:
> as an arena of historical change, the arrival and departure of races;
> as a place where revelations may occur; as a no-man's-land between conscious and unconscious;
> as an arena for sexual adventure

The relationship between landscape and health has always interested me—that European (or maybe it's more particularly English?) notion that contemplation of a landscape can restore health. Hence all those tubercular artists contemplating lakes in Switzerland—taking in the air but also, importantly, the view. Last year I stayed with some people inland from Geraldine in a huge old house that had previously functioned as a convalescent home. The carefully landscaped lawns and gardens, framed by some very occidental arrangements of native trees, with the Southern Alps beyond, were obviously constructed so that the wheelchair-bound patients on the balcony would find themselves seated, basically, in the midst of an arcadian scene.

D: Landscape and health is a fascination of mine, and especially landscape plus health/disease plus literature. My greatest reading last year was Thomas Mann's *The Magic Mountain*, a late discovery. It has it all, tuberculosis (in clinical detail), Swiss mountains and weather, and over all the effect of health-cure on the perception of time. (When tuberculosis was stopped in its tracks by antibiotics, another iconic disease just had to appear. I don't say AIDS appeared to serve literature, but literature certainly grabbed it.) And the beach. You know Baxter's 'Poem by the Clocktower, Sumner', from his eloquent, rhetorical phase:

> Under the shadow of the naked tower
> Play the wild children, stranger than Atlanteans . . .
>
> An Ice Age lies
> Between us; for they know
> The place and hour of the young phoenix' nest
> On the bare dune where we can see only
> Worn glacial stones and terminal moraine.

I don't remember the phoenix' nest but the cliffs at the end of the beach certainly meant seabirds' nests to me, and the brilliant flowers of the iceplants. I didn't of course think of the sand as terminal moraine, but I knew the beach as a healthy place to stay.

The beach as a health resort was a late eighteenth-century discovery as far as I know. Before that the sea-coast was mostly a menace: think of all the shipwreck scenes in art and literature. In my childhood tanned meant healthy, though we did wear sunhats to guard against 'sunstroke' (heat exhaustion, I suppose). The first health camps in New Zealand were in tents on beaches. Sunshine, 'salubrious air' full of 'ozone', salt water, wide horizons, all calculated to ward off 'consumption'. During the 30s young men abbreviated swimming costumes to trunks, in the first stirrings of the surfie culture—as distinct from the surf-lifesaving culture, which was social responsibility on the beach (and retained costumes that covered the chest). Then came melanoma. The sun after all turned out to be the Sumner Borough Council in the sky. Sorry, I'm running away with our conversation, but you touched a nerve.

G: One thing about the New Zealand literary culture: it always seems to be the characters in the stories who get the suntans, not the writers themselves. Persons of an 'artistic disposition' tend to be drawn towards ill health and a pallid, pasty introspection (despite the odd anachronistic outburst of jogging, yachting or some other outdoor pursuit). I've never quite figured that one out, although I think it was

F. Scott Fitzgerald who said that writers should always have bad health except for brief periods of convalescence when they are not writing. Perhaps as the 'sore thumbs of the tribe' (as Baxter—from memory—called them), artists have a duty to keep poor health. Katherine Mansfield was another exemplar in this respect. You mentioned the connection between landscape and health and literature. I'm wondering if we could add the visual arts to the literary arts as a part of that equation. I'm thinking of a story you told me a few years ago about Colin McCahon loaning a painting to you when you were sick . . . I guess that was back in the early 1960s?

D: It was 1949 actually. I was reminded of it last year when I saw *The Angel of the Annunciation* at an exhibition in Nelson celebrating the centenary of the Suter Gallery. I couldn't resist telling a bored young attendant, who was sitting at a table thumbing through a book about McCahon, that the painting had once hung on my bedroom wall for five months. He perked up and wanted to know more. So I described how Ron O'Reilly brought McCahon to see me, at a low point in my invalid years; how Ron characteristically did most of the talking, good talk, but in his slow, relentless monotone; how I became more and more exhausted and finally did a faint, or rather felt faint; how distressed Colin was, and how he came to the door the next morning with the painting and two books on loan, one of reproductions of one hundred great paintings, or some such, and the other a small book of reproductions of Grünewald. I loved that painting. It was the best thing that happened to me in a rather grim year. My parents returned it to him when I went to Auckland the following year for an operation at Green Lane Hospital. I never saw him again. Even after we both moved to Auckland permanently our paths never crossed. But I see the painting from time to time and regard it as in some sense mine.

G: Maybe paintings, like views of Swiss lakes, do have restorative powers. Since I began working at the City Gallery, Wellington, it's been interesting visiting art collectors and seeing how they relate to their paintings. There can certainly be an intensity in the relationship between owner/viewer and artwork. People particularly feel that way about Colin McCahon's work. We were unable to include one of his important Te Whiti-related works in the 'Parihaka' show for the perfectly good reason that the elderly woman who owned it felt the painting was intrinsic to her well-being. She sat in front of the work every day and contemplated it. This was clearly how she planned to live out her remaining days. So, in this day and age, paintings still serve an iconic function, although you could also think of them as mandalas (in the Eastern sense). 'Paintings for people to live by' was one of McCahon's stated objectives and it looks like he achieved that.

One of the most moving experiences I have had of an exhibition was in 1997 when I went around the 'Hotere—out the black window' exhibition with broadcaster Ross Stevens, who was dying of cancer at the time. I have never seen anyone whose experience of colour was so heightened and, I would say, epiphanous. We parked ourselves in front of Ralph's large *Dawn / Water Poem* canvas—with its vast, lush wash of red paint—and Ross was, literally, enraptured. When Ross died a few weeks later, the family reproduced the Hotere painting on the order of service for his funeral. A more beautiful and appropriate use of that image I couldn't think of. In sickness or near death, you could say, we are brought into a close proximity with visual and verbal language. When you wrote *The World Regained*, was it an act of thanksgiving—for health regained—or were you aware of yourself somehow writing your way towards health?

D: Interesting question, and I'm not sure that after more than forty years I know the answer. If it was either, consciously, it was thanksgiving for health regained. But more consciously than that it was thanksgiving for being given a good story to write. I'd thought of myself as a writer since the age of about six—encouraged, I now realise, by my parents, who knew I was unlikely to be able to do anything else. But I have just embarked on rereading *The World Regained* for the first time for ages, in preparation for a new edition AUP is bringing out, and it strikes me that there was a catharsis going on, 'getting it off my chest' or 'out of my system'. I didn't find self-revelation easy, though.

G: Contradicting F. Scott Fitzgerald, you seem to be most prolific when you're in good health?

D: If I am most prolific when in good health, there is of course a simple physical reason for this. People with an infectious disease like tuberculosis are usually running an elevated temperature. They have a fever, in other words, and 'feverish activity' is no mere figure of speech. Whereas oxygen deprivation (which tuberculosis patients also have in their very last stages, when they fall silent) leads to inertia. But I could also turn your remark on its head and say that, within reason, my health is best when I am writing. The thought of not writing induces a kind of panic.

G: I guess I think of my asthma as being more of an asset than a liability in the creativity states. Since that first time I had an asthma attack at Opunake, I've thought of the disease as my 'Taranaki' sickness. On the subject of which, there's a very strange passage in John P. Ward's book *Wanderings with the Maori prophets Te Whiti and Tohu in New Zealand*, published in 1883. When the two Parihaka leaders were imprisoned in Christchurch, to alleviate the asthma from which both men suffered, the jailers generously gave them pipes and tobacco to smoke. So you have this sad image of Te Whiti and Tohu puffing and wheezing away, all those miles from home . . .

But my ailment is comparatively minor and I've probably exploited it: asthma was always a good defence against team sport when I was at Sacred Heart College. And whenever I get it bad these days it induces a kind of literary 'coma', where I lie on the bed in the midst of a pile of books and, sometimes, blank sheets of paper—which probably makes me like the ghastly Tullio in Visconti's film *L'Innocente*: someone who 'indulges his illness'. I mentioned at the beginning of this conversation, how I thought people with Taranaki roots formed a kind of a tribe or gang. I suppose the other tribes I belong to comprise, firstly, asthmatics, secondly, Catholics and, on reflection, I'd throw the literary tribe in there too. What about you?

D: My cardiac condition exempted me not only from school sports but at secondary level from school itself and the whole experience of being a teenager. Obviously this had an influence on my formation (to use a Catholic term) that I can never escape from. But whether it makes me part of a tribe is a different matter. Some years ago a society of heart surgery survivors was set up (or rather imported from America), as a support for those facing surgery. Zoë and I were more or less dragooned into becoming members. We thought we would be visiting patients to demonstrate our survival. But it turned out that doctors and other health workers didn't want a swarm of amateurs in their wards imparting dubious information. So we switched to supporting one another, which meant finding out what we had in common, which turned out to be nothing. We ended up having housie evenings, at which point Zoë and I left.

The literary tribe certainly; I felt I was part of that before I knew any writers. And the McEldowney/Ulster Protestant/Presbyterian Church tribes. I've never severed links with those, remaining an active Presbyterian, though that doesn't tell you much, considering the chasms dividing the wings of that unhappy church. When I was young I enjoyed the company of writers like Louis Johnson and Maurice Shadbolt who were in revolt against the literary and every other establishment, and thought their rebellion was great; but I remained in many respects a petty bourgeois conformist. And I couldn't buy into the primitive green movement in vogue with Cresswell, Sargeson, Fairburn, Finlayson et al—anti-industrial revolution, anti-technology, anti-chemical-farming, pro-compost. Having had the latest thing in heart surgery I was hopelessly compromised, a bionic man. Though I do still compost my organic waste.

But let me ask you something. When there was a spate of multi-author books a year or two ago about the experience of growing up Catholic, I couldn't imagine such a book about a Protestant upbringing (except of the fundamentalist, Brethren type). Few would want to buy such a book or contribute to it, and if they were persuaded to they wouldn't have anything to say. I supposed this was partly because most of us went to state schools, but that probably isn't the whole explanation. What do you think?

G: I've pondered that matter myself. I suppose Catholicism is a religion of extremes—all that darkness and light, spirit and body, faith and doubt . . . That generates a certain dramatic and imaginative potential. I guess there's a widespread interest in things Catholic and, as is usually the case, Gaelic because they are perceived as being somehow 'sexy' or 'mystical' or alluring for other reasons. Irishness offers a pretty convenient alternative to mainstream Anglophile, materialist culture too—although this has been distorted and exaggerated. Apparently W. B. Yeats, when he was editing the works of William Blake in the late 1880s, made an unfounded claim that the Londoner Blake had Irish ancestry, his rationale being that all mystical, visionary, inspired souls must have Celtic blood in their veins. (More recently, there was a local variation on this 'argument' when certain writers started claiming that Colin McCahon was part-Maori—an assertion which has no factual basis, even if it has a kind of 'spiritual' basis.)

Thinking about Blake and returning, again, to McCahon, there's a passage in Ackroyd's biography of Blake which seems relevant. He wrote: 'Many of [Blake's] works begin with a visitation, of a bard or muse or angel who inspires the poet and dictates the words of his song; it is, for Blake, a way of emphasising the divine source of all art.' That makes me think of McCahon's *Angel of the Annunciation* propped up at the end of your sickbed and how that was an angel heralding *The World Regained*. Do you remember when, during your illness a few years ago, I unwittingly sent you a card with that same painting on it? So the image was installed beside your sickbed again. Did you think of writing a sequel at that time, *The World Regained Regained*?

D: No, I didn't. For one thing other people had a more vivid memory of the illness itself than I had, and for another the aftermath was not the discovery of a new world so much as a narrowing of the same one. I didn't see much to write about in that. This was probably a failure of the imagination, of which I don't have all that much anyway. I don't regard myself as at all fey. Without denying the magic of McCahon's angel I would rather ascribe its Second Coming to serendipity than to telepathy. My mind processes tend to be step by step, linear, which is why I write narrative prose and am not a poet. I should confess here that, for all my claimed linkage with Ulster Protestants, my ancestry is about two-thirds English and Anglican. There are anomalies in all these racial or cultural explanations, as you know. Yeats himself was Anglo-Irish, a member of the Protestant Ascendancy and despised the Catholic peasantry. His wife, whose 'automatic writing' of messages from the spirit world confirmed his cyclic world view and supplied many of his most compelling images, was indubitably English.

G: I've always loved the coincidences that life 'automatically' seems to manufacture. Part of being some sort of an artist, as I understand it, is the knitting together of these coincidences—not to make something necessarily coherent from them, rather to orchestrate the chaos and serendipity and complexity so, perhaps, the reader might discover a faintly suggested order or meaning. The poem I wrote while you were very sick in hospital in 1995, called 'In Very Peace', is probably an example of that kind of orchestrated chaos. Maybe I should rename the piece 'The world regained regained'. I feel irrationally fond of that poem these days because, when I wrote it, it was a kind of farewell. And you're still here!

To take the chaos/complexity theory a step further, I think your description of yourself and the Yeats family is proof that a good, rich mixture of opposing genes, ideas, beliefs etc is a good recipe for living and working. Derek Walcott is a great advocate of this kind of mixed, high-and-low lineage. In a recent interview he bemoaned the demise of Latin as a subject in West Indian schools. One of his great memories was 'reading the classics under a mango tree'—an experience he sums up nicely in *Omeros*: 'All that Greek manure under the green bananas.'

D: How right you are about chaos/convergence, and about the use the artist makes of them. That's why poets would be the unacknowledged legislators of the world, if anyone were listening, whereas we logical thinkers can only stuff things up. We are the people who think there is only one answer to every question, and only one question to every answer. But I do have my moments. I love finding serendipitous or ironic coincidences, and to bore friends with them. Maurice Gee's character George Plumb was a fervent believer in eugenics, the 'science' of outbreeding inferior human stock. It was a passion he shared with Yeats, my one-time boss Philip Smithells, Hitler, and Maurice's grandfather James Chapple, on whom Plumb was based. I was delighted when I found that, almost before the word eugenics was invented, James Chapple had married a woman whose second name was Eugenie. And I like to see some kind of convergence, though no one else would, in the fact that *The World Regained* was reviewed when it first came out by one of Yeats's late lovers—though many years after he died, of course. She liked it. And I like contradiction.

I've just been looking at 'Tooth and Claw', the Auckland City Gallery's exhibition of animals in art. Do you know Jeff Thomson's corrugated iron hens? I remember going with Zoë to see his cows grazing in Albert Park, but something as small and delicate as a hen? Yet put them among Robin Dudding's beloved White Leghorns, with which (whom?) I renewed acquaintance on Boxing Day, and they would be right at home.

G: Funnily enough, my brother and I bought our mother one of those corrugated iron hens for her seventieth birthday. It's now installed on the stairway of the parental home, where its beak periodically snags unwitting visitors.

D: As for the classics in the Caribbean, just now I've been reading a letter in the *Listener* from a veteran teacher who still uses the previous generation's graded reading books, based on phonics, because the whole-language books used now contain words and ideas that children of the age they are meant for couldn't understand, let alone spell. She is angry that this deprives children of the mechanics of the language. I sympathise with her. But I also remember that, from Kipling's *Just So* story 'How the Whale Got His Throat', I memorised and relished the phrase about 'the mariner of infinite resource and sagacity' long before I had any idea what it meant, and would have been deprived if I hadn't. Yet does this mean I think the mechanics of language are unimportant? No. So often the best answer to either/or questions is 'both'.

G: Without wanting language to deliberately mystify the reader/listener, I think you don't need to understand to appreciate. Language contains rhythm, music, cadence—all qualities which, these days, are made subordinate to sense and (another quality I was force-fed as a young journalist) 'economy'. Listening to the Mass being sung in Latin at St Mary of the Angels or sitting on the marae at Parihaka as Taranaki dialect washes over you . . . those, for me, are quintessential experiences of language even though I do not understand all of what is being stated—and marae and church are places where 'economy' isn't exactly a top priority . . . I was drawn to reading and writing poetry, initially, as an antidote to the rationalism and utilitarianism of journalism (as I experienced it as a seventeen-year-old newspaper reporter in Dargaville). Poetry was writing that could be as plain or as baroque as it liked; it could improvise and dictate its own terms. It could be obscure or elliptical when it chose to. I've always liked Joyce's idea that literature should 'disrupt the language'. The poets I liked initially were the ones who behaved the worst in relation to the journalistic model. So I loved Dylan Thomas, Edith Sitwell, Manley Hopkins, Stein, Joyce, Kenneth Patchen and all manner of French Surrealists. These people all struck me as great disruptors of the language as they found it. I was also drawn to James K. Baxter and the composer/artist/writer John Cage because they set out to disrupt the social, political and spiritual pattern. I've found myself reading essays a lot more in recent years—perhaps, at best, they mark a reconciliation between the poetic and the journalistic modes?

D: The utilitarianism of journalism . . . yes, but rationalism? (If that means rationality.) I wish. Perhaps in Dargaville. Perhaps that is why Michael Horton has just killed the Dargaville newspaper, presumably the one you worked for. My twenty years as an academic publisher have given me a rather different slant on sense and economy. The lack of either in the convoluted language of many academics is worn as a gang patch, to assert their membership of the currently most powerful faction in their field, when what they ought to be doing is conveying information. Still, I know what you mean, and some (not all) of the language disruptors you mention were early enthusiasms of mine as well. The only poet whose work was primarily intended to convey information and opinion, and has survived, is William McGonagall. Yet it seems to me, looking at it from the outside, that the words in any language you know are inevitably tainted with meaning, by which I mean of course something wider than dictionary definitions. It is the interaction of meaning with sound, the tension between them, as well as attempting to express meaning through rhythm, music, cadence, that makes poetry what it is.

I like the thought that essays mark a reconciliation between the poetic and journalistic modes. It throws me a lifeline, the essay being what I primarily write, even when writing something apparently other. I mentioned earlier that I had known from when I was six that I was going to be a writer. By sixteen I had decided the kind of writer was an essayist, and although I have made the occasional attempt at fiction, that is how it turned out. Though I cringe at the memory of a teenager whose favourite book was called *A Hundred English Essays*, who soaked up Francis Bacon and William Hazlitt.

G: I suppose I've surprised myself, in the last decade or so, by writing more and more non-fiction. For someone whose background is a mixture of Roman Catholicism and French Surrealism (as I remember Karl Stead very confidently pronouncing back in 1983) it's strange, maybe, that I find myself committing to the 'reality'-based pursuit that is non-fiction. (I'm presuming here that our present 'conversation' is 'non-fiction'?)

D: I'm not sure I would describe this conversation as non-fiction; but then the Montana Book Awards put poetry in the non-fiction category.

G: Perhaps between the ages of thirty and forty you start attending and questioning the world in more comprehensive, engaged ways? No more throwing verbal or imagistic molotovs into the foyer of the Reality Bank. More thinking and less imagining, it feels like sometimes. I think one of the great books about being almost forty is a poetry collection that you published, Dennis—*Tales of Gotham City* by Ian Wedde. Between twenty and thirty, for me anyway, were years spent in a very heightened imaginative state. Now, like Ian Wedde in 1983, it's *thinking* and *questioning* and a degree of analysing that would have made my skin crawl fifteen years ago. I remember back in the late 1980s Elizabeth Caffin summing up a writer whose work I admired very much as 'A Thinking Person's Gregory O'Brien'. Maybe that's what I've become: 'A Thinking Person's Gregory O'Brien'! Anyhow, right now I'm pondering a return to the Imagination . . .

D: I should hope so. Forty is far too young to give up on the Imagination.

II

THE SHAPE OF LIVING

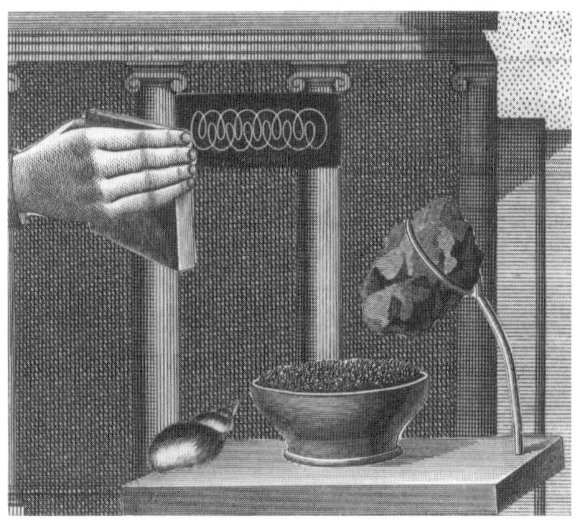

Morning Glory in Springtime in autumn

self-portrait

The delicacy of two herons flying across the surface of a vase, the black and white of their wings beating against the blood-red enamel—a vase baked in Japan, where the herons began and ended their flight, their wings outstretched across their permanent address of sky. As a dream this side of waking remains all day, the blood-red enamel of sky.

My father bought my mother an enamel vase decorated with flowers for their wedding anniversary: *Morning Glory in Springtime*, which he planned to give her in autumn. Under the pretence of a business trip, he drove north to Auckland to buy the vase, leaving his wife with a friend for the day. Careful not to shatter or chip the ornament, my father strapped it into the child's car seat before driving cautiously south. The vase reminded him of the garden his wife so fastidiously kept around the edges of their recently built house. He thought the vase could be left in the garden and not noticed for weeks. It was seven days until the wedding anniversary.

With an hour to spare on the way home from Auckland, my father visited a friend in Matamata, taking the vase into the friend's house for safe-keeping. The two men got to drinking and, in the subsequent tomfoolery, my father's friend balanced the vase on his head while staggering about the room to Tchaikovsky's 'Waltz of the Flowers'. The vase shattered on the hearth and my father's heart sank, although his friend maintained it was nothing that a few more drinks couldn't fix. My father knew he could not return to Auckland for another ornament without his wife suspecting something. And it was to be a surprise. He continued home dispirited.

Three days later, my mother was admitted to hospital, haemorrhaging. The miscarriage of an unthought-of pregnancy. A friend of my mother's looked after my older brother, absorbing him unnoticed into her family of nineteen (all of whom were born before her fortieth birthday and not a twin among them). During the reprieve my mother's admission to hospital granted him, my father drove back to Auckland for another vase.

After the miscarriage, there was still a child inside my mother. The doctors said there had been twins but only one had miscarried, the other was still clinging on for dear life. So my mother spent six weeks in hospital while I spent six weeks waiting for the dark bus that never came.

My parents spent their wedding anniversary calmly and quietly in the ward, my father sitting on the end of the bed, looking exhausted but relieved. He had just driven back from Auckland, this time with a blood-red enamel vase with two herons printed on it strapped to the car seat. He decided not to give my mother the vase until she returned home from hospital.

When it was safe for her to be discharged, my mother was collected by my father and, after plucking their one-year-old son from the fold of my mother's friend, they returned home.

My mother carefully unwrapped the vase and then she smiled and sobbed and placed it on the mantelpiece, where it has remained until this day.

As children we would stare long and hard at the vase with the two herons flying across it, one of them flying parallel to the surface, floating there in a kind of glory, while the other bird flew off in the direction of the inside of the vase. It seemed to be vanishing into distance but somehow never quite managed to disappear from its enamel sky.

My mother later told me the two herons on the vase were the memory of her twins. The one flying away from the world, towards the interior of the ornament, was why she cried sometimes, she said. And there was a sorrow the bird left behind on the surface of the vase, and that sorrow would not permit the bird's vanishing.

The shattered image of *Morning Glory in Springtime* remained with my father, who never mentioned the earlier vase to my mother. The two herons on the blood-red vase were her sorrow and her happiness —they were all that she knew and there was no garden, to her knowledge, preceding them.

An attempt at the first page of an autobiography

A man stands nervously at the top of a tower from which lengths of yellow tubing protrude. These tentacle-like tubes curve downwards, emitting a thin stream of water and, sporadically, ejecting the bodies of small boys above the agitated surface of the heated pools which surround the tower on all sides. The pools themselves look like the oxidation ponds of a sanitation system designed to purify the world.

Standing close by the man, a nine-year-old boy stares upwards. The boy asks what someone the man's age is doing up here. The man replies that he has been told *The Black Hole* is exactly like being born—you plummet through darkness then are expelled into blinding, disorientating daylight—and he wants that experience.

'No,' the boy is adamant, 'it is *Bob's Mistake* that is like being born. If they put a roof on it, it would be exactly like being born.'

'I suppose, aged nine, you remember being born?'

'No, although I do remember when I was a year old . . . Have you been on the *Gut Buster and Squeeze*? I don't think that would be much like being born.'

'Sounds like it might be.'

'You ask anybody. *Bob's Mistake* is the one. Although there's probably too much water for it to really be like being born.'

'I don't know about that. Being born, there's lots of water, apparently. You swish around.'

'If you go too fast down *Bob's Mistake* you'll bang your head where the pipe bends around. Can you see over there at the far end, by the kiosk, those kids sitting on the concrete, clutching their heads?'

'They say every birth is different so I guess it follows they'd need a great many water slides . . .'

'It's your turn.'

'The main difference between *The Black Hole* and being born, it seems from here, is that the children making their way into the world don't yell and whoop and holler as much as all you children on the water slide . . .'

'You'd better go.'

JOWIL
ALAMEIN
Oct. 19th 1951
EMPRESS HALL · LONDON

The shape of living children I

My father was at the battle of El Alamein—this I established as a fact of my childhood. It was a turning point in the war. Looking through my father's souvenirs of that time—a collection of war documents, minute photographs and a bag of buttons—I found the diagram below, which for some years I took to be a strategic outline of the El Alamein campaign.

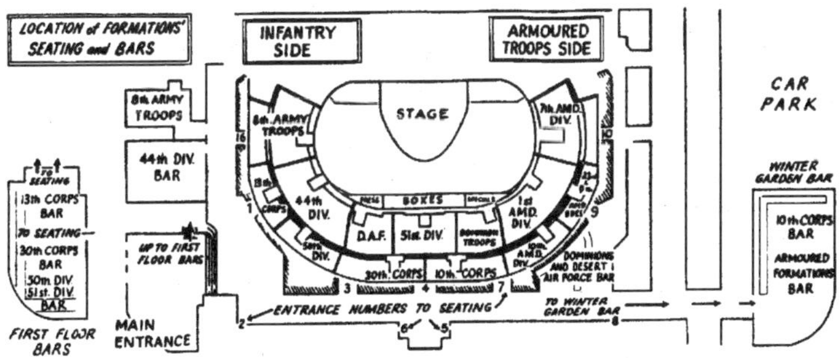

Much later I discovered this was, in fact, the seating plan for the El Alamein reunion night at the Empress Hall, London, a few years after the war.

On this particular evening my father was a member of a haka party which shared the bill with the Luton Girls Choir, who were very big at the time. Guests of honour in the audience included Winston Churchill, Field Marshal Montgomery and General Dwight D. Eisenhower. Many of the men in the haka party had trudged across North Africa and up through Italy. For a time, on account of the Empress Hall performance, I thought my father must have been a member of the Maori Battalion. In actual fact, my father had sat most of the war out at Mechanic's Bay, Auckland, fiddling with wireless components, watching the flying boats disappear first thing in the morning and return at nightfall. The precise nature of his involvement in World War II—maintaining the navigation and communications equipment of these flying boats before they headed off into vast, treacherous areas of the Pacific Theatre—would amaze me years later as I watched him struggle to put a record on a record player and, even later still, throw his hands up in despair over the operation of a compact disc player.

The concert programme included a series of photographs of soldiers in action, the word REMEMBER . . . ? hanging like a banner across various scenes from desert life. The photographs depicted boxes of ammunition pulled by donkeys, men in pith helmets pushing barrels of water up dunes and the shifting sands that were constantly removing traces of human life from the desert, much the same way the tattoos on the soldiers' arms had disappeared from these images at the touch of the army photographic retouchers. There were men standing in the rain—in the desert of all places—like extras in a Hollywood musical.

Reproduced on the back cover of the programme was a coat of arms, the ensign under which the desert army trudged backwards and forwards across North Africa and, finally, forwards and upwards into the horrors of Italy. There was an assortment of animals, heraldic material, a badly drawn fern leaf and a desert rat.

During the weeks leading up to the concert, a fleet of Rolls-Royces, courtesy of one Viscount Kelmsley, was sent to take my father and the other men to rehearsals and deliver them home afterwards. The Rolls-Royces were Viscount Kelmsley's expression of appreciation for what the 'men of '42' had achieved. He also turned on an impressive array of drinks—this at a time when alcohol was scarce—after each rehearsal and at the conclusion of the concert itself.

By the time of the final rehearsal the haka party was impeccably synchronised, but on the night of the concert the men were all over the place. Some were up and some were down. Most of the party were grinning, and throwing their limbs about as if they were rag dolls, not warriors. According to my father, the presence backstage of the Luton Girls Choir was more than the precisely tuned limbs of the men (remember, some had just got back from the war) could cope with. Their performance was further impaired by the prospect of free, limitless alcohol after the function. The men started jumping, my father recalled. (Apparently this also happened at the beginning of battles, despite the best efforts of army discipline to impose stillness and rigidity on these young, overly enthusiastic men.)

While the presence of the Luton Girls Choir certainly made the men jump, it was their singing that most impressed my father. They were in fine voice, immaculately turned out and perfectly tuned, even if, according to one of my father's sceptical co-performers, the choir had largely kept their mouths shut during the war and busied themselves assembling tanks.

In a photograph reproduced in the *Daily Graphic,* the leader of the haka, Inia ('Happy') Te Wiata, is far more airborne than the rest of the men. On account of the organisers' difficulty locating traditional Maori piupiu, most of the performers in 'Happy and the Haka' are wearing rugby outfits left behind by a team that played exhibition matches during the war. On the left of the photograph my father's face is obscured by the upraised hand of an even more hopelessly out-of-time member of the party.

Following the show, the haka party, ecstatic after what they thought had been a pristine and inspired performance—a wrong assumption they based upon the generous applause—partook of drinks in the Winter Garden Bar while, on the wet road outside, their Rolls-Royces waited to take them home. Occasionally the men would cross to the windows and look down on the limousines, as if they didn't believe they would still be there, or that they existed in the first place.

The ample sponsorship of the Imperial Tobacco Company and the Ardath Tobacco Company ensured that a dense cloud of smoke—not unlike a dust storm or the smoking, fuming Battle of El Alamein—expanded to fill the very warm Winter Garden Bar, enhancing the atmosphere of what my father still refers to as the most impressive 'smoke concert' he has ever attended. Small groups of well-dressed smokers stood around like string quartets, he recalls, with cigarettes blazing where you might have expected violin bows.

The lounge was filled with drinks and celebrities—Beatrice Lille, Lester Piggott . . . A steady traffic of savouries resembling miniature landmines issued forth from the kitchen, while waiters with trays rushed about, filling the spaces between dignitaries with drinks. In one corner, surrounded by high-ranking officers, Stirling Moss was making racing-car noises and gesticulating with his hands, as if describing a car cornering at great speed. Vera Lynn was hanging about with some members of the Luton Girls Choir who, unless my father was mistaken, were drinking particularly fiercely. My father remembers Churchill on the evening in question as a little man, Eisenhower a real talker. Both spent time in the foyer commiserating with the Royal Artillery's band of boy trumpeters who, while old enough to be shot at, weren't old enough to drink at the bar.

During the Empress Hall performance I was sitting in the gods, where the unborn are seated, looking down on all of this, silently watching as events drifted past like tracer fire and were lost in the darkness.

We were bemused, you could say, but also troubled. You see, there was another balcony even higher than the one where we were seated. And we could see our own children—another generation in waiting—looking down on us from up there.

And beyond that again, there was a further balcony and I could make out the shapes of yet another generation of children waiting up there, just as the other 'men of '42', those who were not with us on this occasion, once waited, then ran down the silent, sloping expanses of sand to their deaths.

Lost and living children

My father's friend—the one who would have him believe the Luton Girls Choir spent much of the war out of action—related an interesting story about the choir during the years of conflict. Many of the girls were, not surprisingly, married to members of the armed forces and a good number had small children. In the summer of 1943, the tank factory where several of them worked held a combined Sunday picnic outing with an adjoining clothes factory which, since the beginning of hostilities, had been producing camouflage fatigues for infantrymen.

As a treat for the employees with small children, the workers in the clothes factory were granted permission to make tiny outfits for the young ones out of leftover scraps of camouflage material. At the outset of the picnic, the children were presented with, then wrestled into, these outfits. Immediately upon donning the jackets and jumpsuits, the children ran or crawled off across the lawn, some disappearing into the surrounding parklands.

Later that afternoon, with the curfew approaching and the supply of purple fizzy drink (a gift from the People of America) dwindling, it became evident to the Luton Girls Choir and their fellow picnickers that their children were now impossible to locate, their camouflage clothing merging flawlessly with the surrounding foliage.

During the ensuing search, parents inadvertently tripped over their own children as well as those of others. Many of the youngest infants who were thought to have vanished off the face of the earth were found sleeping face down on the grass close by the picnic rugs. It was dark by the time the adults had cleared the surrounding countryside.

Perhaps it was not altogether surprising that, two years later, when the fathers of these children returned from active service still wearing camouflage uniforms, their wives looked suspiciously at them, thinking the men might be off at any minute, that they might simply disappear into the foliage and never be seen again.

My father's friend insisted that, as the picnickers hurried on foot back towards the blacked-out suburbs, and the first air raid sirens sounded, there were still children hidden away out there in the undergrowth.

Aspects of his face

The scapular was a thing of the past, I was told at school, although some of the more devout young Catholics continued to wear this leather strap with two leather tags—a scene from Christ's life embossed on one, a saint's on the other—under their school shirts.

During lunch break or interval, older boys would come up behind any younger pupils foolish enough to have their scapulars visible around their necks and grab the strap, tightening it to form a garrotte. The older boys would scream with laughter at this, but the younger boys were rendered incapable of either drawing breath or issuing a sound.

There are two kinds of men, my grandfather would say: those who have fallen and get up, and those who have fallen and will never get up.

It was during the Battle of the Somme. He was carrying a piece of artillery towards the front line with five other soldiers, their arms and shoulders aching beneath the weight of the cannon. Advancing along duckboards laid across the sodden terrain, they listened to the whine of artillery shells passing above them. (My grandfather would be hard of hearing later in life on account of these bombardments.) Nearing their destination, with the whining more piercing than ever, the men paused to adjust the weight of the cannon upon their shoulders. Then the earth around them exploded.

Shrapnel killed the other five men instantly. Someone said the cannon was blown twenty feet into the air. At the time the shell exploded, my grandfather happened to be wearing a leather scapular beneath his uniform.

When he regained consciousness, he was laid out on a stretcher, his body covered in small wounds, the noise of battle retreating behind him. An unusually large piece of shrapnel had pierced his clothing and embedded itself in one of the leather rectangles, which had been dangling just over his heart. The doctor said that if he hadn't been wearing the scapular he would have been killed instantly. The hospital chaplain said it was a miracle.

Another version of this story maintains that my grandfather had, in fact, removed himself from the cannon a few moments before the explosion to adjust the scapular around his neck, which was causing him some discomfort. The five other carriers had walked a few paces further along . . . In the split second before the blast hit my grandfather, he saw his comrades dissolve in a flash. Not so much fallen, he said, they were sucked down into the earth.

Both stories converge a few days later when my grandfather regained consciousness. Every hair on his head had fallen out and would never grow back (a trait subsequent generations of males in his family would inherit). After some weeks' convalescence he was able to limp back to a troopship, which returned him to his Taranaki farm. (Later he would feel safe in aeroplanes and on ships but was never quite relaxed while walking on the ground.)

You might think this incident would have made my grandfather a devout man, but all he subsequently had to say about such matters was that the five soldiers accompanying him to the front were the ones who had been made 'devout'.

He would always carry with him something of these events in the form of the slivers and chunks of metal that resided within him, affecting his moods and health—one of a generation of men who, half a century later, would set off metal detectors in airports.

What I recall most clearly about my grandfather, in the years leading up to his death, is the peculiar way he went about shaving. In the late morning, he would carry a wooden box into the lounge where he would sit, his eyes intent upon a small mirror mounted inside this box—a mirror in which he would interrogate one or another aspect of his face. His overshot jaw enabled him to exhale upwards, the warm air ascending his cheeks and nostrils, soothing his eyes. Tiny bubbles of air in the shaving foam made a faint crackle as the updraught freed them from the lather.

As my sister recalls, the shaving kit resembled a miniature theatre—a magical assemblage of curves and right angles, of mirrored and opaque surfaces—with which the old man would entertain his grandchildren. When the leather catch was released and the door of the shaving kit slowly opened, the light of the world would enter the shadowy interior like the most contrived stage lighting.

I, on the other hand, recall the shaving box as an ominous, dreadful device from which my grandfather would carefully remove his razor as if he were defusing a bomb. I imagined he must have felt nervous shaving, the length of metal going close by his face, reminding him of the spray of shrapnel that separated him from the other five—metal which, failing at once to kill him, now accompanied him through the long, empty years as far as his death.

East born

I was born in the East and my family was German. Or so I imagined, in the game that went from east to west, from street to street, between Eastbourne and Westbourne Roads and along the moon-shaped crescent connecting them. Skateboarding or walking or most often running between the parallel streets, we would project our muddled Berliner accents over the barricades of hedges and parked cars, pitching our battles, volleys of pine cones, too old or new apples and acorns at each other. As far as we were concerned, as children, the two streets would never be reconciled to each other, just as the world they were modelled on would remain divided into East and West. From the family home in Eastbourne Road, the West was only a stone's throw away so, playing at Spartacists or something, we would throw stones at it.

Home was a place to stagger back to. Beyond the division of each day, it embodied a unity and oneness, with its L-shaped corridor and its orderly progression from one room to the next, each of them linking up with the other, embracing.

Europe, looming in the far distance, seemed to us a continent of longing, whereas home was that which we had been granted and, it followed, had no longing for. And whereas Europe was a place haunted by its past, as children we had yet to discover or construct our pasts—the corrugated iron and weatherboard of our histories. Beyond our embattled neighbourhood, ours was a country of fences as opposed to walls, of skeletal structures, of openings.

On the other hand, East and West were as separate here as they were anywhere and they were destined to remain so, just as we were certain what we had at home would remain intact or, if not exactly intact, then at least in a kind of musical arrangement with itself—an arrangement which included the way light entertained itself in each of the rooms, playing among the frosted interior windows, the crystal wind chimes. Every moment shimmered in the unified world of these four walls—walls that could quietly accommodate all manner of dreams, including dreams of peace and even some of war.

Just as East and West were, for the duration of our childhood, divided, a decade later—not long after our parents sold it—the house we lived in came to be divided. We will come to that.

It was a house in the grand manner. My father bought it because it reminded him of Corfu. He moved his Lawrence Durrell novels (their pages marked by willing yet often uncomprehending fingers), his wife and three children into it. He had named his daughter Justine. He would sit her at the front of the house so she could watch the vines as they grew over the archway, died in winter then were revived again. She learnt to count the grapes rolling down the side path. The vines wrapped around the house like strands of chaotic ribbon.

It was in this house that our parents gained a tenuous hold on their world, a world which centred on the three of us—their three European-looking children—each growing older and more like them. We grew proud of the house, its luxuriant greenery and the cellar full of red and white wines which seemed distantly related to those vines. The imported bottles would invariably be left too long and have gone off by the time our parents came to drink them, but this didn't seem to matter—our parents paid more attention to the years on the labels and how quickly those years had gone by.

One thing our parents said which remains with me is that you should always respect the house in which you were born, that you will always be a citizen of that place.

East/bourne and West/bourne Roads—the places we were born—two streets trickling down the side of Mt Hobson, intent on remaining parallel, some distance apart. Only in retrospect it seems the two streets, like the two halves of Berlin, were ticking like clocks—or perhaps they were the arms of a broken timepiece, laid out side by side, surrounded by all the other broken pieces.

Later I came to recognise two reasons for the ongoing battles we, as children, were immersed in and to understand the nature of that conflict. First, there was the fact that we—the children of the East—were so similar to the children of the West and this similarity was a territory to be competed for. Second, there was the simple fact that if we were ever united then the game would be over—a state of affairs we could neither entertain nor allow.

The subject of my final intermediate school essay was the division of Germany into East and West—as rational and irrational as that, as clear-cut and as chaotic. The essay mentioned our parents watching the Berlin airlift from a small stained window, a sliver of the Gulf in one corner, Westbury Crescent—the street spanning East and West—in another.

I was born the same year as the Berlin Wall and with this fact came a certain knowledge and authority on my part, or so it appeared in the way I justified my essay to the class.

While the haircuts on the Eastern side were severe, I pronounced, the clothes dowdy and the young people too good at sport, far worse than that was the graffiti on the Western side of the Wall. The verges on the West, I pointed out, were covered in television guides and cassettes with their innards unspooling across the ground. Pink Floyd mostly. The young people there clearly did not know what to do with themselves.

The children in the class who hailed from Westbourne Road took my presentation to be an insult. I felt their discomfort but proceeded regardless. As a member of a family from the East, I felt a dogged loyalty to all those tattered Eastern greatcoats, the woollen hats and worn-out generations of gloves even if, as it appears to me now, they were snagged on a kind of ideological barbed wire.

After the class, the teacher took me aside and showed me a photograph of dozens of tiny Russian children, all wearing identical clothes and with identical closely cropped haircuts. The teacher intoned that this was what living in Eastern Europe was actually like, but I replied that they looked like American haircuts to me.

Just as my school essay about the division of Germany could never have anticipated the reunification of East and West, neither could it have foreseen the division of the family home.

Who would have thought that, in our lifetime, East would meet West, the wall between them exploding into a spray of tourist souvenirs and historical mortar? But then who would have thought, at about this time, our family home would be divided in two, sliced clean down the middle and driven off with in the dead of night?

I am standing on the pavement in front of Number 5, Eastbourne Rd, Remuera, staring through the crack which now divides the house into two equal parts. Everything about my childhood is divided by this gap. A couple lying on a bed find themselves separated by a thin strip of sky. A wall on which a world map once hung is torn down the middle, about where the American continent was. To cross the kitchen while drying a plate would now entail levitation or, at least, extraordinary speed.

The house is neatly dissected and will remain, for a few days, divided by a wall of sky a metre thick, a space through which the manoeuvring of distant aircraft can be made out, interspersed with figures and numerals in white—clouds in fact—which look like graffiti in German.

As a matter of course, the letterbox which was a replica of the house itself, small and pink (it would be repainted each time the house was repainted) with the number 5 affixed, has been demolished . . .

Signs of change in the street have been evident for some time—gates have been fitted with alarm systems, power poles have disappeared under the footpath and the dangling lines on which birds thoughtfully swayed are now buried.

The lawn in front of our house has been carved out, along with the skeletons of birds we buried therein and the tunnels we abandoned which pointed in the direction of the Free World or the other side of the world. Our family house has been inscribed with words in chalk, details of its pending removal. We will come to that.

Oh, as the singer sings in the adult songs, *what these streets have seen*.

I notice the vines, recently unfastened from the walls, in a bundle on the front lawn, a few strands growing hopelessly back towards the house. I am thinking, also, about the reunification of Germany and how time, which to me always resembled a flat field, has now become steep, and even, in places, treacherous. The house which we had reasonably supposed would never move is about to travel in two parts from Auckland to, it is rumoured, a small Waikato town where the halves will be reunited . . .

They backed a truck in and drove one half of the house south before the second vehicle reversed into position, a neighbour later told us. The living room, bathroom, kitchen and lounge followed fifteen miles behind the three bedrooms, study and corridor. The neighbour suspected a few rooms went missing, but she was not certain of this. It was past midnight.

I am told there are men—developers—who buy old houses and move them from towns like Taihape and Wanganui—and Auckland, I suppose—to any place they can rid themselves of them at a profit. These men shuffle and reshuffle towns. I have seen settlements of the houses they have bought stranded in the middle of nowhere. Like gypsy caravans, they are set up in camps, stationary in the daylight hours before resuming the road at night.

I can see clearly all these houses travelling by night, in all directions about the country.

North and South.

East and West.

Houses being stolen from their pasts, being driven off into the darkness.

Ghosts.

Wide loads.

Photograph of the author at 5 Eastbourne Rd, Remuera, Robert Cross, 1994.

If I had known then what I know now, my school essay would have been incomplete if it did not mention the empty section that replaced our childhood—the large hoarding that stood over the property, the words suggesting a new development—four bedrooms, a swimming pool, 6000 square feet . . .

It seems probable, when you consider the way the city disposes of itself, that in the fullness of time this new house will likewise be expelled from its surrounds and cast adrift, to end up in a similar situation as our family home—the Waikato River burbling behind it, children with small-bore rifles shooting targets hung against its south-facing wall which was once its west-facing wall. And the clouds above like lettering in white spray-paint, the words in German, likewise cast adrift.

Oh, as the singer sings, *what these streets have watched go by . . .*

All those houses travelling the back roads and highways by night, looking for their previous owners. Driving north and south, hoping to pass us coming the other way, freshly plucked from dreams, wide awake.

I can see the separate halves of my father's daydream of Corfu motoring through pitch blackness, from time to time driving back down Eastbourne Road and surveying the blank façade they have been replaced with. And the collected works of Lawrence Durrell travelling a parallel course around the North Island with nowhere that could be called their home.

We have never ascertained where the house—Number 5, Eastbourne Rd—went, but in the small hours of morning we can hear the wheels of those two trucks driving the length and breadth of the country, looking for each other and looking for us.

Wild horses

1

In the early evenings that amount to so much of childhood, *The Lone Ranger* would follow hard on the heels of the late afternoon cartoons. With Rossini's 'William Tell Overture' booming excitedly, a masked man would ride desperately across an equally desperate-looking expanse of desert. At the end of the title sequence I would turn the television off. The rest of the programme never made any sense to me.

2

Throughout my childhood, my mother would often play at a golf club known as The Grange. Between times she would bash golf balls to hell and gone at the Remuera Golf Club driving range. As a child, I thought of this range as being in some direct relationship with the desert across which the Lone Ranger galloped.

3

The miserable failure of my father's racehorse Kyle Park provided a solemn accompaniment to my teenage years. The horse was named after a village in Ireland where the paternal family hailed from. After coming second in its third or fourth race, our horse's career went steadily downhill. We would spend drawn-out, tragic afternoons at various racecourses around the North Island or waiting outside the Remuera TAB, listening to the accelerated race commentary—the mentions of our horse becoming fewer and fewer as each race progressed. So went the slow march of our adolescent years, accompanied by the Rolling Stones and a whole generation of teenaged males slowly strumming the introduction to 'Wild Horses'.

4

One day at the end of a particularly inattentive and unruly English class, our teacher insisted all the boys stay behind until we had finished reading aloud Chapter Four of *A Portrait of the Artist as a Young Man*. I was assigned the five wretched pages that remained. Aware of our eroding lunch hour, I at once adopted the manner of our favourite race commentator, Reg Clapp (who, incidentally, ran a menswear store next to my father's Mt Roskill legal practice). To my surprise, the English teacher didn't intervene—and later admitted to being quite impressed—as I rattled through Joyce's odyssey, my quick-fire delivery ending with the epiphany on the beach when the youthful James sees a beautiful woman knee-deep in water and, at precisely that moment, discovers Art. The instant my hectic stream of verbiage ran out, the boys erupted from the classroom, released like racehorses out of their starting gates or the soul of the young artist set free to float among the Spirits and Vapours of the All-embracing World.

5

My mother belonged to the Hole In One Club—a select band of golfers, all of whom had scored the big hit. This group had many of the characteristics of a priesthood, its members considering themselves blessed as well as at the height of their golfing prowess.

My father had despairingly given up golf some years earlier, saying that, unlike my mother, he had no luck. Like his foray into the world of horse racing, golf was just part, he said, of life's rich tapestry of injustices.

In 1990 a consortium of these lucky Hole-In-Oners, my mother included, chipped in and bought a racehorse called Rua Rukuna—'Two Under' in Fijian, as someone told us, probably wrongly—in the hope their golfing luck might translate into horse-racing luck.

6

The golf ball with which my mother achieved her Hole In One Club membership was enshrined—as was the done thing—on a gold-plated trophy mounted atop a compact wooden stand on a shelf in the hallway next to my brother's portable cassette player which, from time to time, would eat up tapes. One particularly black afternoon, after the cassette player had devoured my brother's copy of Bob Dylan's *Desire*, my three-year-old son came into the kitchen with a golf ball in his mouth. This initially made us all laugh, until my mother asked him where he had found it. Hardly old enough to speak, mouth full, all he could summon forth was a cheerful, purring sound.

My mother, in a flash of recognition, rushed out into the hallway to discover her Hole In One ball had been wrenched free of its stand and was now having the teeth marks of a three-year-old added to its heroic golf club scars.

A pat on the small boy's back sent the ball flying across the kitchen floor, from where it was retrieved and eventually reinstated on its stand (at a considerable cost), then consigned to the top of the china cabinet for a safe number of years.

7

Jorges Luis Borges, in *The Book of Imaginary Beings*, lifts some 'mythical horses of the sea' from the writings of Pliny. According to his Latin source, wild mares along the Tagus would run or face into the howling west wind and this way they conceived the 'Breath of Life'. This was said to produce a swift colt, but the horse would last no longer than three years.

Like these legendary colts, Rua Rukuna had an extraordinary, albeit short, career, winning its first five races—including the prestigious Magic Million at Trentham. At the prize-giving ceremonies after these races there would be anarchy as, instead of the accustomed well-heeled owner collecting the trophy, over fifty golfers would flood the platform, posing beneath the cup and beside the horse, waving at the crowd and endlessly shaking the jockey's hand. Photographers were kept busy for hours. After a series of these exhausting mass handshakes, the winning jockeys could be seen sprinting off towards the centre-field as soon as the joyous horde started moving towards them.

Rua Rukuna's winning streak exhausted itself by the time the horse was three. You could tell just by looking at him. We visited the horse shortly before a race at Ellerslie in early 1992, gaining access to the stables because of our part-owner status. We were able to walk right up to the horse and stare into his eyes, our noses almost touching. And it was clear, at this stage, the horse was *no longer really there*. He had just tucked into a bucket of oats and extra hay—a birthday treat—and this was to be his sixth race. Later that afternoon, his head thrown back, he let all the hacks run by him.

The exact size of the world

1 *Small world*

'These are my babies,' our mother would exclaim in front of the television set whenever the rock group Split Enz appeared—firstly as part of a Sunday evening talent quest, then later on regular music programmes. 'My little ones, and look at them now . . . ' Scattered about the carpet between her and the screen, my brother, sister and I were never sure whether our mother was appalled or approving. 'These are my babies,' she went on. 'My Plunket babies!'

Our mother had been a Plunket nurse in Te Awamutu during the 1950s and was, she told us, assigned to the members of Split Enz in their early, formative months. (Later we ascertained it was only Tim and Neil Finn she could lay claim to.) This was at a time, our mother explained, when New Zealand was so small you couldn't help but bump into *everyone* at one time or another.

Earlier that decade our mother had spent a year nursing in England, where New Zealand nurses were considered very desirable—even more so than their Australian counterparts, who, she said, were good but always wanted more money. Our mother was the in-house nurse for an elderly gentleman, an affable fellow who lived in a mansion overlooking the cricket grounds at Lords. She recalled watching, in the distance, the Indian side play the English. It was like watching the death throes of the British Empire, as she recalled it. Out there on the immaculate lawn.

The old man, my mother's charge, happened to be a close relative of Benjamin Britten, and the composer would often visit, accompanied by a fair-haired woman whom our mother wrongly assumed to be his wife.

One day, as our mother was watching the cricket through the french doors, Benjamin Britten entered the lounge and introduced himself to her. He shook her hand and said, *Benjamin*. Apparently he had just composed something or other for the Queen—or maybe it was the King—and said he had something else on the way. He asked our mother how the match was proceeding, to which she replied she could not tell from looking out the window, but the depressed tones of the commentator on the kitchen radio suggested the batting of the Home Team had collapsed.

Our mother always thought New Zealand was a small place, until she realised what a small place the world was. It was a small world, she would say, as though acknowledging this somehow made New Zealand bigger. A small world with so few people, she concluded, and Benjamin Britten, Tim Finn and Neil Finn just happened to be one or two or three of them.

Photograph of the author and Sue Healey in Melbourne, 1980, by Justine O'Brien.

2 *Lucky country*

Sporting a dreadful nineteen-year-old's beard, in the photograph I stand with my friend the dancer Sue Healey in an alleyway somewhere near the Victorian College of Arts, Melbourne, in December 1980. We thought Samuel Beckett would have approved of the gloomy, funny graffito behind us: BACK SOON, GODOT.

The beard in the photograph lasted only a few weeks but the leather schoolbag accompanies me to this day. My sister Justine (who took the photograph) and I had tagged along with Sue—a fellow Aucklander—as she auditioned for the Victorian College's dance school. She subsequently studied there and went on to great things in 'the lucky country'.

I've always thought of the Australian continent as the perfect setting for Samuel Beckett's play *Waiting for Godot*—a vast, empty expanse with the odd tree awkwardly stuck in it. (Sidney Nolan's drawing reproduced on the cover of various Faber editions of the play captures perfectly the parched, marginal existence of this tree, and the play whose emblem it is.) If Godot was ever to return, Australia would be the place.

Waiting for Godot has always appealed to actors—maybe because it is such an accurate portrait of waiting for the telephone to ring, the long wait to be 'discovered'. In 1979, during a week in Sydney with my father, I attended the Jane Street Theatre production of *Waiting for Godot*—a brilliant performance in a tiny theatre with an even tinier audience. The actors were complete unknowns—wide-eyed yet assured, genuinely affecting in their existential boredom. It was hard to imagine the actors in this production ever being picked up. They were *too good*, for a start. You could easily imagine the two principals acting out their theatrical careers in the relative obscurity of suburban Sydney.

The venue was so small my father and I were seated virtually under the branches of an artificial tree—the sole prop—right next to the play's protagonists, Vladimir and Estragon. And when the famously silent character Lucky broke into his soliloquy we caught it right in the ear. A character called 'Lucky' in this *Lucky Country* production struck us as particularly appropriate at the time—an aptness which I was reminded of some years later when Kylie Minogue bounded her way onto the global stage singing a song many have since come to consider the unofficial Australian national anthem, 'I should be so lucky'.[1]

Last year in the catalogue of a Sydney rare-book shop, I came across a copy of the programme from the Jane Street production. The item had an extraordinarily high price tag. Why? You might ask. I shuffled through my old papers and photographs to unearth my pristine copy of the folded document. Because the two unknowns who played Vladimir and Estragon on that occasion were Geoffrey Rush (who went on to win an Oscar for his acting in *Shine*) and Mel Gibson.

Notes

1 The sense of teeming nothingness that dominates the play—and is given voice when Lucky, as the playwright instructs, 'shouts his text'—was memorably revived in John Reynolds's series of technicolour drawings exhibited at the Peter McLeavey Gallery in 1994, 'Godot: 100 Drawings around a Beckett Soliloquy'.

The dark plane leaves at evening

some notes on the history of aviation, the aerial perspective, various kinds of elevation and turning 21 in Australia, 1982

1

In all the important, decisive plane trips in your life, it is impossible to think of yourself as a passenger. Rather, from your economy class seat, you are piloting the aeroplane—it is your will power that is lifting the 747 from the tarmac and directing it towards whatever destination you have in mind. My twenty-second year is bracketed by two such flights: the first to Melbourne, a few weeks before my twenty-first birthday, the second back to Auckland from Sydney almost a year later.

The last thing I saw of New Zealand from my aisle seat as the late-night flight departed was a spotlit, billowing windsock—a cylinder of air, a receptacle of glowing colour against the stark blackness of the night sky. Over time, I have come to think of that windsock as a flag flying over my year away—if periods of time can have flags—a three-dimensional ensign containing and representing twelve months as well as one or two Australian cities. I also came to the conclusion, not long after, that the flag of the country to which I belonged (as yet unspecified) was, in fact, a windsock.

2

The summer before I moved to Australia I worked in the research library of the Auckland City Art Gallery, where a painting by the English/New Zealand artist Patrick Hayman (1915–88) hung just inside the library door. Entitled *Atomic Explosion in the Pacific*, the picture is a turbulent assemblage of imagined life forms: above a Gauguinesque nude and a trawler flies the curiously hybridised form of a bird/fish/aeroplane—a flier at once apocalyptic yet warm-spirited and almost awkward in its trajectory—like an origami swan gone seriously wrong.

The skies in Patrick Hayman's paintings are often inhabited by such strange, enigmatic presences, be they animal, human, mechanical, or all these things at once. In the case of his 1965 painting *Self-portrait as a flying machine*, the front end of the biplane's fuselage has been replaced with the bearded, bespectacled visage of the artist himself. Here we have a different kind of 'aerial' view—a vision of the artist as inhabitant of the skies. Beyond nationalistic agendas and the conventions of landscape, portrait and still life (all earthbound by definition), we have the artist as resident of his own imaginative stratosphere.

Patrick Hayman, *Self-portrait as a flying machine*, 1965, oil on board.

3

As a symbol of the voyage, the aeroplane gradually, as the twentieth century progressed, usurped the role previously filled by sailboat or oceangoing vessel. As well as the aircraft that pepper Hayman's skies, depictions of yachts and fishing boats—influenced by the Cornish naïve painter Alfred Wallis—trawl or cruise on through a great many of his paintings and drawings.

In the best Freudian manner, Hayman's marine paintings often include a female figure—eroticised, totemic—whereas the aeroplanes are unabashedly male symbols. Reiterating the Duchampian analogy between machines and the male sex (see Duchamp's *Bride Stripped Bare By Her Bachelors, Even*), the intrusive presence in Hayman's *Woman frightened by a flying machine* is unmistakably sexual in nature. Hayman's aeroplanes are crazed, mechanistic spermatozoa—intruders into a psychosexual landscape of bulbous forms and stalk-like tree trunks.

Patrick Hayman, *Woman frightened by flying machine,* 1976, oil on board.

4

A momentous occasion upon my return to New Zealand in 1983 was visiting the touring National Art Gallery Rita Angus exhibition. Included in that show was *Journey, Wellington* (1962–63), an enigmatic cityscape above which an airliner—reminiscent of Hayman's aeroplane-spermatozoa—floats between two egg-like moons. This connection between aviation and maleness, however, was conveniently disrupted elsewhere in the exhibition by a painting entitled *Aviatrix*—a portrait of the artist's sister Edna, who was the first woman member of the East Coast Aero Club to obtain a pilot's licence. A sad irony of this work was that while Angus's sister managed to master air as a trained pilot she would later die from lack of it, succumbing during an asthma attack in the last month of the 1930s.

*

A great many artists this century have, understandably, been obsessed with aviation: the weightlessness, acceleration, speed and the way it reconfigures the world before your very eyes. The aerial perspective destabilises the natural order—the horizon, for a start, becomes an arbitrary line; foreground and background become redundant, as do conventions of one-point perspective and tonal recession. As well as the speed, however, there is the stillness of being transfixed that far above the firmament—suspended, detached, cut loose, set adrift.

The Russian Suprematist painter Kazimir Malevich's *Suprematism (Eight Red Rectangles)* (1915) is, on one level, a summation of purist abstraction, the world and its orchestrated effects removed, boiled down. All we are left with is geometry, the colour red and the non-colour white. At the same time, however, the painting can be read as an aerial view of a group of red rooftops in the midwinter Russian

Kazimir Malevich, *Suprematism (Eight Red Rectangles)*, 1915, oil on canvas.

snow. Malevich was, in fact, fascinated with aviation and aerial photography, and later became preoccupied with early notions of satellites and space travel. In the art of Malevich and the Dutchman Piet Mondrian, the soaring heights of abstract art and those of technology neatly coalesce. Both artists also shared a belief in spiritual and temporal progress not unlike that espoused by Pierre Teilhard de Chardin, who spoke of 'the adoration of the Upward and the faith of the Forward'.

5

As my flight for Melbourne departed, the windsock pointed back in the direction from which I had come: an extended finger signalling 'go back' or, at least, 'consider again what you're leaving behind'. Hence, the windsock came inadvertently to denote the place I had left.

In Australia I was greeted by another windsock, pointing back in the direction from which the landing aeroplane had approached the runway. Since then I have noticed windsocks around the world, all of them identical and all of them pointing back in the direction from which the aeroplane has just come, pointing towards the past.

In contrast to the backward-facing windsocks of my departure for Australia and all the other destinations, I imagine the windsocks of Malevich and the Russian futurists magically reversed and pointing towards a dizzying, irrational future.

6

An English translation of the fourth volume of Blaise Cendrars' memoirs, *Sky*, appeared in 1992. The book is, for the most part, a memorial to the author's son, an aviator who, having been shot down by the Germans and then imprisoned, survived World War II only to die in a plane crash shortly after the end of hostilities. As was the custom for a pilot, Cendrars' son was buried wrapped in a parachute.

As a means of coping with his loss and commemorating the tragic descent of his son, Cendrars devotes much of *Sky* to recounting the lives of Catholic saints who, during their lives, were supposedly capable of feats of weightlessness, of levitation. To this end, Cendrars quotes verbatim lengthy passages from Olivier Leroy's aptly titled tome *La Levitation* (1928). It's a puzzling literary strategy, although perhaps a necessarily circuitous and distanced one given the immensity of Cendrars' grief. Incapable of finding his own words, he appropriated those of someone else—the saints' lives providing a supporting structure for his largely unspoken elegy.

Sky is, in effect, an attempt to populate the vast empty spaces between people, as well as the space through which the author's son fell. It also embodies the emptiness into which the author plummeted upon hearing of his son's death.

Central to Cendrars' book is the figure of St Joseph of Copertino, the 'New Patron Saint of Aviation'. Coincidentally, a few years before coming upon *Sky*, I had written two compressed lives of St Joseph of Copertino in my novel *Diesel Mystic*, which appeared in 1989. In my book (a work much preoccupied with weightlessness and flight) two adjacent churches with the same name—St Joseph's—have erected billboards on facing sides of the highway. The two identically named churches use these billboards to compete for new parishioners, constantly trying to outdo each other with miraculous tales, most often of a levitational kind. In Catholic saintology, levitation is one of the more common proofs of sainthood; another is bilocation—the ability to be in two places at once (a quality I have St Joseph manifest literally in *Diesel Mystic* by living his 'life' simultaneously on the two opposing billboards).

Some years after *Diesel Mystic* appeared, a friend of mine related an interesting story involving the book. My friend works in the library of a provincial New Zealand city, where the husband of one of her workmates is a prominent land rights activist. She tells me that, while this fellow doesn't care much for books, he does insist on carrying the library's long-overdue copy of *Diesel Mystic* around with him. It surprised me that someone involved in *land* rights should be, according to my friend, so 'involved' in a book which has as one of its central premises the whole business of levitation, of escaping from the land, the ground.

*

Calling to mind Patricia Grace's story collection *The Sky People* and the vaporous bird/humans of the painter Hariata Ropata Tangahoe, in my imagined postscript to the story of my friend's friend's husband, the activist becomes as interested in Air Space as he is in Land Rights and accordingly devotes a sizable proportion of his activism towards that end. 'Where would we be without our air?' he points out. 'We are the people of the sky above the land.'

7

Shortly before I left for Australia, the brother of a friend of my sister's flew me from Auckland to Rotorua in a small aircraft. The machine, parked at Ardmore aerodrome, looked like one of those motorised pretend-aeroplanes outside supermarkets, although with flimsy wing extensions and a FOR SALE sign leaning against the fuselage. The asking price was $22,000 ono. Clambering into the cockpit, I was shocked that the only instrumentation was a speedometer and a dashboard-mounted compass which looked like something from a cornflakes packet.

Soon, miraculously, we were airborne and cruising downcountry at just under 100 miles per hour, which, despite the fact it was the top speed of our machine, seemed too slow for an aeroplane. Looking down on the farmland, I thought of Baxter's 'Cattle like maggots on / Green porcelain paddocks'. Some motorists on State Highway 1 appeared to be overtaking us.

8

Between flying in and out of Australia, the only flights I embarked upon were the intermittent ones into the imaginative airspaces of books. For my twenty-first birthday, my brother Brendan gave me a copy of *For The Birds* by John Cage. The American composer/writer/artist declared that he was 'for the birds, not for the cages in which people sometimes place them'. This belief in creative freedom was Cage's credo, although he did have the good sense to question the romanticism of both birds and flight, noting a few years earlier:

> Artists talk a lot about freedom. So, recalling the expression 'free as a bird', Morton Feldman went to a park one day and spent some time watching our feathered friends. When he came back, he said, 'You know? They're not free: they're fighting over bits of food.'

Ian Wedde pulled off a similar ornithological nosedive in his poem 'Mahia, 1978': 'Jonathan Livingston Seagull gulped worms and shit', while admitting, begrudgingly, 'Oh certainly he could fly'. Despite appearances to the contrary, the French composer Messiaen's preoccupation with birdsong was certainly no decorous affair, as his piano-crunching *Catalogue d'oiseaux* attests.

While I was living in a heavily built-up part of Sydney, the flights certain books offered were the greatest freedom. The year was bracketed at the other end by the gift from my brother of two books: Louis Zukofsky's long, baffling poem *A* and Wassily Kandinsky's collection of prose-poems, *Sounds*. Like Cage, Kandinsky and Zukofsky were great mixers of music, art and literature. Kandinsky developed theories concerning *synaesthesia* to such a literal degree that he believed specific orchestral instruments matched specific colours.[1]

Occasionally during that year flocks of parakeets would swoop down onto our rooftop, a raucous, iridescent pink wave—confirming, you could say, these colour/sound relationships before I had ever really thought about them.

9

It is October 1997 and I am collecting the Japanese avant-garde electric guitarist, 'psyche monster' and 'noise terrorist' Keiji Haino—also known as 'The Prince of Silence and Noise'—from Wellington airport. His concerts are notorious for their extreme volume and the violence of his approach to his instrument. Haino is accompanied by an interpreter who knows only fractionally more English than he does. Driving past the end of the runway, I hear a guttural murmuring from the back seat (Haino, I am told, prefers speaking an ancient Japanese dialect), then the interpreter beside me gestures towards the runway and asks: 'What . . . is . . . that?'

'A windsock.'

He translates that for the backseat passenger and I hear them both laughing and saying, '. . . wind . . . sock . . .'

The following day, delivering the two men back to the airport, I notice as we approach the runway their conversation in Japanese is punctuated by the English word 'windsock', accompanied by breathless laughter and an enthusiasm counter to their usual cultivated gloom and high seriousness.

10

Two large collections of poetry accompanied me to Australia: *Collected Writings in French* by Jean (Hans) Arp and James K. Baxter's *Collected Poems*.[2] On the return flight, these weighty volumes were again consigned to hand luggage to lighten the significantly overweight suitcases in the hold. Travelling east, I remember reading Baxter's 'Air Flight North':

> I do not like this chariot. It gives me
> Faustian dreams. Undoing the seat belt
>
> And lighting up a smoke . . .
>
> . . . I meditate the doom
>
> Of Icarus, while the hostess brings
> Coffee in trim red mugs. A calm flight.

These lines rang true for a twenty-one-year-old with only a suspicion or intuited sense that all was not right with the world, and an emerging belief that poetry might almost make up for that. In hindsight I think that the year 1982, to start with, was a runway we taxied out onto. The rest of the year was one long plane trip, from the time I took off until I landed twelve months later.

11

How do we record a flight? We have a few Baxter poems, Smithyman's 'Flying to Palmerston', Stead's sequence 'Yes, T.S.', which links Auckland with England, and Bill Manhire's 'Breakfast', which brings us back home via Singapore . . . We have Colin McCahon's North Otago and Canterbury landscapes with their cubist-inspired, tilted planes of landscape—views which would be inconceivable without air travel. There's McCahon's famous (now destroyed) 1953 canvas entitled *International Air Race*, the artist looking down on two aeroplanes and through sporadic cloud to the earth beneath; also McCahon's 'Jet Out' works of the early 1970s.

We have the aerial cityscapes of British/New Zealand painter Robert Ellis, who was an aerial photographer in the Royal Air Force during World War II, then spent the rest of his life painting roadways and urban geometries from that same viewpoint. There is John Drawbridge's euphoric painting *Flight* (1968). Even Ralph Hotere's abstract paintings of the 1960s were influenced by his training as a pilot in the air force during the previous decade, Bill Manhire suggests.[3]

12

'Windsock', that orange word flapping in a breeze that is constantly leaving and arriving, reaching as far as Australia then returning.

Our two-year-old son Felix has been obsessed with windsocks for some months now. We drive him across town to observe the windsock at the end of the Wellington International Airport runway as it tenses and relaxes, sways then is still. 'Windsock' was the third or fourth word he learnt to say.

13

The aerial viewpoint has dominated post-World War II painting in Australia to an even greater degree than in New Zealand. The painters Sidney Nolan and Fred Williams were both, at various times, preoccupied with aerial views, having experienced epiphanies while flying over the Australian landscape. Some of Nolan's best earlier drawings are either of Icarus or of an aeroplane crashing in the desert (an event he actually witnessed while stationed at Wimmera during World War II). In 1949, after flying over the interior, he began painting the unpopulated central Australian landscape. While Nolan's paintings were the first sustained series of Australian aerial landscapes, they were prefigured by Margaret Preston's small masterpiece *Flying over the Shoalhaven River* (1942) with its flattened space and Aboriginal-inspired pictorial rhythms.

'The flat canvas became the perfect way of realising the experience of looking down on the landscape from an aerial viewpoint,' Patrick McCaughey wrote of Fred Williams in 1981. 'Just as the landscape flattened out below Williams, so he made it do so for the viewer.' The denuded language of the Australian desertscape, as depicted in particular by Williams, also conveniently echoed, in the late 1950s and early 60s, the pictorial strategies of Post-Painterly Abstraction as embodied by the work of Barnett Newman, Mark Rothko and Ad Reinhardt.

14

Towards the end of 1987, I read extracts from my then-unfinished novel *Diesel Mystic* in the lounge bar of the now-demolished Gluepot Hotel in Ponsonby, Auckland. Just as I was concluding the title chapter, in which a Maori flamenco guitarist/diesel mechanic from Ruatoria attains an illuminated state and starts levitating, the painter Tony Fomison stood up in the midst of the audience and said: *I know that man*.

The guitarist/diesel mechanic's name was Robin Williams—the same as the Hollywood actor—and Fomison had heard him busking at the Otara market. I would later record that moment of recognition in the published version of *Diesel Mystic* in a chapter entitled 'The verge of losing somebody':

> The park is located on the verge of the highway south and on the verge of losing somebody.
>
> Can I tell you a story a diesel mechanic from Ruatoria once told me? Johnny Ruatara asks.
>
> I know that story, I reply. I know that man.[4]

Kevin L. Jones, photograph from *Nga Tohuwhenua Mai te Rangi: A New Zealand archaeology in aerial photographs* (VUP, 1994).

15

An archaeologist or geologist stands on the ground and looks down into it—an aerial view, if you like—staring miles downwards into the earth, his attention plummeting, free-falling through the clay, rock and layering of whatever else. He is also, of course, staring down through time.

Fred Williams's landscapes are archaeological in their register of underlying patterns, textures and forces. Their nervous twitches of imagery, their recesses and moments of detail are similar to those that permeate an important series of aerial photographs of New Zealand taken by Kevin L. Jones. Not unlike microscopic or atomic photographs, Jones's landforms are full of suggestiveness: a reclining figure emerges from the Northburn herringbone tailings. The landscapes often look like the human nervous system or X-rays. Or a child's drawing—a feathered or string man, even. At other times the surface of the land looks like human skin under a microscope: porous, bathed in light. (The way the land continues out beyond the borders of the photographic image reminds us that photographs can only ever be fragments of a viewpoint.) This is close to the territory of Paul Klee and, for that matter, early Gordon Walters—an organic mythology of insinuated and oblique forms.

While Colin McCahon was drawn to the mass and structure of the primordial hill country and coast, the inessentials which he usually removed—such details as trees, roads and buildings—are essential to Kevin Jones's photographs. Out of these he creates a sparse, puzzling calligraphy. And whereas McCahon's aerial view revealed an 'order' which paralleled that of Old Testament Christianity—a land permeated with darkness and light, suffering and redemption—Jones's photographs offer a far less simplified or generalised reading. They are hymns to the particular and the disordered. Instead of the changeless, primordial landscape, we are presented with one that changes by the minute, the time of day, depending on the season—or depending on the speed, height and angle of the aeroplane in which we are travelling. It is like the landscape in Andrey Tarkovsky's films *Andrey Rublyov* and *The Stalker*—it is a place of inscriptions, inferences and traces. It is strewn with human history, with relics.

16

A warm afternoon in early September: I am standing at the top of Auckland's recently completed Skytower. The city recedes into the distance in every direction; however, there is one direction in particular I find myself returning to—my eye travelling up Remuera Rd, past Mt Hobson and on towards Meadowbank. It is nearly twenty years since I lived in Remuera, on what is now known as the 'northern slopes'. Driving through the suburb in recent years, I am struck by how much the area has changed. It's an amazing thing how money can run a suburb down.

The resonant spaces of an unassuming childhood have been replaced by the bleeping of automatic car-locking devices and the constant ringing of malfunctioning burglar alarms. Travelling through the suburb by car or on foot, there is nothing left of my childhood. Our family home at 5 Eastbourne Rd has now been replaced by a heart-stoppingly monstrous million-dollar condominium. I visited the street in 1995, by which time our house had been deemed unworthy of its location and shipped off in the middle of one night. All that was left was a life-size floorplan of the basement where much of my childhood was spent. This was another kind of aerial perspective: the floor of the rumpus room, workshop and wine cellar rendered as a sequence of connected two-dimensional planes, the sheltering walls and roof gone (see photograph p118).

*

From the top of the Skytower, the light is golden and washes over the seemingly flat landscape (the elevation renders undulations in the landscape inconsequential). My ostensibly detached and distant gaze is drawn into this landscape with its memories of a childhood spent on bicycles, tunnelling through bush or knee-deep in the tadpole-laden creek beside Portland Rd . . . It is not a 'realistic' view per se—it is the distanced, 'formalised' view from a height. It is the aerial perspective of a Malevich, a Fred Williams, a Kevin Jones. The most surprising thing, however, is that, although I have never before seen the suburb from this perspective, the view appears *familiar*. In fact it feels exactly the same as the diagrammatic floorplan of the suburb which, as a child, I constructed and was constantly drawing up in my mind.

This experience of sighting or recording some intimate 'truth' from such a detached and unlikely vantage point has an analogue in the artist's need to find or create a necessary height or distance (in time or space) so as to see afresh past experience, to unearth its patterns and meanings, its street formations and floorplans. The poem, a case in point, needs this kind of space—it can't be formed while nestled hard up to its originating material.

My year in Australia, at the age of twenty-one, was an attempt to construct this kind of distance and vantage point, then to furnish it with imaginative materials. The future of the creative enterprise, as far as I was concerned, hinged on this manoeuvre. It was as if everything had been thrown up into the air and allowed to hover there for a time, awaiting whatever might eventuate.

17

I have seen with my own eyes one of the levitating saints cited in Blaise Cendrars' *Sky*: Gerard Majella (1726–55), a Redemptorist lay brother who fell into an ecstatic trance one day while listening to a blind beggar playing a popular canticle on a flute. For five years (1989–94), I lived beside a monastery named after that saint, overlooking Oriental Bay in Wellington. During this time, the monastery chapel, which had been a regular venue for Sunday Mass, was closed. On the wall above the altar, there was a large nineteenth-century oil painting of the monastery's patron saint, levitating outside a church above a bewildered gathering of women and children.

With the chapel no longer in use and the future of the monastery buildings uncertain, it was decided that the painting of St Gerard should be returned to the Italian town of Mater Domini, just south of Naples. The picture, by Gagliardi, had been gifted to the Wellington monastery around the turn of the century and was now worth millions upon millions of comparatively worthless Italian lire which, surprisingly enough, when the figures were rounded up, came to roughly one million New Zealand dollars.

I sighted the levitating saint crossing Hawker St, carried by two workmen who were struggling to steady the canvas against the prevailing northerly. The saint, his arms outstretched, appeared to be flying parallel to the pavement, after the fashion of a missile or a child's drawing of a jet. Or a migrating bird heading for the northern hemisphere. (The seasons were changing and the saint's trajectory could quite accurately be described as a kind of migration.)

The last I saw of Gerard Majella, he was gliding head first into the back of an O'Brien Removalists truck (the legend *Don't Risk It, Let O'Brien Shift It* emblazoned on the rear door), to reappear, I imagine, some months later in Mater Domini amidst great celebration and solemnity, the one leavened by the other.

Cyril Wright with St Gerard in Ecstasy. Measuring three by four metres, the painting will have to travel on its side.

After 80 years, St Gerard goes home

18

Building a structure, a vantage point—that is the business of the poem: to lift itself beyond subjectivity and sentimentality by an inherently irrational process involving sounds, echoes and tremors, as well as sense. The end result: such towering yet immensely vulnerable structures as the poems of Guillaume Apollinaire and Blaise Cendrars. Like the small boy in Allen Curnow's poem 'Survivors', we are lifted onto the shoulders of the effective poem. We are held up there as the wind 'freshens across the park, the crowd begins / thinning towards tomorrow. Climb up and see.'

Which brings us to that most humane yet difficult objective of poetry: the recapturing of time, the repossession of past experience—

in particular, childhood—and, beyond that, the unravelling of history, the renewing of its significance.

As a book by Louis Zukofsky, read on the floor of the Sydney apartment, December 1982, puts it:

> Strange
> To reach that age,
> remember
>
> a tide
> And full
> for a time
>
> be young.

Poetry, then, can be an opportunity to 'be young', to re-experience that which is familiar as though it was fresh, newly awakened.

19

In the belly of the aeroplane taking off there is a moment when we are all children again, defenceless, silent, our language (and all its reassurances) lost to us. And then, a moment later, we are safely off the ground and the drinks trays and dull magazines separate the adults from the children once again.

James K. Baxter offered a disgruntled account of such a trajectory in his poem 'The Chariot', the banality of the aircraft offset by the 'unreal vantage' it offers:

> Though the god Technology has lifted
> Me above myself in the dead metal belly
>
> Of the thunderbird, over the winding silted
> River bends and grey feathered willows . . .

20

In one of Patrick Hayman's last dated paintings—perhaps his last—*The dark plane takes off at evening* (1988), a black aeroplane flies upwards directly into the sun. Left behind are the figure of a woman, a hybridised bird/human and one other. A valedictory symbol, the dark plane is a crucifix. No longer the sexualised mechanism of earlier paintings, here the aeroplane—like that in McCahon's 'Jet Out' drawings or in Malevich's Suprematist works—prefigures and enacts the flight of the human soul leaving its earthly garden. Having shed the quirky particulars of Hayman's earlier motorised inventions, this Dark Plane, in its stark, universal symbolism, can be seen as a reprise of D. H. Lawrence's 'Ship of Death', the aeroplane supplanting the vessel in Lawrence's poem while inheriting its function:

> Oh build your ship of death, your little ark
> and furnish it with food, with little cakes, and wine
> for the dark flight down oblivion.

This painting is the beginning of Hayman's dark flight, the creatures of earthly desire at once left behind yet somehow involved and implicated in whatever might eventuate.

21

From this height looking down, I watch a ridiculous twenty-one-year-old with far too much luggage struggling along Williams St towards Kings Cross, Sydney, where he will soon be installed, just around the corner from a delicatessen which does a brisk trade selling Lemon & Paeroa and banana bikes to homesick New Zealanders, a few metres along from the largest Coca-Cola neon in the Southern Hemisphere, or so we were told, or so I am telling you now.

*

> . . . the vast, shimmering moment.
> The contracted, pearl-like year . . .

*

There are threads that one is left holding at the end of every year. In the case of my twenty-second year there is a succession of windsocks, a series of meditations on air and aviation. Also, a suitcase full of books—including Teilhard de Chardin's *Letters from a Traveller*, the Yale *Gertrude Stein* and the Penguin edition of Blaise Cendrars' *Selected*

Poems—which I am still unpacking, There is also an acquaintance with the New Patron Saint of Aviation, Joseph of Copertino, standing there amongst all the other statues at St Canice's, Kings Cross. Into his good company I would commend Patrick Hayman, with his strange, airborne society; McCahon, with his flying crucifixes high above Muriwai Beach; Keiji Haino, with his one word of English; and Blaise Cendrars, the poet of youthful intoxication and delirious elevation, whom I would nominate as the patron saint of high-spirited youth—and the patron saint of all of the above.

Patrick Hayman, *The dark plane takes off at evening*, 1988, oil on canvas.

Notes

1 This correlation between music and colour he took even further to encompass literary expression as well. In the preface to his book *Sounds*, Kandinsky stresses the interdependence of all the arts and complains on behalf of artists intent on breaking down barriers between genre: 'In the past the painter was looked at askance when he wrote—even if it were letters. He was practically expected to eat with a brush rather than with a fork.'

2 Two reasonably accurate accounts of how much of my twenty-second year was spent were published in *Sport 13* as 'Disasters in Splendour', and as 'Flying Wall Café' in *Man with a Child's Violin* (Caxton, 1990).

3 These comments were included in an interview I conducted with Manhire, 'Some paintings I am frequently asked about', published in *Landfall 191* (Autumn 1996). *En passant*, Ralph Hotere, according to various sources, continued to fly after his training and piloted a small plane around Northland during the late 1950s while working as a school arts inspector. On occasion these school 'visits' to remote rural areas consisted solely of a fly-past—with Hotere, in goggles and flying cap, waving from the open cockpit, then continuing on his way. Later, you could only assume, the real challenge for the aviator was somehow convincing the Department of Education that this did in fact constitute a 'visit' in the best bureaucratic sense.

4 Travelling around the East Cape on the *Words on Wheels* tour in February 1998, I read out the aforementioned chapter of *Diesel Mystic* at the Uawa school and mentioned Fomison's response. The local Maori nodded in recognition and later pointed out that the Williams family—many of whom played flamenco guitar—extended all around East Cape. 'The place is crawling with Josés,' one woman said, and went on to explain how, in the nineteenth century, a Spaniard called José had been shipwrecked on the Cape and settled there, subsequently taking fifteen or so wives. 'His descendants are everywhere,' I was assured. Many of the Maori also happen to be citizens of La España Peregrina (Wandering Spain) and, not surprisingly, have inherited this original José's passion for flamenco guitar. 'The hills are alive with the sound of Josés,' someone else remarked.

North Piha bach with typewriter

1

Spending a good part of the 1980s living in a tiny bedsitter close to a busy Epsom intersection, I would regularly escape to Frank and Pat Jones's beach house overlooking the surf at North Piha. As a kind of therapy, I would ride my motorcycle out there, usually—as befits someone in his twenties—in a state of worry, elation, bewilderment . . . While, in hindsight, these solo excursions appear as much a form of 'crisis management' as a concerted effort to clear space in which to write, once I had settled in at the beach house I would spend virtually all my time at the typewriter. (My novel *Diesel Mystic* was drafted in four days during one of these sojourns.) My Suzuki A100 motorcycle laden down with typewriter, paper, books and as little food as possible, I would descend the hill to Piha Beach, sometimes detouring along Garden Road, passing LITTLE SAINT ANNE'S and HANK SCHUBERT'S, to arrive finally at the Jones's bach, which had been less than memorably christened by the previous owners KELVINGROVE.

Within the orderly enclosure of the bach, with its flat, dusty surfaces, magazine covers had been made crisp by the sun, dried flowers slowly reduced to dust, sunlight had faded the Michael Smither print and dried out the glue that held together the table and chairs, making them extremely frail, prematurely aged.

2

For two decades Nicholas Jones and I have sat on either side of the bach teapot, with its upholstered helmet to keep the warmth in (which also has the effect of making the innocuous object look like a miniature tank). The bach is the site for and centre of lengthy conversations about the most vexed of topics: religion, art, music, the emotional life—ah, the emotional life!—matters which, year about, are dealt with in a sincere if muddled fashion inside the warm, wise sanctuary of the beach house.

On these joint outings, a cumbersome old stereo takes up most of the car interior, along with boxes of records. After unloading the sound equipment, we listen to music non-stop for days and nights on end, from John Coltrane to Claudio Monteverdi, from Palestrina to John Zorn to Funkadelic. The bach becomes, accordingly, a carefully maintained acoustic space, the music blending with the roar of the sea from beyond the verandah.

Any description of the bach would be incomplete without mention of the typewriter, the stereo, the militaristic teapot, the fridge that sounds like an avalanche in a car wrecker's warehouse . . . Neither can the building be considered as distinct from its surroundings, the view being very much a part of the architecture: Lion Rock filling one side window, the Waitakeres looming like a wall behind the bach, a pine tree growing up through the deck, a layer of sea salt covering the entire structure.

When, aged about thirteen, I first visited the Piha bach it had only two rooms. On that occasion, we children slept in a flooded tent pitched out front, peering up through the rain at the fibrolite structure. A year or two later, an extension was built, adding a second bedroom and enlarging the living and kitchen area. The dimensions are still not large—I worked out that wherever you are inside the bach you are never more than three steps away from the central point. Also added was a deck, without railing, which jutted out above the lawn, a launching platform for the eye, carrying us beyond the dunes and out across the water. (Happily, no one ever misjudged the edge of the deck and plummeted the three metres to the sand below, even on the darkest of nights while returning from beach walks between the fluorescent waves and that vertical black cloud, Lion Rock, which advanced towards us or receded, depending on the atmospheric conditions.)

For a time, as teenagers, we moved away from the bach, preferring to pitch a tent up in the Waitakeres, somewhere we could drink our under-age beers in secret, bottles buried under rocks in the riverbed to keep them cold.

3

The brittle, sunbaked furniture: every year it grew lighter and paler, closer to dissolving into air. While, during writing stints, the table in the living room functioned as a desk, between drafts I would sit outside on the deck with my notes, moving around the house so as to remain in sunlight or, depending on the time of year, out of sunlight. Similarly, furniture would move around inside the house, followed by small piles of reading materials, teacups and, towards evening, wine glasses.

There were other literary activities. One summer I worked alongside the actor Teresa Healey clearing lupins from the property, taking turns at slashing while the other read lengthy tracts from the epic Australian poem 'The Nightmarkets' by Alan Wearne. (We left one clump of lupins standing overnight so a family of frogs that had made their home *sub-lupin arboreus* in an ice cream container full of stagnant water could vacate their residence under cover of darkness.)

Another time I arrived at the bach to find a huge, dead swan lying by the back door. After dragging its surprisingly hefty bulk across the sandy lawn the following day, I buried it under a mound which, to the neighbouring bach-owners arriving from town that evening, must have seemed of human proportions. It was the kind of symbolic moment a young writer might have made something of. Although, in this case, I never worked out exactly what it was a symbol of.

4

Asleep in our single beds, the Piha bach is a constant, unmoving reference point while the elements swirl around us: the wind, the hills and always the sea, 'the sea', in Louis Zukofsky's words, 'fishing / constantly fishing / its own waters . . .'

What surprises me now is that such an unassuming and only occasionally visited structure should have come to embody, more than any other place, both the levity and gravity of growing up, of friendship, love, disappointment, sadness and always the returning connection to the natural world. It still serves as a model for the kind of books I hope to write: the jaunty structures, without decoration or anything extraneous, teeming with human life and alive with the *romance* of it all.

Certainly during the years I 'worked' at Piha, there was a *romance* about the bach. As if it was Frank Sargeson's hut—the way sunlight soaked into the fibrolite—or the Trappist monk Thomas Merton's hermitage, or Dylan Thomas's study staring out across the Irish Sea. It was also the room overlooking the Seine where Simone de Beauvoir and Jean-Paul Sartre sat in tandem at their desks. The structure contained a dream of becoming a writer and, beyond that point, a dream of continuing writing.

The chair. The faded cushion. The dining/writing/*everything* table. The sliding glass doors opening on the view. In that order. For a time.

The second Ada

She was Holly Hunter's double in the underwater scene in *The Piano*. Imagine spending days on end being thrown off the side of a Maori canoe—well, that's how, she told the class, she had spent the last fortnight. The geology tutorials and field trips proceeded as usual during her absence, the students excavating volcanic rock from around the Auckland isthmus, chipping away at the dry, brittle surfaces like prospectors looking for, well, prospects.

When she went off 'on location' to a bay in the Bay of Islands, she could not tell anyone—not even me—where she was going or what she would be doing there. The crew and cast had been sworn to an effective kind of secrecy which would quieten things down for a short while to make the subsequent noise even more dramatic. It would also enable a mythical quality to enter and inhabit the project at an early stage, to fortify it for the grandness of its future.

The rehearsals were few and interrupted by the weather. She had to practise following the grand piano into the water and being jerked over the helm by a rope with the cameraman all but perched on her shoulder like a bird. The first few times she was allowed to wear a modern swimsuit, but once they started filming 'proper' she had to don full period costume, which made her feel, as she disappeared overboard, like the nineteenth century personified.

Needless to say, when the filming was completed the secrecy to which they had been sworn dissolved in a blaze of publicity and chatter. She would proudly—but never quite arrogantly—announce that she had, in fact, been Holly Hunter's double while the American actress sat in a far-off caravan talking American on the telephone to America. It wasn't that she didn't like Holly Hunter and she didn't mean to be difficult, but because they were so similar-looking she did wonder, from time to time, if they could have made the entire film without Holly Hunter. She could have been one hundred per cent Holly Hunter's double—a thought which made her think of the dictator Hoxha's double in a travel book she had just read set in Albania. The similarity between the two names made her laugh: Holly

Hunter and Hoxha (pronounced *Hodger,* she was quick to point out)

Recounting to the geology tutorial her aquatic adventures, she made her classmates feel decidedly washed up and undistinguished by comparison. Hopeless, boring and without glamour. One rather tragic student in his early thirties proffered that he had once appeared in a film called *Talkback,* engaged in a kissing scene with a woman twice his age in the back of a taxi driven by a woman three times his age. They were filmed driving back and forth along Karangahape Road while the director lay across their laps with a walkie-talkie instructing them when to start kissing for the camera (which was mounted to the bonnet of the Holden Belmont and operated by remote control) . . . But no one from the tutorial seemed interested, they were all too busy interrogating his rather more interesting classmate as to when they might be able to see this film, *The Piano.*

Some months later, the tutorial went on an outing to see the movie. They wore their funny geologists' clothes. They stared enviously down into the green water as Holly Hunter's double was dragged, dramatically, into it. The boyfriend of Holly Hunter's double (who was the only one who knew all along how she had been spending the weeks away from class) looked especially pleased after he had seen the film.

The student who was in *Talkback* later tried to start up a conversation about screen kissing and the anguish this topic had obviously caused him, but this only made the others more fixated on *The Piano.* They were so entranced by the flickering keys, the flickering tongues, it was as if it had all been *real.* One geologist was quick to point out that Holly Hunter had played the real piano bits—a note at the end of the film had said so.

The double was asked if she had had to do the grotesque underwater scene where Holly Hunter is suspended, billowing, full of air, above the sunken piano. But she said they hadn't needed her for that scene—a dummy got the job. Which was fortunate, as it took them days to get that one right, she added.

Being Holly Hunter's double gained her privileges around the university. The cafeteria staff would refuse to take money from her for the many cups of coffee she embarked upon with many acquaintances, all of them weighing her up, checking details, all of them with their differing opinions as to whether or not she looked like the

American actress. They sought her silent, antique gaze. She retreated back into history before their very eyes. They placed her on tracts of coastline. No matter what she was wearing, she knew her attire was being transformed into Victorian skirts and bonnet. A dress like a cage. And when she left them, driving off in her cranky Volkswagen, she imagined that in their eyes she was being spirited away by ship's boat or waka or, at a pinch, by horse-drawn cart.

She rode the crest of this particular wave for a month or two before it beached itself finally and with, on her part, some degree of relief. It was during a party at Piha Beach attended by students and media persons, a smattering of fashionable types all drinking ferociously and mulling about in the luminous interior of a bach hard up against a backdrop of blackened hills. Her geology classmate—the tragic one—was there also.

He immediately launched forth into his accustomed diatribe against the film industry.

That movie he was in, he mumbled, the one called *Talkback,* well he didn't get to utter a single word in it, let alone talk back to anyone. Even though he was continually opening his mouth. And what sounds there were in *that scene*, he pronounced, and this was really meant to shock people, well they were added later.

For once, the cast of *Shortland Street* were left in their own little corner of the party, talking amongst themselves. The activity centred on the opposite end of the room where a woman who looked like Holly Hunter was holding court.

It took only a few overheard comments for the woman from my geology tutorial to realise that the woman in the corner of the room had, in fact, been Holly Hunter's double in *the beach scenes.* It was the back of *her* head as the soundtrack gushed and the piano stood, isolated, on gloomy Karekare beach. It was her moving at speed along the sand with the camera tracking, or just standing still. There could be any number of doubles, the young geologist mused. Doubles and triples and quadruples. At first she felt upset, robbed, but gradually a sense of relief came over her. She had *never been* Holly Hunter's double—Holly Hunter's double *didn't* exist—just as in Albania it was discovered that the dictator Hoxha's double, after all the fuss made about him, didn't exist. Even if, in that case too, a considerable number of such paid imposters wasn't an implausible idea.

It was at that moment during the Piha party—this she told me some time later—that she ceased to be Holly Hunter's double. She would refuse, from that evening onwards, to talk about her role or entertain such thoughts in the heads of those seeking her acquaintance. She would no longer cultivate the glances of men who stared at her face as if they were staring back into history.

Later in the evening, after deciding to drive back to the city, she lingered long enough on the lawn to watch the sun go down over the water. The romantic glow reminded her of the end of a film. *Damned, redundant stretches of coastline,* she thought, and for once the volcanic plateau and the geology class didn't seem such a bad prospect.

Warming her car's engine, she sat back and watched the party-goers—an unruly troupe—as they carried Holly Hunter's other double down to the beach, where they had positioned a portable stereo just below high-tide mark. The theme music from *The Piano* was gushing forth across the iron sand, tumbling upwards over the dunes, crossing the beach road then reaching as far as the bach. Stumbling, collectively, over the dunes, the men bore the double down onto the sand, crushing the small sea things underfoot while, overhead, 'Holly Hunter' was held in their upraised hands. Someone made a joke about Thomas Bracken and Thomas Marram Grass, but no one got it. Some of the men must be professional actors, the geologist thought, they managed such convincing impressions of drunken men. Many of them were quite carried away by the pageant and mumbled nautical things—*land shakes, avast, blinking brine, blasten damnation and bugger me days*—although these utterances, like the sound of the sea, were subsumed in the lush score, the trickling piano and the overpowering strings. In the middle of this music, the men lowered Holly Hunter's double down onto the hard wet sand. While, at that precise moment, the other double accelerated along the waterfront road in her Volkswagen 1600 Fastback which dated from 1972, and refused, now, to go back any further than that date.

Radio Birdman

A child's guide to aviation

Of his childhood, all he remembers is the model aeroplanes, the sky heavy with them, their wings like birds' wings, gently colliding or brushing against one another. He would read the aeroplane manual over and over, memorising it, like the words of a song, words that had the capacity to transport him:

Power is derived by the twisting of strands of elastic rubber which extend from end to end of the body, and although the winding up is a rather tedious process, when the tension is released they drive the propellers at astonishing speed for quite a long time. Thus the tiny planes can cover long distances and rise to big heights as long as their equilibrium is not disturbed by eddying winds.

While his childhood was the heyday of both the model aeroplane and the transistor radio, it was well before the days of radio-controlled model aeroplanes. It wasn't until years later that, driving through the Waikato, he suddenly realised that the model aeroplanes of his youth had also grown up.

The photographs that accompany this text are by Brendan O'Brien

An adult's guide to (the history of) aviation

That which he most feared as a child finally happened. The long, lethal arm of the Russian airforce reached the Waikato. The hammer and sickle waved above paddocks grazed by ambivalent cows. Tents were pitched alongside State Highway 1; men in Russian hats raced across the road for cigarettes and ice creams from a nearby service station.

Presumably to intimidate the local population, an extraordinarily life-like mannequin was placed outside the main tent, the figure dressed in the infamous Gravity Suit.

A teenager's guide to aviation

The band existed from 19. . . to 19. . ., when it died without ever having compromised. We were close. We lived together, shared food and clothing. We went on long journeys. We fought all sorts of enemies, real and imagined, and amongst ourselves . . .

Underneath the barbarian surface there was a serious heart. When we were playing our music it was life or death. Giving total concentration and maximum effort was a matter of personal honour. We would sometimes experience a transformation within ourselves while playing. We went somewhere beyond day to day existence. The feeling was like something I got later from flying in a jet fighter extremely low over the desert. We lived for this experience.

Deniz Tek, guitarist, *Radio Birdman*, 31 December 1987

End of the history of the Waikato

One of the locals has taken a potshot at the mannequin in the Gravity Suit, the bullet entering through the visor and blasting a neat hole in the mannequin's head. Now the bullet is rattling around in the back of the helmet or inside the plastic skull.

The locals are lying low, anticipating the Russians' reputedly unquenchable appetite for retribution. Already they can see rows of burning haystacks and civilians herded like cattle into holding pens. They imagine their television transmission being interrupted by men who cannot speak English.

Be your own pilot

The cockpit of the faster-than-the-speed-of-sound jet fighter in which you sit is remarkably similar to the interior of a Ford Anglia. The same crude metal fittings and lack of finish. Mounted on old milking shed fittings alongside the aircraft are one or two missiles and an assortment of smaller bombs, their interiors removed, like mangoes with their innards scooped out.

A brisk souvenir

The Russian Mig-21 supersonic jet is touring the Waikato on the back of a truck. The aeroplane, in flying order, is said to have been bought by a farmer for $40,000, a sum he recouped within a month of going into business, charging eight dollars a head just to sit in the cockpit or watch a video of the jet flying across long, gloomy stretches of sky in supposedly happier times. A formation of scale models in various sizes, to suit various tastes, follows 'the real thing' around petrol-station towns in the Waikato, a part of the brisk souvenir trade.

A new world order

The first Mig has been so successful, a banner announcing the arrival of a second jet fighter is attached to an abandoned container some distance down the highway.

The jet fighter in which the rock guitarist would fly low over deserts and expanses of ice has become a children's entertainment.

Long-range guidance system

The ball in the tip of the ballpoint pen is a miracle of modern technology, the teacher explains to the child. When someone is writing by hand at a normal speed, the ball is reputed to rotate between three and four thousand times per minute. The teacher is trying to interest the child in becoming a writer instead of the pilot of a jet fighter.

Postlude

Early morning in the Waikato. A woman prods a frozen puddle with a stick, then lifts the flat, transparent disc from the driveway. Her gloved hands carry it indoors as far as the freezer, where she will stack the sheet of ice on its side. Returning later in the day, her son will remove the puddle from the freezer and discover his face reflected in it, his eyes staring back at him, frozen there between twigs and leaves, three wooden clothes pegs and the tiny figure of a plastic soldier running, bayonet bent around 180 degrees.

A long sentence in Czech ending in English

Jenny has followed the two Czech writers out onto the verandah after dinner at a Lower Hutt marae. Moments ago the novelist and the poet were staring bewildered at a plate of kina—now they face each other in the half-light out front of the whare kai. The glowing twilight above the Hutt Valley has reminded the men they need a cigarette—two cigarettes, in fact, which are now burning a few feet apart like the headlights of a vehicle. It is early autumn and the valley between the silhouetted ranges is punctuated with the sweeping high and low beams of cars and the intermittent glow of house lights. The sun has only just gone.

Looking up at the golden sky which is flecked with pink remnants of clouds, Ivan Klima says in reasonably articulated English, that it must have been on an evening like this that The Beatles wrote 'Lucy in the Sky with Diamonds'.

The poet Josef Hanzlik, who is also staring upwards through the cigarette smoke, replies, not quite comprehending, *eh*?

To which Klima responds with a long sentence in Czech ending in English:

. . . .
. . . . *The Beatles, Lucy in the Sky with Diamonds.*

At the end of which Hanzlik nods approvingly, *Ah, The Beatles.*

Ah, Lucy.

Of course.

The shape of living children II

I

We go back there only for funerals—or for the music of funerals, the brass band rallied around the flagpole or the karakia. Maybe once or twice just to watch the cows grazing around the volcano or the horses swimming in the river. But it is in funerals we are returned to this place. And one day our own funerals will restore us, finally and absolutely, to this point, this promontory, with what few strands of music remain, running like rivers down the mountainside and vanishing into the ever-undulating sea.

Thinking about old Mrs Tito, whose farm adjoined ours, it wasn't hard to believe that Yugoslavia was, as we were then told, run by a Maori, a relative of hers. We were convinced that General Tito was a local boy who had made good in Europe, just as similarly indisputable sources later informed us that Jimi Hendrix was also—at least in part—a local boy who, in that instance, had made good in North America then England then North America again.

The most capable Mrs Tito looked after my mother's family when they were small. She would send them down to the river for eels. The river ran through the family farm, under a bridge, then through the Tito's farm. There was a certain respect concerning the river, as well as the mountain, that she would teach the children. She told them a river had to be maintained, that you had to *feed* it—although they were never told with what.

As children, we were unsure if General Tito had made a mess of Yugoslavia or if he had held the country together. Much later, of course, Yugoslavia fell apart completely, which, you could argue, confirms the latter view.

The word 'communism' confused us no end. While we were supposed to equate it with a cold, harsh climate, the children in photographs of Yugoslavia looked happy enough, even if, in some of the images, they were marching in what seemed to be unnaturally straight lines—the nuns never made us line up like that, deeming such militarism appropriate only in state schools. Even more incongruous with communism were the newsreels of life in anarchic Yugoslav villages where the adults sat around drinking oily red wine while their children played cricket with fruits that appeared to be so hard they could stand such treatment for months.

II

One morning in May 1989, my three-year-old son and I are sitting in a parked car by the cemetery gates. He insists on remaining in the car while I walk along the promontory to where my grandfather is buried. Jimi Hendrix is playing on the car stereo and my son's two great passions are, at this moment, Jimi Hendrix and trampolining. And trampolining isn't an option at the graveyard, except in some remote, abstract sense.

Weaving between the headstones, the guitar of Jimi Hendrix follows me the length of the wind-blasted headland—'The Wind Cries Mary' then 'Killing Floor'. When the tape has run out, my son comes running from the car, scuttling down among the gravestones, some of which are exactly the same size as him. 'Who died for what and why these children?' he asks, dodging cheerfully from aisle to aisle, jumping out from behind the overgrown statues, some of which are the shape of living children and mark the graves of children.

III

1833 was the year of the last great battle over the pa. That was how the year was described to us. A war party of over 800, many with rifles, traipsed down from the north and laid siege to eighty families with only one rifle between them, stuck out here on the headland.

While the attacking party was fearsome and murderous—or so the defenders had every reason to believe—the southerners surprised even themselves during the month-long siege, repulsing all of seven assaults. The final attack was on the night of a full moon. Reaching the palisades under cover of musket fire, the warriors were turned around with stones and spears and one rifle which—it was related to us with much pride—was fired by the chief himself, who, after the engagement, changed his name to 'Clear-Eyed' on account of the fact that sixteen of the enemy dead were found to have shot in them. The retreat became a rout, the southerners pouring out of the pa. Sixty-eight of the attacking party were left dead for the loss of only one of the defending tribe.

The pounding of a thousand feet, the patter of shot hitting the palisades—I imagine rivers of such music descending the mountain on all sides, like the spokes of a wheel.

IV

1982. Expatriate New Zealanders in Sydney are organising the annual 'Kiwi Night' in an inner-city club. This year the highlight is going to be the Jimi Hendrix Memorial Unaccompanied Electric Guitar Solo Competition. The organisers send out a press release announcing the recent discovery that Jimi Hendrix was one-quarter New Zealand Maori. The *Sydney Morning Herald* runs the story, which, it soon comes to light, is a hoax—and not a particularly elaborate one at that. Heads roll, a journalist friend later tells us, in the *Herald*'s George Street office.

The Kiwi Night is a high-spirited affair, the organisers riding the crest of the wave of the *Sydney Morning Herald*'s gullibility. The club is jammed. Neville Purvis, aka Arthur Baysting, is the compere. A music shop has lent a Fender Stratocaster and Marshall amplifier. Chocolate fish, flown in for the occasion from Auckland, are selling steadily from the bar, along with banana bikes and 750 ml bottles of DB Double Brown. Fuelled by drunken nationalism and anticipation of the imminent competition, the evening's euphoria increases.

At one point early in the guitar solo contest, organisers have to rush on stage to stop a particularly ardent contestant from smashing the brand new Stratocaster to pieces on the floor. It is a moment of some tension as they wrestle the instrument from the musician, then hand him over to the bouncers, who are already rolling their sleeves up. He appears to be just the material they have been waiting for.

During the interval our friend John Carrigan wins a hot lamb sandwich after answering a long string of questions concerning the exact location of certain takeaway establishments around New Zealand. But the real prize-winner of the evening, after further heated competition, is a Maori bass player from Bondi who breaks into a stirring, unaccompanied rendition of 'God Defend New Zealand', a local variation on the Master's 'Star Spangled Banner'.

V

After my grandmother's funeral in 1994, we follow the children as they run between the gravestones, leaping over them or flinging their arms around them, the sleeves of their jerseys stretched so they dangle and flap like wings. (As children, we were forever being told not to stretch the sleeves of our pullovers, that it was *not natural*—it was like trying to grow wings. Our hands always had to be visible, hovering at the ends of our sleeves.) Still resounding from the last time my son and I were here, the guitar of Jimi Hendrix wends its way between the elongated arms and wings of gravestone angels. It occurs to me that the enormous sleeves of Hendrix's psychedelic shirts were probably an attempt to approximate such wings.

And I imagine all the generations of our family that have been and that are to come . . . Like the stone figures that stand in irregular lines, that are eased to the ground by the offshore winds, we too are the shape of living children, running down the grassy bank as far as our deaths. And carrying on running, beyond even our deaths.

The man who wrote the book about the weather

This morning I was standing outside a service station, soaking up the cool, autumnal blueness when, at a nearby petrol pump, Erick Brenstrum, meteorologist and author of *The New Zealand Weather Book*, emerged from a blue car. I was leaning against a lamppost, wondering why and how it was that, unlike the Hispanic poets, we cannot sing love songs to our country. You would have thought the literary self-image might have improved since Dennis McEldowney, fifty years ago, spelt out the national belief that 'New Zealand is a dreary (some say a drizzly) wasteland, in which we try to escape from our puritan consciences . . . by the aid of the six o'clock swills and the banknote dreams of the Totalisator Agency Board . . .'

Why is it that we still cannot *sing* a song of this place, like Lorca—'oh how the city sings'—or Neruda in his fecund odes to fruit and vegetables, in his paeans to every moment of his life in Chile. Bearing in mind that the word 'stanza' derives from the Italian for a room, why is it that the rooms of New Zealand poetry are still so dank and fuggy? And why don't we do something about this: throw open the windows, slap some fresh paint on the wall, talk the place up?

It was into this reverie that Erick Brenstrum walked, wearing a blue shirt—in keeping with the general appearance of the morning. On such a day, employees of the Meteorological Office look pleased with themselves and proud of their station in life. The only grey in the sky was the underneath of my Subaru station wagon, which had been jacked high up into the air on account of a suspected oil leak.

I complimented Erick on the impressive security card affixed to his person. He said that these days at the Met Office you needed a security pass to get through just about any door in the building. I have a security card too, I proffered, showing him my City Gallery ID, which bears a handsome photograph of a woman who doesn't work at the gallery any more. Art museums need security—they are always worried someone is going to swipe their pictures—but what on earth did the weather people have to worry about, I asked. Were they afraid someone might break in and tamper with the climate?

He laughed, then said, rather more seriously, that they had recently had a 'stairdancer'. Erick then asked me what the book was that I held in my hands.

Selected Odes of Pablo Neruda. I said I was going to be talking with Kim Hill about the Chilean poet on the radio the following morning. Erick then announced he was off to South America the following week on business. He had been re-reading Neruda himself, brushing up on his Spanish by way of bilingual editions. Last time he was on the continent, he had placed flowers on Neruda's grave. This time he planned to visit one of the poet's houses as well as make another pilgrimage to the gravesite.

I said this struck me as not only appropriate but thoroughly necessary Met Office business. Then we considered for a moment the question of trans-Pacific traffic and how New Zealand and Chile were, basically, neighbours. In Pablo Neruda's 'Ode to the Voyager Albatross', the *magna avis* traverses the oceanic boundary fence:

Desde Nueva Zelandia
cruzo todo el oceano
hasta
morir en Chile.

From New Zealand
it had crossed an ocean
to die
in Chile.

While a cloud in Chile translates, literally, into a cloud in Wellington, the words don't cross the Pacific quite so easily, the distance between Spanish and English being yet another ocean to cross. Erick Brenstrum and I agreed it was the *translator* who makes all the difference, especially with Neruda.

Margaret Sayers Peden did a great job here, I proffered, waving my book around. The odes coming across as clear and sharp as the weather, which, needless to say, speaks both English and Spanish.

Ben Belitt, we agreed, tied the poetry in knots. Erick recommended the translator of *Extravagaria*. Who was it translated

Extravagaria? Erick had left his copy at the office and couldn't remember off-hand. Then the conversation proceeded onwards, more generally in the direction of this partially enlightened world we go about in—a goodly place in which the Meteorological Office will support its emissaries to lay flowers on the graves of poets. That Chilean meteorologists might one day bestow garlands on the graves of New Zealand poets!

Alistair Reid, that's it. The Met Office recommendation! *Extravagaria.* Translated by Reid. It finally comes to us.

Erick Brenstrum's petrol tank is now full. He bids me a good day then drives off, leaving me staring up into the grand expanse of sky, this blueness that stretches between New Zealand and Chile, English and Spanish, Pablo Neruda and the two of us, his enthusiastic readers, heads held high in the blue air, upraised in the pure breath of his verses.

Electricities

I am sitting in an Auckland dealer gallery pondering some paintings by Michael Smither. One in particular holds my attention—a New Plymouth public garden scene called *Poet's Bridge*, the title of which strikes an encouraging note: there can't be too many such places dedicated to poets. The owner of the gallery then shatters my meditation, informing me that 'The Poet', in this case, was a racehorse that won the garden's benefactor a whole pile of money.

In recent months I've found myself moving from one sphere of employment to another. After spending, as a television company employee, hours on end in a room with as many as eight videotape machines going at once, I now stand silently, my face a few inches away from an oil painting. Concerning these different confrontations, these different kinds of engagement, there's a quality in the latter encounter which I find myself overwhelmingly drawn towards and which, for want of a better word, I'll call 'the poetic'.

Before the television arts series *The Edge* went to air in early 1993, I sat with a group of involved parties in the Ponsonby restaurant Praego, collectively trying to think up a name for the imminent programme. Not only did the TV3 executive not want the word 'arts' in the show's title, he thought it would be ideal if the word was never mentioned on the programme itself lest it 'turn off' the audience. That attitude summed up the network environment in which our ugly duckling was supposed to learn to swim.

Towards the end of the second and final series, we succeeded in sneaking a few moments of serious arts commentary onto the programme, in the form of Jane Sayles talking about the 'Voices' exhibition at the Museum of New Zealand Te Papa Tongarewa. She

---

This text was written late in 1994 when I had just finished working on the television arts programme *The Edge* and was in the middle of writing *Lands and Deeds; Portraits of Contemporary New Zealand Painters*. Commissioned for a series of essays in *New Zealand Books* focussing on what writers were currently working on, the exercise allowed me to be (in Justin Paton's words) 'an emcee at my own poetry reading'.

used the word 'aesthetics' at one point of her disquisition. I was certain at the time that the network would cut this segment from the broadcast programme. Using a word like 'aesthetics' on television was a transgressive act the equal of saying 'motherfucker' on the six o'clock news. Miraculously—or so it seemed to me—the word sailed through the network screening process and resounded uncut and un-bleeped on the late Sunday afternoon broadcast.

Depressingly, Barbara Kruger was right when she described television as 'an industry that manufactures blind eyes'. Baudrillard also maintained television was 'directly destructive of meaning and signification, or neutralises it'. My job in television was a decisive factor in my decision to undertake the project I am working on, *Lands and Deeds*—a book based on interviews with eighteen New Zealand painters. My objective was to rediscover how alive the eye and mind could be after a time spent in what I often found myself thinking of as a kind of 'twilight' zone.

Recently, one of my workmates on *The Edge* wandered into the video-editing suite and, as she stood there talking, her long hair extended horizontally from the side of her head to touch the door frame, which must have been alive with static electricity. Her hair remained there for some time, just like that, reaching for the door frame. Somehow this image sums up, for me, the milieu in which I found myself. The digitised, electromagnetic environment, as far as I can make out, is a zone in which 'the poetic' is generally absent, or at least neutralised. Regardless of the purchase television has on the public eye and mind, I now find myself moving off into smaller, quieter, more cherished things.

Alongside *Lands and Deeds*, I have been working on a satellite project, a series of short poems about painting and painters. These poems are fragments of real and imaginary conversations with artists—my chance to touch upon the mysterious commingling of seeing and doing which is the act of painting.

*

Some way into the sequence of poems, Toss Woollaston is standing in his living room, contemplating an unfinished painting of the white shed in front of his house. (1) Minutes later we are standing in front of the shed itself, the afternoon light almost too bright to look at, radiating off the side of the structure. (2) That evening we find ourselves discussing a photocopy of a drawing of his mother—c.1934—hanging in the living room, and (3) the following morning I am holding a tube of titanium white in one hand while writing the following with the other. This sequence of whitenesses—(1) to (3)—led to this poem:

TITANIUM

There is only one white. The end wall
of the garage at five in the

evening. Her face against the glass, lips
moving as though she was

talking. A white you could see
all the way through,

as far as the ground
beneath. But she

was not talking.

The woman's face in the poem is that of Woollaston's mother. Her face is the whiteness of the sheet of paper, the window her face presses against is the glass in the picture frame. And I am left sitting there wondering if I will ever get around to writing an essay about the three important female presences in Woollaston's life: his mother, the poet Mary Ursula Bethell, and his wife, Edith.

The next day, I write the following during the short plane trip back from Nelson to Wellington.

Cover of *Sage Tea*, by M. T. Woollaston, Collins, 1980 (featuring portrait of the artist's mother, c.1934).

Toss Woollaston at Upper Moutere, photograph by Gregory O'Brien, 1994.

COMPOSITION

The clearing in the centre
of the thing—

isn't that the subject of
all painting? Let me explain:

the white square
in the middle

of the thing—a cup of tea
with a grain of salt

or how an insect, floating, resembles
a tealeaf. To put it

another way: I was
to spend the day painting

but a horse on a long rope
caught my attention, going

around and around
a man in a blue hat.

Woollaston spoke fondly of the English expatriate Robert Netterton Field, who taught him during the 1930s and exemplified, for the young painter, the role of the committed artist. For years, as I was growing up, my family owned an oil painting by Field—an earthy river valley reminiscent of Woollaston, yet predating him:

RECOGNITION ONE

Field or valley, Robert,
we watched you walk,

your colourbox overwhelmed
by daffodils,

the day's paintings
watching as you approached them.

My father met Field once and thought him the perfect gentleman. There is a sense in which all of Field's paintings contain my father's observation.

My ruminations continue while flying from Invercargill to Christchurch—a clear winter's day:

RECOGNITION TWO

There was a moment, Robert, you realised
the two great mysteries:

contentment and friendship. Also what
Dante said: 'art is

to god like a nephew'—you recognised
so much in that, how
    so much

of the country was covered
by riverbeds, mile upon mile

of snow and how it melts
sometimes, the isolated animal
    man.

*

As a teenager, upon finding a painting of Dunedin by George O'Brien (no relation) in an early issue of *Art New Zealand*, I was disorientated at seeing my own name—G. O'Brien—on a pebble in the foreground. It was at that moment I began entertaining the possibility of making some kind of entry of my own into the conversation that is New Zealand arts and letters. Up until then—in a house that, to my great good fortune, always had pictures on the walls—I had always thought it was someone somewhere else who was responsible for the primary production.

FOR G. O'BRIEN, PAINTER, 1821–1888

George, I once saw my name on a rock
in one of your pictures,

the distant town's windowframes packed
with crumpled newspapers

against the cold. You had drunk
the family heirlooms,

the miniature bottles of vodka, in one of those small
Dunedin residences, your shadow falling

through one side of the house and
out the other.

Sketching the city from the Southern Cemetery,
arguing with the wind over a watercolour

your hands had slowed, eventually
lost it. A matter of days

later you were laid flat, across town, in the
Northern Cemetery with your daughter

and wife, the grave unmarked. But
you put my name on a stone, George,

and I owe you that, among other things—
how the town in the watercolour

became a city. Also, on earlier, colder mornings,
the way a woman held

your jar of painting water between her hands to stop it
freezing. And how it was

one day the inquisitive townsfolk discovered
you had finally

married her. Your little bag
was gone.

If the work of the painters in *Lands and Deeds* communicates something to me, then the short poems are my end of the conversation, something in return. A number of artists the poems address are no longer alive: such dazzling figures as Patrick Hayman and Rita Angus.

MAN OF HAY

Standing on
something
living,

Patrick,
the pulse
in my foot.

DIRECTIONAL

Where they meet
the estuary,

Rita, creeks build monuments
to themselves. But

the imagination doesn't need
monuments, it needs

more imagination.

Not surprisingly, while writing *Lands and Deeds*, I find myself going around and around that mulberry bush of New Zealand painting: Colin McCahon. He crops up throughout the interviews—as omnipresent as Baxter appears above the firmament of New Zealand poetry.

PAINTER WITH CLOUDS

I see my paintings
reflected in lakes

like billboards hammered up
against blue sky,

between the colours of earth
and heaven

although I am not
a religious man,

believe me.

Last August I travelled to Invercargill to interview the eighty-six-year-old painter William J. Reed, who painted extraordinary works upon his return from the Pacific Theatre, where he had served as a medic during World War II. The fact that his work has hardly even been acknowledged underlines the need for a number of retrieval jobs within the local art historical record. Art institutions and criticism often seem obsessed with the distant past—the 'historical'—on the one hand, and with the present—the 'hot new thing' so beloved of television—on the other. Much recent work falls through the gap between.[1]

One of the poems that followed my meeting with Reed inadvertently picks up the marching rhythm you feel in his nightmarish summaries of the Pacific war. The poem sets the 'music' of a watercolour brush on paper against that of a military marching band.

A CENTURY OF MARCHING

They tried to interest you in
the trombone, saying

it was an instrument with a future.
It was almost

the twentieth century—they were
going to be needing

brass bands. That was the future
they anticipated for you,

the trombone
slide a long arm

extending beyond the immediate
present. Rather than those

twitching brushstrokes, your infuriating
paintbox. That was

the wrong direction
entirely.

A mood of apocalyse dominates William Reed's productions. His memories of the Solomon Islands have remained chillingly present to him and, through the paintings, present for us.

SOLEMN ISLANDS 1941–45

Five more hours painting
until dusk.

We have the light, Bill, and
the means

to extinguish
the light.

The exhibition 'Fomison—what shall we tell them', curated by Ian Wedde, which was recently at the City Gallery in Wellington, is now touring the country. It's a show that casts a strange, at times bleak light on the twentieth century. There was a story Fomison told about how his father, upon his return from fighting in World War II, brought back a watercolour box which he had salvaged from a German army base they had captured. This token he passed on to his small son. Somehow that watercolour box epitomises, for me, the history that can be contained in paint, in these smallest vestibules of colour, these colours awaiting form. I wrote a sonnet which recounted events from the point of view of the previous owner of the paintbox, the man from whom, indirectly, Fomison was to inherit his colours:

ORIGIN OF A WATERCOLOUR BOX

Painted hands, he recalled, the hurry to leave school.
Marching in single file to watercolour class. Many ponds

approaching an ocean. One name in German sounded
like the Pacific, went the circumference of a tube of water-based colour.

Far from the meaning of art, the commentary was about
art, pretending not to notice the running colours. Later

bicycles disappearing into the oncoming cloud, water flowing
towards the opaque borders, a brigade advanced towards him

through Italian sheets. Water soaking the paper, running down
the falling roof, as they were over-run—1944—the door kicked open,

coffee spilled over their boots as they ran between gardens,
the trees of smoke. Who would have, dying, thought,

fifty years later, deeper in water—the Pacific—the faces
of these men still drifting through schools of fishes.

So Art is about inheritance, about that which is handed down—be it the Grand Tradition or a small wooden paintbox—which points to another difference between Painting and Television. While painters, no matter how radical, are answerable to so much that has gone before, television producers are answerable only to the evening's ratings. And here, I suspect, ends my career in television.

Notes

1 Author's note, 2001: This situation has improved markedly since the early 1990s. Recent exhibitions, in both public and private galleries, have 'rediscovered' such artists as Helen Stewart, Adele Younghusband, Janet Paul, Juliet Peter, Charles Tole and Sam Cairncross, to name a few.

III

FRINGE DWELLERS

Blue Monk, Black Light
Ralph Hotere and Thelonious Monk, a notebook

1 Standards

Named after one of the quintessential jazz standards, Ralph Hotere's stainless steel artwork *Round Midnight* (1999) is an appropriately stark, beautiful creation. Completed just before the turn of the year 2000 and first exhibited at the Dunedin Public Art Gallery in the new year, Hotere's *Round Midnight* is steeped not only in night-time but in the midnight of the twentieth century. It is a pristine panel of darkness, cut into by a cross-shape—the mast of a ghost ship, perhaps, moving through the black water of Otago Harbour as seen from the artist's house at Carey's Bay.

Thelonious Monk's 'Round Midnight' has been recorded thousands of times by an extraordinary array of jazz musicians—from traditionalists to the avant-garde. As a standard, it is constantly reinterpreted by young and old, by the respectful and the dissident. It is a haunting melody—in most versions it is shot through with nostalgia, although at times it can swing and, occasionally, deconstruct. The tune has had words set to it but the greatest renditions are the wordless ones—like Monk's original quintet version from 1947, with its melodic, harmonic and rhythmic extemporisation.

The tune 'Round Midnight' is that paradoxical thing, a rhythmical structure that is almost emptied of rhythm, hence the transfixed, ethereal feel of it—a mood echoed in Hotere's *Round Midnight*. In fact, you could think of Hotere's artwork as another wordless version—a transposition from one art form to another, from the key of 'Monk' to the key of 'Hotere'.

2 *'Mr Jazz' in New Zealand*

Thelonious Monk flew to New Zealand in 1965, one year after his face appeared on the cover of *Time* magazine. He was the fourth jazz musican to be thus honoured, being preceded by Louis Armstrong, Dave Brubeck and Duke Ellington. At the time he arrived at Auckland airport his international profile was at its peak and he was referred to, in all seriousness, as 'The High Priest of Jazz' and 'Mr Jazz'. Accompanied by the Baroness Pannonica de Koenigswater and his wife, Nellie, Monk was taken on a Royal Tour of the country, complete with Maori concert parties and boiling mud pools.

Coinciding with this degree of fame, however, there was a suspicion in critical circles that the pianist/composer had become erratic and his talent, particularly as manifest during concerts, was falling apart.

3 *Olivier Messiaen:*

> Music is a perpetual dialogue between space and time, between sound and colour, a dialogue which ends in a unification: time is space, sound is colour.

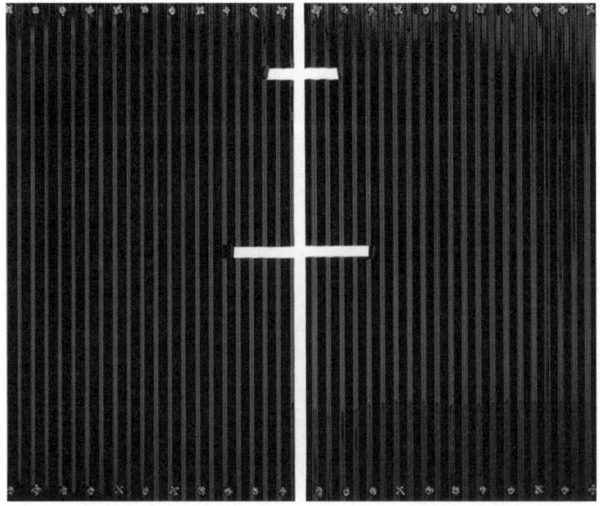

Ralph Hotere, *Round Midnight*, 1999, painted steel with lead nails.

Photograph of Ralph Hotere, Marti Friedlander, 1979.

4 Carey's Bay and beyond

On 19 May 2000, I gave a talk entitled 'Carey's Bay and Beyond—Landscape and Spirituality in Ralph Hotere's Art' at the Dunedin Public Art Gallery, to coincide with the exhibition 'Hotere—Black Light'. The lecture examined the artist in relation to three 'monks': the American jazz musician Thelonious Monk—known as the 'Blue Monk', after one of his most famous tunes; the painter Ad Reinhardt—who was nicknamed by his friends the 'Black Monk' on account of his other-worldly aspirations; and the Trappist monk and poet, Thomas Merton. The lecture touched upon a number of concepts central to the monastic or ascetic life, while acknowledging that the artistic life is inherently 'monastic' if you go along with Keats's famous remark to Shelley: 'My imagination is a monastery and I am its monk.'

5 In praise of memory, playing by memory

Often, during concerts, Thelonious Monk would leave the stage for disconcertingly long periods. Or he would sit silently, listening to what the other band members were doing, his head resting in his hands. He would change a tune halfway through or he would mix fragments of various tunes together, leaving the rest of his quartet

'audibly confused'. As a somewhat befuddled Peter Keepnews observed after one performance: 'It's hard to tell whether Monk actually forgot what tune he was playing, or whether he was trying to see how closely his sidemen were paying attention, or whether he just decided he'd rather play "Rhythm-A-Ning" than "Evidence".'

There is something of this channel-switching, improvisatory manner in the work of Ralph Hotere as well. Like Monk, the painter is quick-footed and fleet, jumping around within a single artwork—a tendency particularly apparent in his printmaking. As an artist who has produced works of a purist abstract manner, then returned to figuration, then gone on to work that is completely word-based, his printmaking of the 1980s is an exuberant mixing-up of these elements. In the lithograph *Night Window* (1992), he brings together not only a disorientating array of formal motifs but also verbal fragments. The 'voice' in the artwork is musical and lyrical rather than rational or consistent. The viewer is left wondering whether the work is a 'Black Window', a 'Night Window', a 'Black Union Jack', a 'Dawn/Water' work or something else entirely. It contains elements specifically from all these series—and others—but refuses to settle into any of them.

Perhaps, like Monk's music, Hotere's painting is an art of remembering things *differently*, a routine in which memory is a dynamic force. Rather than rediscovering a pre-existent order or form, he is trying for new figures, new *sounds*.

6 *August Kleinzahler:*

> Not very long ago the music identified with Monk was considered to be weird or esoteric, grating, probably a joke or affectation. The man himself did little to alter this view . . . dancing around in little circles at performances, grunting and humming . . . he was consumed by the sound of the world around him, principally its rhythms, silences, discords . . . 'Mad Monk' they called him . . .

7 *Beyond and back*

Both Ralph Hotere and Thelonious Monk are masters of the subtle variation. In series such as 'Black Paintings', 'Requiem' and 'Port Chalmers', Hotere has painted suites of minutely modulated black surfaces, playing on the slightest variation or inflexion—much the same way as the pianist would replay the same simple phrases night after night, making tiny adjustments, most of them imperceptible to the listening audience. 'Jazz is my adventure,' Monk would say. 'I'm after new chords, new ways of syncopating, new figures, new runs. How to use notes differently.'

'Beyond' is a word used to describe both Monk's artistic trajectory and his destination. It will do for Hotere's as well.

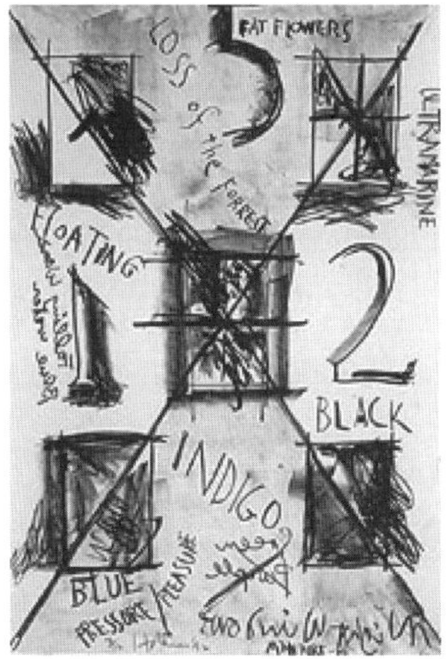

Ralph Hotere, *Night Window*, lithograph, 1992, courtesy of Marian Maguire and PaperGraphica.

8 Monk's months

The year after he completed the 1999 *Round Midnight*, Ralph Hotere produced a series of twelve lithographs that improvise around the vertical cross motif that bisected the stainless steel piece. In the 'Round Midnight' prints, the cross motifs occur two or three times in each image—like the masts of midnight boats down at Carey's Bay.

Both Hotere and Monk walk a line between order and chaos, between composition and improvisation, between fullness and emptiness. New combinations are forever being arrived at. You see these manoeuvrings throughout Ralph Hotere's oeuvre, but particularly in the works of the 1970s and 80s. Texts such as Bill Manhire's 'Pine', 'Dawn/Water Poem' and 'Night Windows, Carey's Bay' are constantly being re-voiced, just as Hotere's own geometric motifs and archetypal symbols are reshaped and re-integrated. For an artist who subscribes to Ad Reinhardt's belief that the 'essence of art is to have fixed rules, regular routines', Hotere's rules are, by their very nature, flexible and mobile.

Confronted with what are, then, such inconclusive productions, the viewer and listener are drawn into an active involvement. We have to negotiate the collisions and shifts in meaning. For Hotere, the audience is the backing group, moving from tune to tune as the 'composer' dictates, or observing the silence that he opens up. This evasiveness is the crux of his work—just as it was for Thelonious Monk sitting silently at the keyboard, listening as the other three members of the quartet improvised around the silence which was the very centre of the music. This way, the audience was drawn to that empty space at the heart of what was unfolding before them. Hotere, too, stands back and looks silently at his work, observing what has been offered. In the case of both 'Round Midnight' and *Round Midnight*, there is a blurring of the roles of performer and audience.

9 How to Distinguish Decadent Songs (The People's Music Press, Peking, China):

> The rhythm of jazz is against the normal psychological needs of man.

10 Misteriosi

The persona of the 'Misterioso' Monk as performer/artist suggests a few ways of considering Ralph Hotere. Both have been cast as priest, shaman, cerebral abstractionist; both are Men of Few Words, ardent individualists, yet individuals drawn to collaboration with like-minded and -spirited friends. Both are wearers of remarkable hats. By the 70s, Hotere had a leather floppy-brimmed hat permanently up top—this was replaced most recently by a classic beret sporting a small Cuban flag and Che Guevara badge. The hat, in the case of Monk and Hotere, is a useful form of self-expression—or perhaps subterfuge. It is also an emblem of 'guerilla' resistance, a compounding of artistic and political freedoms very much in keeping with Monk as seen on the cover of his 1968 recording *Underground*.

Despite a legendary reluctance to explain themselves, Monk and Hotere have often been photographed—in situations of their own making, it should be noted—so the primary historical record of them, aside from this art itself, is the photographic one. Usually we see Hotere in the presence of his artworks (which tend to overwhelm his slight frame) and we find the hatted Monk play-acting as postage-stamp profile or French Resistance fighter. On one occasion Monk refused a request from Riverside Records that he be photographed for the cover of a forthcoming album dressed as a monk swigging from a bottle of whisky while leaning on a church pulpit. Instead, he insisted they photograph him in the seat of his three-year-old son's pedal car (which, he told them, was where he composed most of his music anyway). That is the image that appears on his epoch-defining *Monk's Music* (see p189). As an assertion of being seen on his own terms, it's unbeatable.

Both Monk and Hotere have been depicted in the cockpit of small aircraft. Solo Ralph appeared in *Landfall* a few years ago in the single-seater he learnt to fly as a territorial in the early 1950s. And on the Columbia recording, *Solo Monk*, the pianist is a lone flier in the cockpit of that great motif of Modernist adventure, the biplane.

Thelonious Monk would start each gig alone at the piano and then, at some unpredetermined moment, the other band members would materialise. The solitary statement came first, then the collective

one. While at the beginning of his career, Hotere was, like early-evening Monk, a solo act, refining his singular voice and statement, more and more since the 1970s the work has been collaborative, with the ensemble comprising figures as various as Manhire, John Reynolds, Bill Culbert and Mary McFarlane.

11 In search of a lost concert tour

Visiting from San Francisco in 1992, the poet August Kleinzahler was intrigued by various reports of the Thelonious Monk Quartet's legendary New Zealand tour. He imagined Monk and entourage the morning before the Rotorua Town Hall engagement, looking for their reflections in the thick, impenetrable mud ponds, or pondering the geysers, those outpourings at once mythical and real. Monk would have felt close to them, Kleinzahler was certain . . .

Charlie Rouse on tenor, Larry Gales on bass, Ben Riley on the drumkit—the three of them holding the music together as Monk wandered on and off the Rotorua Town Hall stage. Wearing his funny hat. Clapping his hands. And an audience, by some accounts, numbering as few as a dozen, scattered around the expanse of the hall.

12 Defining moments

Somewhere out there in those less than full auditoriums the length of New Zealand, a generation of Young New Zealand Poets was being entertained and, quite probably, altered. Among the audience at Rotorua was poet Bob Orr, Ian Wedde was in Auckland, Alan Brunton somewhere else . . . Two decades later, Orr relived the event in his poem 'Thelonious Monk Piano':

> Thelonious Monk does the talking
> the piano does the playing
> Thelonious Monk does the listening
> his life begins to play
> the memories are in his hat
> the music is in his head
> the ivory is in his heart
> the elephant is in his fingers
> walking out of Africa into the New York snow

Not only did Monk find a captive audience of New Zealand poets, overseas he had been long established as the Poet's Pianist. As the Australian poet Laurie Duggan riffed in 'Five Spot', from his 1990 collection, *Blue Notes*:

Monk's Coming
on the Hudson's
about appropriate
for breakfast.
White frost. Trains
in the clear air.
Discrete piano notes . . .

Kleinzahler himself dedicated a book to Monk: *Earthquake Weather* (Moyer Bell, 1989), the opening poem of which concludes in mournful Monkesque fashion. A nocturne to play before Duggan's aubade.

Poor Monk, dying at the Baroness's
on the hill above Weehawken
night after night
cars sluicing into the tunnel below

in the city, fanning lights
across the broad river,
the West Side throbbing
across black water

out of notes, dying.

Before returning to San Francisco, August Kleinzahler asked if I could dig up some more about Monk's antipodean tour. I wrote a formal letter to the United States Information Service in Wellington, asking them to send me any information whatsoever. Some time later a reply arrived in the mail. The Service could not help with my inquiry because, in their words, 'our records do not go back that far'. Judging from the tone of the letter, the Information Service had never heard of Thelonious Monk. Whereas the pianist, so famous for forgetting which tune he was playing or even, apparently, which city or country he was in, could 'remember' countless elliptical compositions, it would seem the official 'memory' of the American state was incapable of traversing a handful of years to retrieve a few dates.

13 Wagner:

> Music blots out our entire civilisation, as sunshine does lamplight.

14 Concrete practice

Like Ralph Hotere, Thelonious Sphere Monk was an expert at giving nothing away. John Mansfield Thomson recalled the pianist's arrival in this country for his 1967 tour:

> Monk arrived at Wellington airport wearing one of his famous hats—the 'High Priest of Bebop' or 'Mr Jazz'. 'Mr Monk, how would you define jazz?' asked *Dominion* reporter Graham Rhind . . . 'He turned his warm liquid gaze toward me, started to tug at his frizzle of beard. He tried to pluck the words out of the air. Then they came to him and his huge, intensely-dark face broke into a dazzle of teeth. "Jazz . . . when you hear it, I guess you know."'

Still reeling from the experience, Ray Harris in the *New Zealand Listener* (30 April 1964) recalled the conclusion of the Wellington Town Hall performance:

> There were many at the Town Hall who openly denounced Monk's well-known wandering after 'vibrations' as a gimmick, an egotistical means of drawing attention away from the other instrumentalists . . .
>
> . . . when the audience clamours for an encore at the end of a concert he ignores applause until it has reached deafening proportions, and then makes one brief appearance at the stage door, more or less as a token gesture. As one fan aptly put it, 'Monk has spoken.'

Monk's reply to the journalist and his silence at the concert's conclusion will do as a statement on behalf of Hotere and his painting as well. Hotere, in what must be his only utterance about his priorities as an artist, stated in 1968:

> I have provided for the spectator a starting point, which, upon contemplation may become a nucleus revealing scores of new possibilities. No object and certainly no painting is seen in the same way by everybody . . . It is the spectator who provokes the change and the meaning in these works.

You could say Hotere is a Monkesque absence or elusive presence on the contemporary art stage. It's a position you could associate with Zen Buddhism. The Zen masters, with considerable brilliance, always refused to rationalise or verbalise their experience. If questions had to be answered, the reply would invariably have the effect of further vexing and frustrating the interrogator. Such rebuttals were of course an eloquent way of stating that Zen was a *concrete practice* rather than a study or form of intellectual exercise. Using this as an analogy, the art of Monk and Hotere also makes a stand as fundamentally 'concrete practice'.

15 Wassily Kandinsky:

> Colour is the keyboard, the eyes are the hammers, the soul is the piano with many strings.

16 A map of this land (1992)

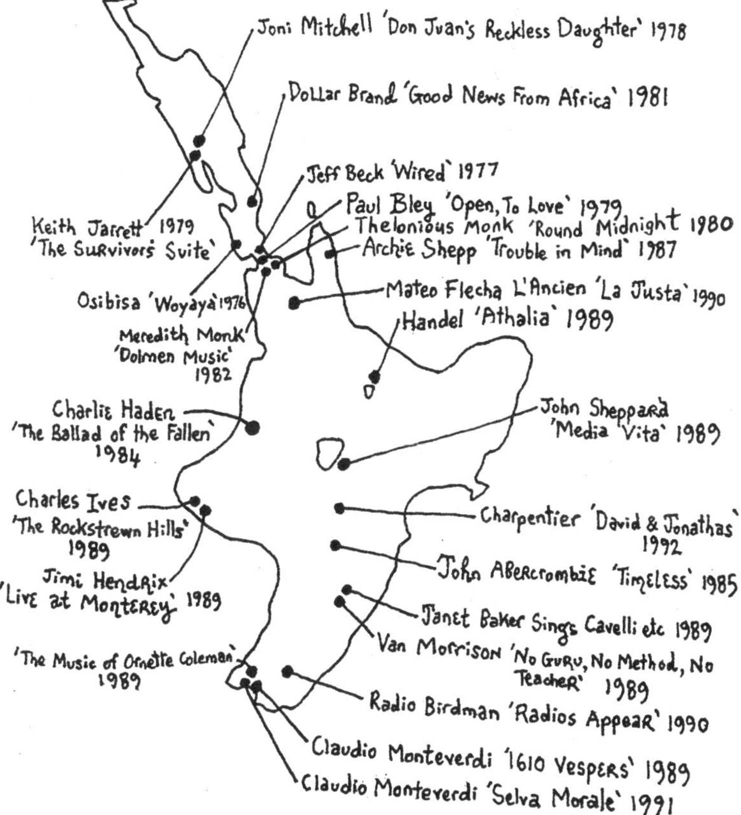

A few years ago, Alan Brunton asked me to contribute to a proposed issue of *Landfall* devoted to music. Instead of writing a piece, I prepared the map of the North Island reproduced here. The diagram was an attempt at placing pieces of music in the landscape according to where either I first heard them or they attained an especial significance for me. Since drawing the map I have whenever possible revisited the sites specified on it, ensuring the upkeep of this 'large, living museum', which is also, inadvertently, a fragment of autobiography. The map also takes me back to the apparition of Thelonious Monk on stages around New Zealand. And an imprint of music, his music, left on this landscape.

Coda

He was standing in the middle of the stage as everything moved tentatively, nervously around him. His hands curved in on themselves, fingertips reaching back until they touched his forearms.

From this point, he could proceed.

Thelonious Monk spent some time adjusting the height of the piano stool, then just sat there in silence, hands pressed together, index fingers running the length of his nose. An attitude somewhere between prayer and thought and something else entirely.

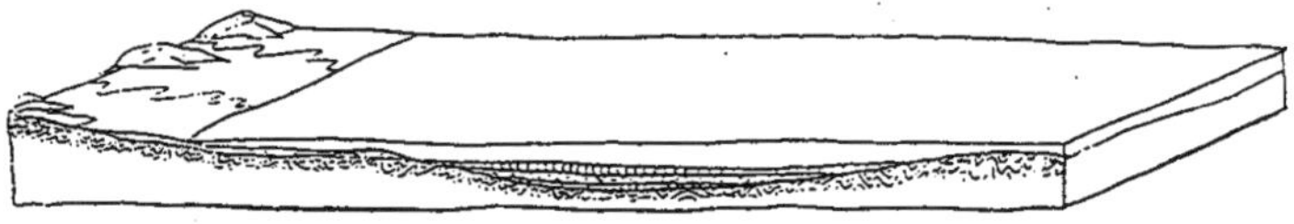

The lines crossing the landscape were electrical cords leading towards and away from the microphone stands which were positioned at the outer limit of his field of vision. The cords were rivers through which the precious notes coursed.

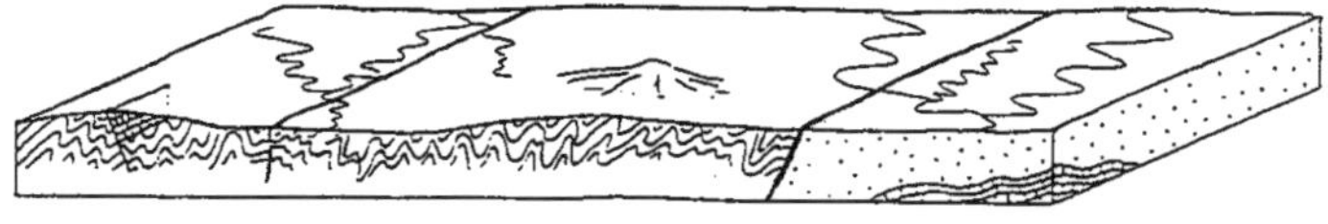

The wavering lines beneath ground level were the intonations of Charlie Rouse's tenor saxophone, straining the surface, or holding it up, or managing to do both at the same time.

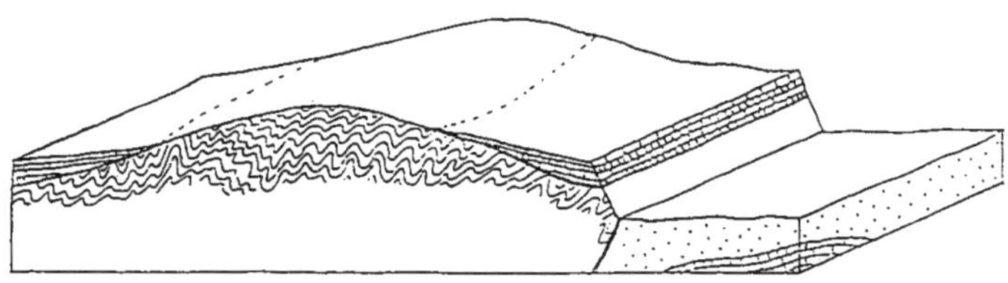

It must have been like this—rivers winding freely across the land, hills broken down by weathering and the passage of water—the natural agents, an erosive music. A world which, if it existed, hardly existed at all, except as a vapour, a music, a remnant of its own past. Uplifted, warped and faulted.

Thelonious Monk, mid-concert, looked as if he was trying to find shelter or running for cover. Or he stood in the middle of the stage, a long way from the piano.

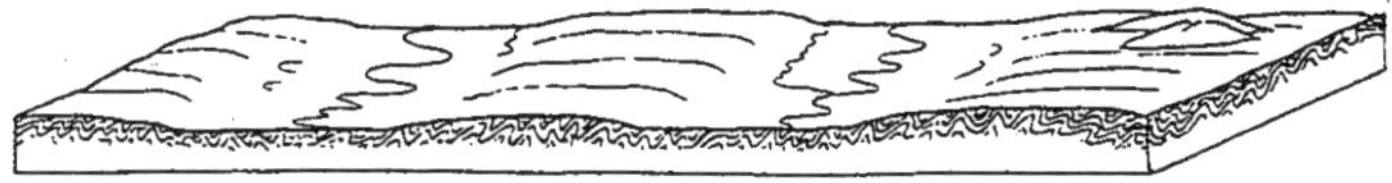

The undermass as it rose—the rhythm section attempting to break through the surface. Only Monk had left them no surface to break through. They had become the surface themselves, moving deeper and deeper into themselves.

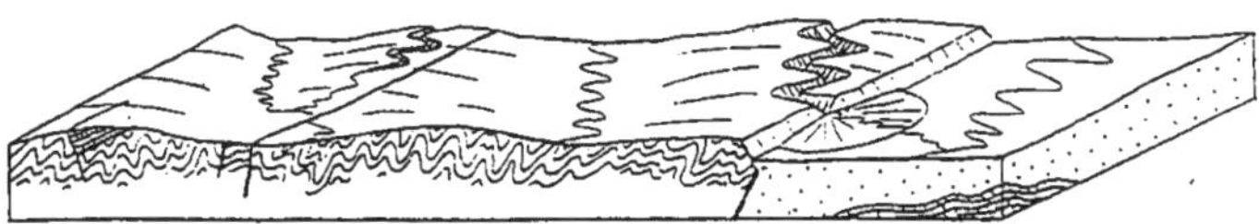

Such a folding and fragmenting of rocks can occur only in what geologists refer to as Great Mountain Building. These specialists agree that around this time there must have been a Great Mountain System. And several great pulses, raising the valleys into higher land.

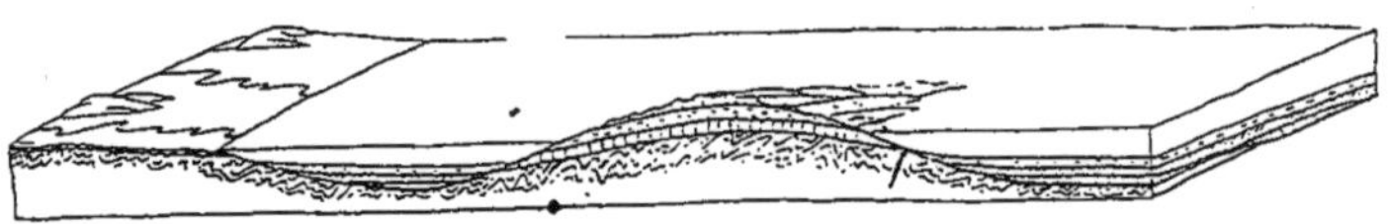

Here, they said, it was starting to break up . . .

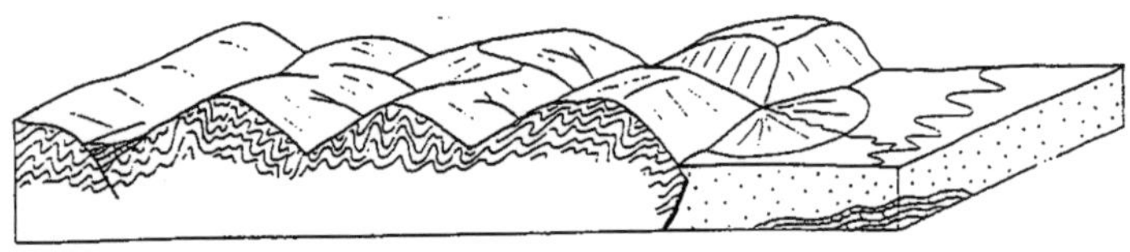

Thus we have a great rhythm, Monk said. And so it was said of him.

No road to follow

Eric Lee-Johnson

After Eric Lee-Johnson's funeral in 1993, his widow apparently placed a box of shells the artist had collected by the door and asked mourners to take a handful each as they left. The gesture was very much in the spirit of Lee-Johnson himself, acknowledging the forms and objects that inspired his best work. A handful of these shells from Lee-Johnson's studio has resurfaced in Michael Smither's recent painting *Little Muddy Rock* (reproduced in *Art New Zealand* 69), registering, in a small way, the persistence of Lee-Johnson's concerns and forms.

Born in 1908, Lee-Johnson occupied a central position in the emerging nationalistic art of the 1940s and 50s. Paralleling his friend A. R. D. Fairburn in the literary world, he was a major figure on the art scene, both as a practitioner and an ideologue. Since then, however, his reputation as a painter has diminished, although the Auckland Art Gallery's 1992 'Fifties Show' established Lee-Johnson as a crucial figure in New Zealand photography.

If it does nothing else, his autobiography, *No Road to Follow* (Godwit, 1993), will reopen the file on Lee-Johnson the painter. Avoiding any theorising or in-depth apologetics for his art, the text and its accompanying illustrations (which include photographs and examples of his painting and drawing) form a convincing enough document to make a major study the next logical step.

No Road to Follow is a lively, readable account with the immediacy of an oral history. The book is not so much an excavation of a life as an episodic re-living of it, avoiding any probing examination of the self and its various relationships. It is a memoir of times and places, people and environments.

While Lee-Johnson's life unfolded against a backdrop of the Depression, the Second World War and its aftermath, it is the immediacy of day-to-day life that preoccupies him, which isn't surprising given the extremely primitive living conditions he and his family encountered—in places like Piha, Mahurangi and Pakanae (near Rawene on the Hokianga Harbour). Just how backward Northland was as late as the 1950s is still alarming. And even more so the lengths to which Government agencies went to suppress depictions of the living conditions of the Maori.

The book is full of wonderfully observed detail, recalling affectionately but unflinchingly a time when a Lyttelton waterfront café would have only one teaspoon in use and that was 'securely chained to the counter next to the sugar bowl'. Or a time in Northland when Lee-Johnson went outside to investigate why his telephone wasn't working and discovered 'someone with no conscience had cut several metres out of a low-hung section [of telephone wire]—most likely, I thought, in this "do it yourself" district, to help tow some broken-down vehicle back home'. Lee-Johnson emerges as a good-humoured, independent spirit (who bemoaned the fact that critics often overlooked the humorous nature of some of his work).

Packed with anecdotes involving such cultural icons as Maurice Duggan, A. R. D. Fairburn, John Weeks, Charles Brasch and Opo the Dolphin, the book paints a vivid, high-spirited portrait of an era when the artist (usually male) could get by on next to nothing, could travel (usually on two wheels) and immerse himself in a life of physical engagement with the world and with art. It was also a time of struggle against indifference, when the likes of Lee-Johnson and Fairburn could put on a major exhibition and the *New Zealand Herald* would send down its racing reporter 'to assess the merits of the works on display'.

Lee-Johnson's impressive eye for the telling detail reflects the visual intelligence that drove his work as both painter and photographer. Many of these details seem almost emblematic of their time and place:

> There was the hillbilly farmer . . . who carted his cream cans out to the main road in a rusted old wreck of a pick-up. On his way out one morning one of his cab doors fell off near Mrs Froggett's front gate. 'But he didn't stop,' she told us. 'He didn't pick it up on his way back either—drove over it.' And apparently he continued to do so until, as a patch of rust, it became a colourful part of the road.

Out of extreme living conditions, and the extreme condition of Lee-Johnson's health (he was plagued throughout his life by TB-related illness), the artist was able to paint up his vision of life and death, growth and decline. Lee-Johnson criticises art historians who have tried to pigeonhole him as an artist 'preoccupied merely with the broken-down reminders of our romantic past'. He berates critic Francis Pound for his assertion (in the 'Fifties Show' catalogue) that the artist saw 'little else worth painting but ruin and decay'. It is, however, these painted images of decline that constitute Lee-Johnson's most enduring statement in paint. Far surpassing his often illustrative works chronicling life in small-town New Zealand, his best works embody a surreal view of nature and damaged life forms derived from a childhood spent 'among the gaunt remains of carelessly torched King Country forests'.

Taken as a whole, his painting epitomises both the best and worst aspects of regionalism, demonstrating the limitations as well as the strengths of art that is nurtured in isolation. The widespread criticism of regional or provincial art is that too few ideas are taken too far (as opposed to cosmopolitan art where too many ideas are not taken far enough). In the 1960s, Lee-Johnson's work did expand to accommodate a more primitivist and abstract style, but this written account—unfortunately as far as any overview is concerned—closes before that period.

Apparently Lee-Johnson finished working on the autobiography only three days before his death. His widow has produced an epilogue which sketches in the details of his life from the 1960s onward. Maurice Shadbolt adds to the book an enthusiastic foreword which, quite rightly, acclaims Lee-Johnson as a 'pioneer nationalist'. The work of Lee-Johnson (and other underrated pioneers such as T. A. McCormack, John Holmwood, Charles Tole and John Weeks) suggests a number of potentially fruitful directions for contemporary artists to take note of. It would be a good sign if all the 'heroic' Jackson Pollock biographies in the Elam and Ilam libraries started gathering dust, and accounts like *No Road to Follow* were absorbed by younger artists.

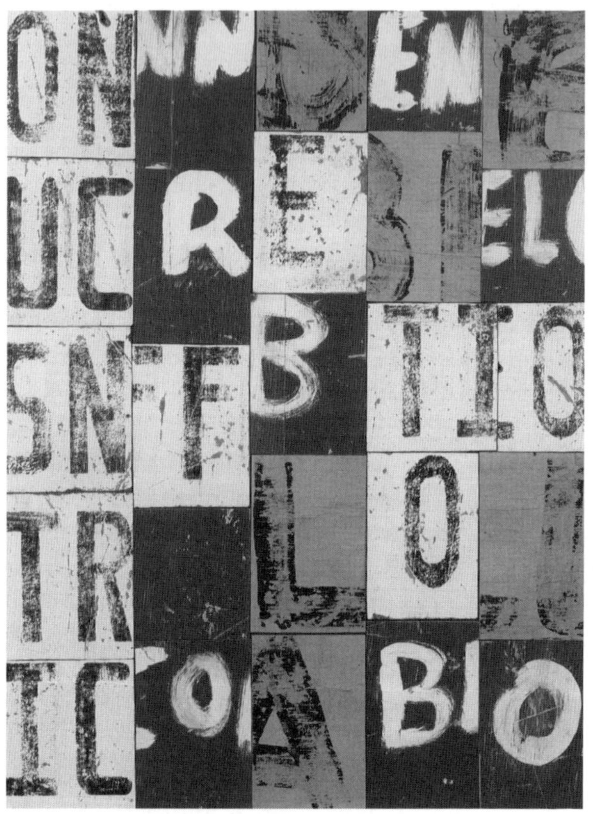

Rosalie Gascoigne, *Honeybunch*, 1993, wood.

These May Mornings in October
Rosalie Gascoigne 1917–1999

'Artists are like the bards of old,' said Rosalie Gascoigne, 'they sing a song of their district.' This brief remark encapsulates some intrinsic qualities in Gascoigne's art. She thought of the artist as a *bard* and the artwork as some kind of utterance, as a song sung. The specific use of 'district' underlines the provincial nature of Gascoigne's project and its origins in the pastoral or bucolic tradition. The works remain close to, and speak of, their place of genesis: the landscape outside Canberra, a sunbaked and bleached expanse of flat lands, gum trees, sun-dazed sheep and signage denoting LAKE GEORGE, DRIVE SLOWLY, DOG TRAP ROAD. These are Gascoigne's geographical co-ordinates; alongside them you would find another set of reference points at the Australian National Gallery—in the vicinity of Pollock's *Blue Poles* or McCahon's *Victory Over Death*. Or you could look into the *Selected Poems* of her friend and artistic ally, Rosemary Dobson.

While, in antiquity, the archetypal bard was expected to be literally blind, in recent decades there has been an expectation in certain circles that the painter be deaf or illiterate, impervious to the spoken or written word. Both requirements are based on an unnecessary but current notion of purity or self-containment in an art world where, as Jonathan Williams has noted, 'product and career have wiped out vision and character'. As one look at any of her creations will tell you, Gascoigne is an exemplar of the artist who is not particularly at home in an art world presided over by (to quote Williams again) 'the Four Horsemen of MacPainting: *Glitz, Chic, Hype & Schlock*'. While, superficially, her works are easily co-opted into formalist arguments—a co-opting to which she gave short shrift on many occasions—ultimately they insist on standing their own idiosyncratic, unapologetic ground. And like the best 'provincial' art, it has to be said, they transcend their particulars. Such is the vision and character of these artworks that can also be considered as concrete poetry or, to use Paul Klee's term, 'visual music'.

Like the art of McCahon and Hotere, Gascoigne's merging of language and form affirms Charles Baudelaire's belief that 'the arts aspire, if not to take one another's place, at least reciprocally, to lend one another new powers'. It was Rosemary Dobson who, in the 1970s, introduced Rosalie Gascoigne to the American poet Denise Levertov, after whose poem 'The May Mornings' she named a work.

> It seems the May mornings
> are a presence known
> only as they pass
> lightstepped, seriously smiling, bearing
> each a leaflined basket
> of wakening flowers.

As well as exploring the same pastoral tradition as Dobson and Levertov, Gascoigne shared their love of the verbal, the 'poetic'. Perhaps even more precisely, her constructions can be thought of as phonetic or syllabic. Traditionally, poetry was based on 'measure'—on the poetic 'foot'—a fact which places the poem in a surprising proximity to maths and geometry. Spanning the distance between the poetic and the geometric, Gascoigne's art is, in effect, a return to poetry in its original state. Her works are rhythmical structures, full of echoes, accents and beats. There are rising and falling cadences—at times there are even rhymes. Here I would like to posit Gascoigne in the company of Edith Sitwell, in whose mind rhythm was the one way modern poetry could hitch itself up to the twentieth century and make something of the ride. 'Rhythm,' wrote Sitwell, 'is one of the principal translators between dream and reality. Rhythm might be described as to the world of sound, what light is to the world of sight. It shapes and gives new meaning.' A further affinity might be noted between Gascoigne's works and numerous musical sources—you need only look at the scores of John Cage, at player-piano sheets, serial music notations or early computer musical scores.

Rosalie Gascoigne grew up in the Auckland suburb of Remuera, then studied at Auckland University, where she gained a BA in English and Latin in 1937. After a time as a schoolteacher, she moved to Australia in 1943 and married Ben Gascoigne, an astronomer based just outside Canberra. She had no formal art training, although she studied the

Japanese art of flower arrangement, Ikebana, prior to making her first 'assemblage' in the 1970s—by which time she was in her late fifties.

'I have a real need to express my elation at how interesting and beautiful things are and to see them arranged,' she said in a 1997 interview. Her own comments on her work are an absolute delight: one large construction, *Plenty*—reproduced in Vici Macdonald's remarkable book, *Rosalie Gascoigne*—bears the following explanation from the artist:

> It's the countryside round Canberra when the yellows are out—yellow daisies, gorse—and it's like a great unmade bed. Terrific. When I started making that, I thought, 'It's got to be big enough for a horse to roll in.' And it was.

The artworks resurrect such familiar objects as road signs, packing crates and pieces of formica, taking them, in the words of Levertov (who dedicated a poem to Gascoigne), 'out of their past' so that they are 'transfigured by being placed, / being seen'.[1]

Like Rita Angus (who was, remarkably, less than a decade older), Gascoigne recorded in her work what Angus called 'the alive, constructive and courteous spirit of the age'. You can trace that spirit through these keenly felt yet humble constructions, and observe an instant of it in a photograph reproduced in Vici Macdonald's book. It is a cool morning—perhaps in May—and Rosalie Gascoigne is 'negotiating' for some corrugated iron at a rubbish tip near Captain's Flat. Out of this kind of informal, matter-of-fact exchange her work came into being.

Rosalie Gascoigne died on 17 October 1999. In the bleached, weathered and reflective surfaces of her work, she remains a beguiling presence. Like the poems of Edith Sitwell, these works of 'gaiety and veiled sadness' linger in the memory, suspended in time and space. These May mornings.

Notes

1 Working in the great New Zealand tradition of the bricoleur—the artist as cultural recycling plant—Gascoigne manifests in her work an affinity with other contemporary practitioners, including Don Driver, Ralph Hotere, Edward Mackenzie and Lauren Lysaght; with poets Ian Wedde, Bill Manhire, Michele Leggott and James Brown; and with composers John Cousins and Greg Malcolm

Big tree transmission
Colin McCahon's tau cross

What is thought to be the biggest pohutukawa tree in the world can be found at Te Araroa, near East Cape. Some of the branches of this ancient tree—called Te Waha o Rerekohu—have grown so heavy they touch the ground. Over time, these branches, at the point they make contact with the soil, have developed their own root systems so that water, instead of being drawn from the tree trunk, is taken directly up into the branches and flows back from there towards the main body of the tree.

The process of give and take embodied by Te Waha o Rerekohu is particularly relevant to McCahon's *Urewera Mural* (1976), a work which drew its inspiration and subject matter from Te Urewera and its inhabitants, the Tuhoe people. Today, we find McCahon's painting has itself become a source, a form of enrichment (albeit, as is now well known, a contentious one) and a means through which people from beyond the Urewera region have come to an awareness of the place and its significance to Maori.

McCahon's *Urewera Mural* has at its centre another big tree: a kauri-like pillar with the nearby inscription 'Tane Atua', the forest god. Like a Maori pou or land-marker, it tells us where we are. Another inscription, 'At the boundary can I forbear from turning back my head', aligns the motif with the traditional pou whenua, which was used to mark out boundaries. Accordingly, the pillar stands between the viewer and the stylised Urewera landscape, asserting the integrity and ownership of what lies beyond it.

In the lower right corner, McCahon foregrounds the words 'TUHOE / UREWERA / THEIR LAND' in a manner reminiscent of the classic New Zealand farm-gate notice, with its hand-painted imperative to 'KEEP OUT' or 'SHUT THE GATE'. Like the pou whenua, the words on the mural must be acknowledged before the viewer can proceed into the verdant darkness beyond.

The crossbar at the top of the central pillar in the *Urewera Mural* transforms it into a T-shaped Egyptian or tau cross. In fact, the tau

Colin McCahon, *Urewera Mural,* 1976, used by kind permission of the Colin McCahon Research and Publication Trust.

cross runs like a sequence of telegraph poles through McCahon's paintings of the 1960s and 70s. Spoken and written words amass on either side of—or above—these poles. It's as if McCahon has intercepted André Derain's 1901 letter to Maurice de Vlaminck, with its exhortation: 'The telephone wires must be made enormous, so much goes on along them.' McCahon's weighty communications are transmitted from canvas to canvas, the voices shifting from Maori to English then back again. This epic, collaged narrative includes a passage from St Paul's 'Letter to the Hebrews', passages of Maori poetry (and English translations), some 'found' pieces of language, a few phrases by the artist himself, and poems.

A symbol of divine power used by the Israelites in Egypt, the tau cross was later assimilated into the Christian tradition as the crucifix.[1] In the *Urewera Mural*, the motif also embodies the downward fall of light (representing grace and enlightenment) and the upward journey towards the light (salvation). McCahon's friend James K. Baxter went on to describe the vertical beam of the cross as a symbol of the relationship between Humanity and God, while the horizontal beam symbolised caritas, or communal love, between people.

In *May His Light Shine (Tau Cross)* (1978–79), the tau cross is suggestive of an altar or table on which the products of the land and of human labour are either offered up or consumed, whereas in *The Days and Nights in the Wilderness* (1971), the T-shape is a body of light above and between two bluffs—'the constant flow of light passing into a dark landscape'. The tau cross in *The Care of Small Birds, Muriwai* (1975) is more oblique—a block of sky seen between two cliffs, this time on Auckland's west coast, where McCahon had a studio.

Colin McCahon's interest in the formal and symbolic qualities of the tau cross (which derived from both the letter T and the crucifix) stemmed from two childhood encounters. Born in Timaru in 1919 and raised in Dunedin, as a boy McCahon watched a signwriter painting HAIRDRESSER AND TOBACCONIST on a shop window and was struck by 'the grace of the lettering' which 'pointed to a new and magnificent world of painting'. The cross as a symbol of mortality had a darker advent, arising from an incident near Oamaru: 'I remember the death of a parachutist whose parachute failed to open and the white cross was erected against the low North Otago hills where he fell.'

In *Toss in Greymouth* (1959), the cross is a silhouetted structure—reminiscent of a figure with outstretched arms—set in an evening landscape. For McCahon, the tau cross was an intensely human symbol—referencing the shape of an aeroplane, a power pole, and the first letter of Toss Woollaston's Christian name, just as readily as it did Christ's Passion.

McCahon referred to the tau cross as his 'load-bearing structure', accentuating its practical applications as the girder of a bridge or foundation/pillar of both Maori and Pakeha dwellings. A 1978 series of small paintings, *Truth from the King Country: Load Bearing Structures*, melded the famous Mangaweka Viaduct with the tau cross. The motif was hinted at much earlier in McCahon's work: in both the human-built structures of *Triptych: On Building Bridges* (1952) and the word paintings of the same decade. Underlying all of the potential readings of the motif is its formal presence as an emblem of support, balance and robust symmetry.

A form of activism and, in the artist's words, 'a potent way of talking', McCahon's Urewera works uphold Maori attitudes to the land and the enduring significance of the indigenous language as well as specific Maori texts. In this respect, the *Urewera Mural* is both an elegiac and a hopeful work. While the inscriptions on land and sky seem to imply that the Maori language has been banished to such hinterlands as the Urewera—a poignant observation at the time the work was painted—

on the other hand, the landscape is also presented here as cradle and nest of the language.

The commission to produce the *Urewera Mural* for the Department of Conservation centre at Aniwaniwa was taken up by McCahon in 1975, two years after he had produced his other major reflection on Maori spirituality and social history, the *Parihaka Triptych*. Asked to explore the theme of 'the mystery of Man in the Urewera', McCahon was immediately drawn to the story of the nineteenth-century leader Te Kooti, who founded the Ringatu religion, integrating elements from the Old and New Testaments with Maoritanga. His follower, Rua Kenana, saw himself in the role of Maori Messiah, as prophesied by Te Kooti, and established a community at Maungapohatu in 1905. Like other millenarian prophets, Rua equated the Maori with the Israelites (hence the particular aptness of the tau cross in the *Urewera Mural*) and believed they would achieve their rightful status and land rights with the advent of the Maori millennium.

The words on the mural are excerpted from a traditional Maori poem which McCahon translated as:

> The stone mountain and the South Wind.
> Hear me! O South Wind:
> The stone mountain is the mountain.
> Come—prepare food for our illustrious men:
> The time has come for food and games.
> Hear me! Tuhoe are the people and Rua is their prophet.
> See the stirring of the lake.

Colin McCahon, *Toss in Greymouth,* 1959, used by kind permission of the Colin McCahon Research and Publication Trust.

Standing at the boundary of Te Urewera—a threshold of understanding as well as geography—McCahon is listening to the words of the prophets and acknowledging the Tuhoe ancestors. He is not presuming to speak on their behalf. Instead we listen, by way of McCahon's 'transmissions', to 'nga reo ora o tangata mate'—the living voices of dead men. Works like the *Urewera Mural* and *A Letter to Hebrews* (1979) are paintings for the prophets, be they Maori or otherwise. McCahon underlined the words 'It is for their faith that the men of old stand on record' in the latter work—an apposite statement in relation to the *Mural*, in which Te Kooti and Rua are seen to stand as equals of the 'men of old' recorded in the Bible.

Painted three years after the *Urewera Mural*, *A Song for Rua: Prophet* (1979) and *May His Light Shine (Tau Cross)* witness a further grounding of McCahon's prophetic vision of New Zealand. Francis Pound has written of the fixation of the latter work on 'the soil as the site of consecration to the Spirit . . . the soil as the site of nativeness—marked here by Maoriness (the "Kumara Patch"); the soil as the site of roots and rootedness, at once of agriculture and belonging . . .'

Metaphors of growing and regeneration, which underlie the *Urewera Mural*, are to the fore in *May His Light Shine (Tau Cross)*, which depicts, in the artist's words, the 'TAU CROSS AS KUMARA GOD'. Both spiritual and material sustenance are implicit in the words of Gerard Manley Hopkins, inscribed at the foot of this work: 'MINE THOU LORD OF LIFE SEND MY ROOTS RAIN'. Like the teachings of Te Kooti and Rua, McCahon's works are idiosyncratic yet immensely powerful reconfigurations of Maori and Pakeha symbolic systems.

'I sing my paintings to myself,' wrote Colin McCahon in 1972. And so he sings them for us—whether it be the emphatic score of St Paul's epistle, or the lyricism of Toss Woollaston's poem which appears in *Toss in Greymouth*: 'Alit on the flax, a tui at dusk / and broke the / late evening / open / with / song.'[2] The song of Woollaston's tui had appeared the previous year in McCahon's *Northland Panels*, in which the word TUI is repeated three times on one panel. Birds, as graphic notation and symbol, resurface in *The Care of Small Birds, Muriwai*, which is a stylised depiction of the gannet colony at Muriwai. Here McCahon pictorialises the nurturing impulse common to all living things, as well as the forcefulness needed to get the young out of their nests and into the air. This work sums up two principal functions of McCahon's art: to nourish and protect the spirit, and to challenge and breach the limits of the physical world. It also encapsulates the need, as Gordon Brown relates, to 'respect certain rules but, at the same time . . . take chances'.

Stolen from the Visitors' Centre in Aniwaniwa on 5 June 1997 as an act of political protest, the *Urewera Mural* was returned fifteen months later. During that time the theft fuelled an extensive public debate about the work and the issues it embodied. Since then, the painting has continued to puzzle, astonish and even antagonise viewers. Painter Shane Cotton wrote at the time the recovered painting was exhibited at the Govett-Brewster Gallery:

> Our perception of the work is forever changed. While McCahon will always be acknowledged as delivering a message that Tuhoe are the Tangata Whenua of the Urewera, Tame Iti and Te Kaha Karaitiana [two figures involved in the removal of the work] will always be acknowledged as Tuhoe artisans who literally took McCahon at his word, imbuing the work, through their infamous interaction with it, with the ihi (power), the wehi (awe) and the mana (prestige) that is Ngai Tuhoe.

Paradoxically, the *Urewera Mural* addresses the past and present of a communal people without depicting any figures. If the painting reflects something of the essence of the Urewera it is by allusion. McCahon does not assume the right to 'represent' the spirituality of the people or to speak on their behalf. The artwork makes, in Jean-François Lyotard's words, 'an allusion to the unpresentable', the unpresentable in this case being the soul of a people, their history, mana, sadness and joy. As Shane Cotton suggests, McCahon delivers a message but he is not the source of the message. What he does is take us as far as the boundary—the poi whenua—and leaves us at the intersection of indigenous and imported tradition—a place of inspiration and hope, as well as anxiety and regret.

Turning from that place, we follow the rueful logic of McCahon's tau crosses, arrayed across the rest of the country like the conductors of some other-worldly electricity or communications system. While the argument of these paintings is as central as the Main Trunk Line to New Zealand's self-definition, when we look closely at the geographical co-ordinates of McCahon's works, we find they are also a paean to the far-flung and the provincial. They assert the centrality of such locales as Muriwai, Ninety Mile Beach, Parihaka, Westland and, importantly, the Urewera—for it is on the edge of Tuhoe Country, Te Urewera, that this particular power-grid is sourced and where some of the crucial voices in McCahon's art begin their transmission.

Nga reo ora o tangata mate.

Notes

1 Gordon H. Brown writes that the tau cross was 'frequently associated with Moses: first, as a sign with which the Israelites marked the doorposts of their dwellings in Egypt on the night of the Passover, and secondly, as the shape of the staff, with the brazen serpent, lifted up by Moses while in the wilderness'. Brown, *Colin McCahon: Artist* (Reed, 1984), p.166.

2 Not untypically, McCahon made two minor errors (or were they conscious alterations?) when rendering Woollaston's poem, the original of which began 'lit on the flax', and the operative verb was 'shot' rather than 'broke' (correspondence from Woollaston to G. O'Brien, 1996).

Breaking open the luggage
Denis O'Connor's 'concrete poetry'

At 11 pm on the last night of his stay in Wellington as a guest at the 1992 International Festival of the Arts, the Irish poet Paul Durcan rang me to say he had padlocked his passport inside his suitcase. He was booked on the early-morning flight home and all attempts by hotel staff to break open what they referred to as a 'fortress of a suitcase' had failed. They said the bag was bombproof.

Arriving at the poet's door a short while later, bearing a file and a hacksaw, a friend and I were ushered over to the suitcase and immediately set to work. An hour later, with my friend sitting atop the suitcase, the hacksaw was a little over halfway through the metal bolt. During the proceedings, we talked with Durcan about notions of Irishness and how Irishness might be arrived at (although, in hindsight, the poet seemed more concerned with placing himself on an aeroplane the next morning than placing himself in relation to our muddled ideas of pan-nationalism).

With an impressive pile of filings on the floor beneath us, finally we made it all the way through the padlock. The suitcase sprang open and, from amid the neatly folded shirts, Paul Durcan extracted his passport—the object of our mission—a passport which, he lamented, these days wasn't exactly an 'Irish' passport any more—it was a dark red EEC passport.

It occurred to me later that the act of hacksawing into the suitcase of that most Irish of poets, Paul Durcan, provided a useful analogy for the striving for Celtic roots so prevalent throughout the English-speaking world. And then the inevitable disappointment, finding that the imagined 'authentic' green Irish passport had been transfigured into something more general. At that moment our Irishness was, if you continue with the analogy, exposed as a case of homesickness for a place we not only romanticised but had, for the most part, dreamed up.

I was reminded of this incident twice while reading the book about Denis O'Connor's sculpture—*BIG AITCHE LITTLE AITChE*—firstly when I found the sculptor using words by Paul Durcan as a title for one work: *Ua (out of, or from). 'The blindness of history in my eyes / the blindness of history in my hands / the blindness of history in my name'*. A couple of pages further on, I found a Durcanesque padlock etched into the relief, *Tenebrae / Pendulum for an emigre.*

Anyone familiar with O'Connor's work will be aware of the recurrent Irish cultural references. Unlike the aspiring pan-Irish suitcase-breaker, however, O'Connor is secure in his own status as the son of an immigrant, an individual negotiating his cultural past and present, exploring its emblems, physical materials and words. His work is an acknowledgement that culture is perpetually being generated by people and by nature. 'In the poetic universe of Denis O'Connor,' as Allan Smith writes, 'the governing condition is that of being embedded: embedded in stone, soil, mud, swamp, region, family, language, dream, history, myth.'

Over the past two decades, O'Connor's sculptural production has been very much the embodiment of the sculpture/culture nexus. The argument of the work seems to go: You approach the notion of culture in much the same way as you walk around a three-dimensional object—there are sight-lines, points of contact, a long and a short view. From some angles things look better than from others. Rather than attempt exegesis, the visual and verbal materials gathered in *BIG AITCHE LITTLE AITChE* sift through and revel in their conflicting but necessarily related realities.

As well as quoting Durcan, O'Connor's recent titles and inscriptions have come from Irish writers including Durcan, Seamus Heaney, Derek Mahon, Paul Muldoon and Ciarin Carson. Their voices echo in O'Connor's increasingly sound- and language-fixated artworks. The title of the current book underlines the centrality of the spoken word—*BIG AITCHE LITTLE AITChE* refers to a detail of pronunciation, a quality of 'voicing' that the sculptures also, in their own way, emulate. O'Connor writes:

> The Irish tongue will not allow the sound we know as 'aitche' to pass across it . . . Today I think of the exhaled and vocalised 'H' as the sound of the unspoken stuff—you know, the stuff that haunts. The voices of ghosts with their books of knots, palmistry and ventriloquism.

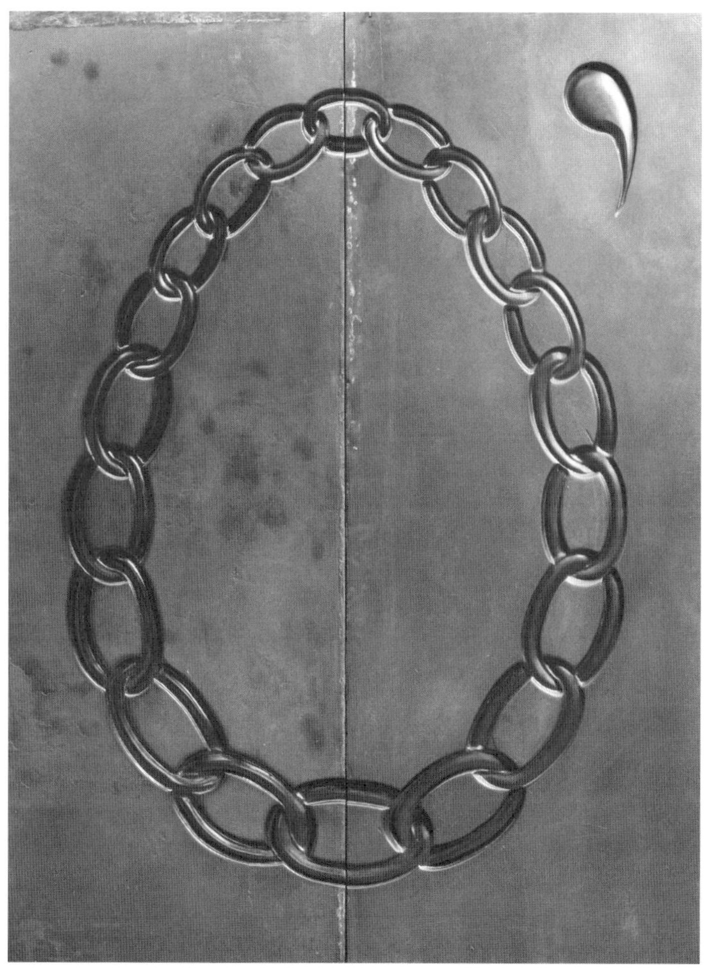

UA (Out of, or from)
'The blindness of history in my eyes
the blindness of history in my hands
the blindness of history in my name'
Denis O'Connor, 1994, oiled slate.

Alongside, and to some degree against, the epic narratives of colonialism and immigration—the broad sweeps of cultural movement which dominated O'Connor's work from the 1980s—the subjective voice of lyric poetry has lately been establishing itself as a predominant ingredient. Recent acts of sculptural ventriloquism or voice-throwing use texts by James Brown, Michele Leggott, Bill Manhire, Geoff Cochrane, Vincent O'Sullivan and Canadian Anne Carson.

The emergence of poetry as an integral component in the work coincides with this shifting emphasis from objective or communal history to subjective history or, more particularly, autobiography. At the same time it should be borne in mind that out there in the broad universe of creative expression, the artist's quest for individual identity has often been considered an offshoot or even a microcosm of the nationalistic impulse—so 'inner' and 'outer' are far from mutually exclusive. In fact, as Alexa Johnston writes, 'poetry forges the links between personal memories, family myths and the larger myths of history'.

Beginning with the book's front cover—an upside-down photograph of O'Connor's Irish immigrant father in Auckland, 1945—we enter a resonant cultural space. As well as evoking both the documents and emblems of empire and industry—from the Blarney stone to the nautical insignia of Old Blightey—O'Connor's works have drawn more and more on his immediate family history. O'Connor has constructed a lexicon of elusive, allusive Irishness, as seen from the vantage point of Waiheke Island, c.2000. He memorialises both communal and individual histories while acknowledging their inscrutability, the fact that some meanings will always be locked away, always out of reach. Individual and collective identities—the work argues—exist to be negotiated, argued over, pondered and momentarily understood. The current book is a sensible habitat for this sort of activity, enriching rather than resolving the arguments it contains.

In the best Irish literary tradition, O'Connor's artworks are at once fragmentary and monumental, seemingly practical but eminently impractical. They are absurd, sad, quizzical and virtuosic. Perhaps O'Connor's 'true fascination' lies—as Flann O'Brien observed of yet another Irishman, James Joyce—'in his secretiveness, his ambiguity (his polyguity, perhaps?), his leg-pulling, his dishonesties, his technical skill . . . His works are a garden in which some of us may play.'

First on the left past the art supermarket, the magic theatre

Martin Edmond's The Resurrection of Philip Clairmont

Having just finished reading Martin Edmond's penetrating, often brilliant new book, I did the kind of thing I imagine Edmond himself would have done: I got in the car, popped a cassette of 1970s guitar legend Sonny Sharrock in the stereo and drove out to the Dowse Art Museum in Lower Hutt, where Clairmont's 1974 *Crucifixion: a triptych* was on display.

Maybe it wasn't such a good idea. While Edmond's book attempts, as its title suggests, a kind of resurrection, Clairmont's *Crucifixion* depicts a Christ-figure a million miles from any possible afterlife. In this agonised, gruesome triptych, Christ is bound, drawn and quartered, and plummeting downwards. It is a painting about spiritual and physical death—a Sam Peckinpah-esque revision of early McCahon.

An equally shocking aspect of the work is the way in which the very pigment of the painting seems to be dying—Clairmont's characteristic palette of explosive reds and yellows and blues is turning grey. The painting is not as I remember it from the 1984 'Anxious Images' exhibition at the Auckland Art Gallery. While the paint itself is well applied—Clairmont certainly could paint—it looks as if the hessian beneath it is decomposing. Edmond's book draws attention to Clairmont's use of ephemeral, fugitive art materials, which, he argues, stemmed from his obsession with physical life and its end.

Edmond's 'resurrection' of Clairmont is centred on a biographical essay, which constitutes nearly half his book and, presumably, would have been the text for the illustrated monograph he had hoped to produce but, for reasons we will come to, could not. He has added to this a personal account of his own journey into the life and work of his friend. These overlapping narratives are full of sad, curious insights, taking us back into the Clairmont family history then on to his birth in Nelson in 1949, his time at the University of Canterbury School of

Fine Arts, his meteoric rise to fame, then the events that led to his suicide in 1984.

The opening section, entitled 'The Morgue', is a compelling 'biography of a biography', in the tradition of Janet Malcolm's *The Silent Woman: Sylvia Plath and Ted Hughes* (Edmond himself made an earlier foray into this sub-genre with *The Autobiography of My Father*, which appeared in 1992). Unlike Janet Malcolm, who was trying to save Sylvia Plath from all manner of partisan and unbalanced appraisal, Edmond sets himself a more fundamental task: to rescue his subject from art historical oblivion.

Clairmont's paintings fell from critical and commercial favour during the last years of his life, when he ended up, to use Nigel Brown's phrase, 'an organic painter shut out of the art supermarket'. Since his death, arguments over copyright ownership and other issues have dogged efforts to document his work adequately. Edmond's planned monograph fell victim to such circumstances. Permission to reproduce works in the present volume was, similarly, withheld. The artist's work is a chilling absence from the book and raises the question: can there be a resurrection without a visible body, a corpus, an oeuvre?

One work was exempt from the copyright issue: a commissioned painting for the Janne Land Gallery, Wellington, which is reproduced on the cover of the book. It's an instructive work, if not a first-rate one. Entitled *Magic Theatre*, it was painted directly onto the gallery doors and depicts a nightmarish stairwell. Apart from a couple of ghostly hands groping a doorknob/lightbulb, the artist himself is notably absent. In fact, Edmond's book is as much a magic theatre as a resurrection. In the illusory world of the magic theatre, figures vanish, only to reappear at the beck and call of the conjuror. If the author is right, we have witnessed the disappearance of Clairmont from New Zealand art. Now we find ourselves waiting outside this magic theatre for the reappearance which Edmond, as conjuror, might well be part of instigating. But, for now, all we are faced with is the empty, hallucinatory stairwell.

The book does, however, include a selection of black and white photographs which impart a strong sense of Clairmont as a person. Tellingly, Clairmont's paintings actually look like him—or, alternatively, he looks like his paintings. The bearded, lank figure of the artist, with his oft-raised eyebrows, has a physical presence we also find in the paintings. Edmond's book convincingly links the man with the art, sketching in his motivation and manner, taking us into the magic theatre which was his studio and home. 'Painting the rooms he lived in,' Edmond observes, 'he laid bare a map of his psyche and the structure of reality.'

The paintbrush and the hypodermic needle were both integral to Clairmont's attempts to broach other realities where, as Edmond says, 'time is different from our day to day experience of it. Through holes in the fabric of reality you can go into these other dimensions. Death is only one of the exits. Others might be found in drugs, in music, in painting.'

The 1970s—when Clairmont was at his peak—are now distant enough for the period to be seen with some detachment. Since the death of Bruno Lawrence (and the 1999 biography), the decade about which people have tended to be either scathing or sentimental now becomes a cultural watershed of increasingly mythic proportions. (Perhaps, if a resurrection is taking place here, it is as much to do with the 1970s in general as with Clairmont's art in particular.) Edmond is a well-qualified tour guide through those often misguided times. He introduces us to the various substances that were being abused, details a wide range of behavioural problems and anarchist tendencies, and—to his credit—is capable of such feats as differentiating between 'hippies' and 'freaks' (Clairmont was the latter).

Upon concluding the book I was struck by a certain irony. Whereas, generally, artists are said to live on through their art, here we have a case of the art—which is absent from this book and disintegrating out there in the physical world—living on through the recounted life of the artist.

In the final analysis it is up to the art itself to establish its exact status—and there I remain intrigued by, but in no way sure about, Clairmont's standing. That said, a while back a friend who was marking Universary Bursary art examinations asked me to look through some of the portfolios. What I remember most strongly is the influence of Clairmont on many of the submissions. The students had obviously studied his work and, I would say, been entranced by it. Clairmont's passion and visionary intensity continue to strike a chord with the young. For better or worse, he is our Van Gogh. In the eyes and minds of the next generation, then, lies the evidence that Clairmont will come up; that he will resurrect. In fact he is doing so as we speak.

Michael Parekowhai, *Lamentations 5:10, 'Our skin was black'* (detail), 1993.

I am a shepherd

Although I look more like police in my blue uniform with hat and stick, standing most hours of most nights out here in the city square which is busy with exquisite wooden sheep, their long legs dug into the soil. I am paid to ensure no one damages these sheep or makes off with them into the darkness—the darkness about which I have now become an expert. The carnivalesque darkness, teeming with life.

I have watched men traverse the square carrying windows stolen from public buildings, the leading string quartets of the day cross in formation and, the night after St Patrick's Day, the square crammed with pigeons gobbling green bread. But that isn't a fraction of what I have seen. How could I forget the Russian composer stumbling past, hands clamped over his ears, or the German infantryman banging on the door of the City Gallery, demanding his watercolour set back. Once there was a woman with the most beautiful name in the world. Monserrat Figueras. After that there were no other beautiful names.

I have seen men crushed under the astonishing weight of balloons and I have seen stolen bicycles chased across the square by a cloud of the most finely glazed china. But I have never lifted a finger, a single leaden finger. Because I am a shepherd and a finger is such a weight to lift.

I stand and watch young and old blurred together in a dance. Feel the wind from their skirts and sleeves as they spin across the pavement and onto my lawn. But should any of them start dancing among my sheep, unsettling them, then I will tell them I am a shepherd and if they so much as brush against one of my sheep I have my instructions and my instructions are to disperse them.

Written at the time of Michael Parekowhai's installation outside City Gallery Wellington, 1994.

Chunk of landscape, chunk of memory
the paintings of Euan Macleod

Deep water man

Seeking shelter from a storm at sea, the protagonist in the children's book *Bert Dow: Deep Water Man* allows himself and his vessel to be swallowed whole by a whale. Not a particularly original plot device, you would be forgiven for thinking. However, some time later, inside the creature, the sailor has to figure out a means of escape, and here our narrative breaks with convention. His solution involves flicking all sorts of paint and gunk from the bottom of his fishing boat up at the ceiling and walls of the whale's stomach. This he does, by the light of a gas lamp, with great gusto.

To the sailor's surprise, he finds this task immensely satisfying—at last he has discovered a way of 'expressing his innermost feelings'. Before long, the interior of the whale's stomach has become a mock-Jackson Pollock. Then, on account of the irritation all this gunk is causing the whale, our hero is relievedly burped back out into the world.

The paint-splattering episode is a deliberate jibe at Abstract Expressionism. Our boots-and-all seaman/workman hero is the Male Expressionist par excellence. The reader can only assume that the whale, at the moment it regurgitates Bert and the *Tidily Idly* (his ironically titled vessel), is passing judgement on the artistic misadventures taking place in the sanctuary/studio of its belly.

Chunk of paint

Expressionism, at the end of the twentieth century, is a mode that has certainly been put through the hoops, beginning with the Fauvist and Blaue Reiter artists and on through the mid-century Abstract Expressionists. With the advent of minimalism and earth art, expressionism might have seemed not only cast out but washed up, the subjective gesture of the paintbrush an archaic trope of a discontinued/discredited modernist experiment. Then, by the late 1970s, Neo-Expressionism had been born.

These days expressionism is most visible in art from developing countries, where it still has a freshness, urgency and potency often aimed at alerting the public to issues such as injustice, racism, historical grievances and the environment. Accordingly, it is a prominent mode in Asia, South America and Africa—also, for other reasons, in Italy and even more notably Germany, where the public function of the expressionist artist is epitomised by Anselm Kiefer. (Expressionism also remains a prominent mode in women's art, for example the work of Robyn Kahukiwa, Jacqueline Fahey and Lily Laita.)

In contrast to these recent, often didactic permutations of expressionism, however, the canvases of Euan Macleod are neither political nor public. This is not to say that Macleod's painting belongs, on the other hand, to the predominantly 'private' school of New Zealand expressionism as epitomised by the art of Philip Clairmont

Euan Macleod, *Striding Figure—Hyde Park*, 1990, oil on canvas.

and Jeffrey Harris. Lacking the 'heroic' angst of these stalwarts (and their predecessor, Rudi Gopas), Macleod produces works that are a hybrid of New Zealand and Australian influences—along with a few from further afield. Macleod's walking figures have an affinity with Alberto Giacommetti's gaunt pedestrians, their limbs like trees or sticks planted in the ground or water. If the figure-in-landscape tradition in this country was to yield a local version of Giacommetti, Macleod might well be the outcome. Importantly, Macleod's figures have been nurtured and shaped by what is largely a landscape rather than a portrait tradition. He uses the entire field of the painted surface even when doing a conventional head and shoulders (usually self-) portrait. Rather than being explorations of identity, in the soul-searching manner, these are explorations of how human figures are contained in landscape and how figures carry landscapes inside them, framed or coloured as memories or epiphanies.

Despite their expressionist marks and flourishes, the paintings of Euan Macleod reconfigure expressionism. Instead of being forged by overt feeling—with its register in the present tense—the paintings are closer to the workings of memory. Yet while the paintings have a metaphysical element, they are never bathed in the stillness characteristic of metaphysical painting. These are 'eventful' paintings: their impasto surfaces are constantly on the move, responding to the light falling upon them. A change of lighting can render a work unrecognisable. Layers of underpainting and hefty applications of pigment imbue the works with a shimmering, unstable life. Some of the paint is applied at speed; at other times it is brushed on slowly, more thickly. Achieving simultaneously a kind of fullness and incompleteness, these works create a visual vacuum. Having looked at a number of these paintings in domestic as well as gallery settings, I have observed the way these sculptural blocks of thick knotted pigment can dramatically alter the atmosphere of a room. Like compressed matter, they have an almost radioactive quality.

Chunk of landscape

While the Australian landscape has shaped much of Macleod's art since he moved to Sydney in 1981, more recent works—following a sojourn back in Christchurch in 1993—have revisited the coastline of a childhood spent around Banks Peninsula. The 1993–94 'Remembrance' works, produced during and after this return home, set out to memorialise the artist's deceased father. These paintings are elegiac—a quality not exactly at the heart of expressionism, although manifest in expressionist works as disparate as Robert Motherwell's *Elegy for the Spanish Republic* and some of Jeffrey Harris's paintings from the late 1970s. The 'Remembrance' paintings are landscapes in which the body of his father is laid or through which the ghost of his memory wanders. If these works are ancestral meditations, they are also, as is this artist's habit, self-portraits at one remove. A comparable lone figure is evoked in fellow Cantabrian J. R. Hervey's 1949 poem 'Man on a Raft'—an appropriately Bert Dow-esque scenario:

> Not out of the war, not out of the agitated
> House of life and wearing the brand of love,
> He is yet no more than the diving bird between
>   Wave and wave

In *Remembrance (Blue)* (1993–94), Macleod's father is the 'man on the raft [of the canvas]' drifting through the pictorial possibilities, never quite coming to rest. The 'Remembrance' paintings are 'funereal landscapes', a sub-genre synonymous with English Neo-Romanticism, in which human mortality is conflated with the temporal nature of the physical world. Ruth Dallas's poem 'Driftwood' proffered an eloquent version of such a melding of human and non-human 'nature' three decades earlier:

> I am the bleached dunes lying
> Beside the uncaring sea.
> Ah,
> But the sea's wind smooths
>   the hoof-scars,
> The sea's voice
>   silences me.

Macleod's paintings contain something of this pantheistic sense of Man as Nature and Nature as Man. Just as vegetation is washed from the landforms, human flesh is washed from the bones. Washes of

Euan Macleod, *Remembrance (Blue)*, 1993–94, oil on canvas.

memory cover these canvases; corrosive rain falls on both landscape and humankind.

The first ships (out of here)

Who is this lone man who strides or stumbles through the last half-century of Canterbury art? Or, more accurately, how many such figures are there, all treading their separate paths?

Now might be the time to start defining a Canterbury School post-Rudi Gopas. This 'Expressionist'-derived lineage would include Tony Fomison, Philip Clairmont, Richard McWhannell, Bill Hammond, Joanna Braithwaite and Jason Greig. The collective vision of these artists is remarkable for its inversion of the Anglophile Cantabrian character—an upside-down reflection, if you like, of Christchurch Cathedral in a black, oily pond.[1] Also notable is the rapidity with which a good number of these artists—Euan Macleod among them—exited the city, and the way the ones who remained have come to resemble a terrorist cell.

Chunk of memory

What kind of air do these figures breathe? And how, in these paintings, does the light fall? Macleod's figures are themselves like downpours of rain or shadows without sources. They enter and emerge from water in a succession of gloomy yet not entirely hopeless baptisms. Macleod's 'Everyman'—at one with his *doppelgänger*s, shadows and Frame-esque mirror-selves—is incapable of drowning or vanishing; he reconfigures, he revives. A contemporary rendition of the Green Man, if you like—but also a granite man, a man of mist and light and falling water. The paintings step outside historical time: the artist and his father meld on the canvas—the paintings are a reconciliation, then, of memory and observation, of past and present. These paradoxes are worked into the very fabric of these paintings in which solid blocks of light appear alongside thin washes of land or human flesh. At once monumental and transient, the works are a meditation on time and matter. To quote Hervey again:

> Yet I have made friends with time,
> Having taken his cloud-burst of pain
> As earth takes the rain,
> And in the threatening twilight
> Have been as an evening lark in whose throat
> Day lingers though lost over the mountains.

Although Macleod's paintings often contain a number of scenes and a veiled narrative sequence, his work is neither cinematic nor literary in any overriding sense. Paintings this seriously brushed demand to be seen first and foremost as paintings. If their lushness and dynamism are uncharacteristic of New Zealand painting, the Australians Albert Tucker and Arthur Boyd offer something of a precedent, as do Jack B. Yeats and Frank Auerbach.

Outside the whale

An expressionist who hasn't confined his explorations to the 'inside of the whale', Macleod has left the mammalian interior—the studio/ sanctuary—of the mythologised expressionist self and taken the intensity of that methodology and aspects of its visual language to some wider-open environments. The stormy metaphysics that rattle these works—as well as a Fred Williams-esque eye for natural order—is at a considerable remove from the essential egotism and subjective emotion of much expressionist painting. There is an allusiveness and an ambivalence in Macleod's ongoing transactions between figure and ground. The closer we are to these paintings, the further we are from any conclusive reading of their imagery. And right up close, the imagery disappears entirely: a landscape becomes the bark of a burnt tree or the porous surface of seaweed, the head in the self-portrait breaks up into chunks of landscape, chunks of memory.

Notes

1 This phenomenon is detailed in Lara Strongman's 'Degrees of separation', *Art in Asia Pacific 23* (1999), p.33.

Changing the light
Noel McKenna in Taranaki

I As they are

'To create is not to deform or invent persons and things. It is to tie new relationships between persons and things which are, and *as they are*.' So wrote Robert Bresson, suggesting a manner of invention which could well be the model for Noel McKenna, a Sydney-based painter who has long been concerned with the many layers of interaction/ communication between figures, objects and their ground. His paintings are, it follows, a transcription of what Bresson called 'the visible parlance of bodies, objects, houses, roads, trees, fields'.

In their painterly language, their metaphysical cast and the psychological interplay between their often-displaced subjects, the paintings take their cue from Carlo Carrà or Giorgio de Chirico. They might also be a contemporary, antipodean reworking of Samuel Palmer's clipped, intensified visions of rural England—the compacted environments John Berger likened to 'furnished wombs'. For years McKenna has painted enclosures: birds in cages, people in houses, houses gridlocked in suburbs, trees or horses contained in fields. His compositions are poetic renditions of these psychological spaces or locations. Only occasionally are these environments comfortable. They are the dreamscapes of an unsettled sleeper.

Memory is a crucial component of these most unsentimental of creations. The majority of McKenna's human subjects are small children or adults presumably in their twenties. Our view is tinted with both nostalgia and, quite often, an almost-parental anguish.

Refusing to articulate specific narrative content, however, the works are ambiguous in their mood. The paintings often appear frozen between two quite distinct emotions, embodying transitional states between, for instance, cheerfulness and ennui (*Waterloo Corner*), anxiety and black humour (*Untitled—two houses*), contentment and boredom (*Queensland Home*). The paintings also often find themselves at the point at which childhood topples helplessly into adulthood.

If Robert Bresson was right when he wrote 'the sight of movement gives happiness: horse, athlete, bird', then these uncomfortably stilled paintings are dominated by its opposite, sadness, and a melancholy which at times borders on desolation. Against the pull of this dark gravity, however, the internal logic of these paintings—these mechanisms in which charm and good humour are also integral parts—provides the necessary uplift to counter any collapse into maudlin self-analysis.

II Parihaka / despatches

Of the many narratives that can be threaded through Noel McKenna's recent paintings, his visit to Parihaka in November 1998 is a surprising but nonetheless illuminating one. Subsequent to that visit, his paintings—which, in accustomed McKenna fashion, were often the size of postcards or photographs—presented vignettes from the journey melded with other more familiar sources.[1]

Parihaka was an important site of Maori passive resistance against the encroachments of the colonial forces from the 1870s onwards.

Noel McKenna, *Man changing lightbulb*, 1999, watercolour on paper.

The village (which is also an important 'site' in New Zealand art history on account of Colin McCahon's pivotal *Parihaka Triptych* (1972)) brings a number of resonances to these paintings, these chambers where meanings are struck and allowed to reverberate.

McKenna's iconography, for a start, suggests some poignant associations. Take the cat in *Fat Cat*. In the writings of Te Whiti o Rongomai (the spiritual leader of the Parihaka people), the cat was emblematic of the Pakeha settler government. The Maori he portrayed as the 'ruru'—or native owl—falling prey to the newly arrived predator.

McKenna's *Fringe Dwellers* (see p177) brings to mind the Parihaka settlement itself—an isolated conglomeration of small houses located at the base of two peaks, Pouakai and Mt Taranaki (Egmont). Elsewhere, the electric light bulb and figure changing the street lamp sit neatly alongside the historical account of Te Whiti's enthusiasm for electricity. By the start of the twentieth century the remote settlement of Parihaka had an electricity system better than that of the province's main centre, New Plymouth. In a manner not untypical of Maori prophets and leaders generally, Te Whiti embraced positive aspects of European culture, seeking to integrate them into an evolving, 'modern' Maori culture.

McKenna's untitled paintings of a caravan lit up by a cross-like power pole suggest various narratives of dispossession. The caravan as metaphor for exile and intransigence strikes a chord in New Zealand, as it does in North America and Australia. For unemployed rural Maori the caravan also frequently becomes a whare or permanent dwelling.

Noel McKenna's paintings are a curious variant on the inherited model of history painting. His sense of 'history' centres on the pauses, the gaps or ellipses between dramatic events. Again, we find ourselves posited in an intermediate zone—between characters, emotions and events. McKenna's landscapes are very much places awaiting people, or from which people have fled or been removed—another poignant association for the Maori people of the Taranaki province.

So, Parihaka opens up a vista or two into these works. Not that the paintings need to be seen in any such light—however, the painting/location nexus does give us a sense of how active McKenna's narrative ingredients can be, without prepackaging a response from the viewer.

III 'Take me out tonight / because I want to see people / and I want to see lights . . .' (The Smiths)

The eye, as it sets out across the shelf-like perspectival space of a Noel McKenna work, is drawn into a curious kind of communion with the inhabitants of these strangely denuded settings. The viewer joins the seated woman at her table, occupies the moon-lit chair, climbs the tree, enters the caravan . . . Integral to this tenuous scene setting is McKenna's way with light. Undermining the obvious connotations, the blocks of light emanating from windows and doorways of buildings and caravans are as filmic or psychological as they are symbolic. Human-made light is juxtaposed with natural light, providing a resonant formal and metaphorical interaction. Like the works of Paul Klee (the 'comic Mozart of modernism', as Octavio Paz labelled him), McKenna's paintings play off the geometries of the world with the disorderliness of the human mind. And they play off the geometry of the mind with the disorder of the outside world.

'There is a light that never goes out,' the Smiths once sang. So the inner and outer light that has obsessed both Australian and New Zealand painters for well over a century burns on undiminished. McKenna's is a particularly compelling essay in illumination and gathering darkness. In these works we also experience the surprising, resounding flash of the illuminated moment—whether the light be from a landing spacecraft or a caravan window.

As Te Whiti o Rongomai said, 'Lightning is not seen from one place only, but from everywhere.' These moments of imparted vision can be seen from many vantage points, offering as many angles as there are viewers. Whether McKenna's paintings are bathed in Perpetual Light or the flickering bulbs of a city's cars and buildings depends as much on the beholder as on the painter himself.

Notes

1 Early in 2000 McKenna gifted an untitled Parihaka-related painting to the Parihaka Pa Trustees. The work was subsequently exhibited in the 'Parihaka' exhibition at City Gallery Wellington, August 2000–January 2001, and reproduced in the exhibition catalogue.

The outsider within

1 *All Our Own Work: New Zealand's Folk Art*, Richard Wolfe (1997)

Charles Brasch wrote in *Landfall* in December 1950 that Colin McCahon, 'hampered at every turn by an inadequate technique . . . was not well enough taught to meet the demands of his vision'. This lack of sophistication and training Brasch considered symptomatic of New Zealand art in general. At the same time, there were aspects of McCahon's paintings Brasch admired unreservedly: 'Their harshness, their frequent crudity, may seem shocking at first; but if we are honest with ourselves we have to admit that these qualities reflect with painful accuracy a rawness and harshness in New Zealand life . . . '

Perhaps more than any other major New Zealand artist, McCahon adopted the techniques and priorities of the naïve or folk painter. Wanting a vernacular painterly quality at odds with the mainstream Western 'fine art' tradition, he often used everyday materials such as commercial paints, tarpaulin and reams of brown paper. His technique was roughly hewn and direct—Dulux rather than Winsor & Newton—a conscious critique of academic or traditionalist art with its one-point perspective, chiaroscuro and refinements of colour, tone and surface. McCahon's art was preoccupied with religious faith and the Christian tradition—just as much naïve art is—and, like many so-called naïve artists, he used handwritten lettering in his work. He was obsessed with the narrative capabilities of image-making, at first in the direct storytelling manner of his religious paintings, then later in his stark mindscapes made up of numbers and words.

An absence of conventional 'fine art' technique or, in McCahon's instance, its deliberate eschewal, characterises much of the artwork discussed and reproduced in Richard Wolfe's *All Our Own Work: New Zealand's Folk Art* (Penguin, 1977). Wolfe, however, doesn't bear the burden of Brasch's Eurocentric notion of technique; indeed, if this book is anything to go by, he relishes the opportunity not to be bound by notions of 'excellence' or 'resolution'. Within the space of a few pages, we are presented with an acrylic painting by Teuane Tibbo, a 'crazy' patchwork dressing gown and a lampshade made of ice-block sticks. Wolfe is happy not to differentiate between the 'high' art of oil on canvas and the 'low' art of the paua-shell ashtray. This approach makes the book wide ranging and often surprising.

That said, the book's breadth and generosity are also its biggest drawback. Such a high-speed tour across a wide cultural landscape allows us little opportunity to dwell on truly exceptional individual artists. The book is more concerned with mapping a folk art 'heartland'—a broad, inclusive, sociologically defined space—than with locating specific 'outsider' geniuses. The very title—*All Our Own Work*—establishes an informal, congenial relationship between the reader and the contents: these productions are part of 'us'—of quirky, democratic 'New Zealand' folks like ourselves. The pleasures are those of recognition, domesticity and acquaintance. We're invited in. It's 'Our Place'.

*

Wolfe writes in his introduction: 'Because of folk art's "outsider" status, the usual rules for evaluation cannot apply. It can hardly be judged using yardsticks it does not recognise: perspective, composition and modelling, for example. But if an evaluation is necessary, it may simply be a matter of deferring to those ingredients which define its very essence: originality, honesty, directness, unpredictability and unconscious humour, for example . . . '

Any book purporting to be about 'folk art' runs into problems defining its exact ground. Wolfe says, rightly: 'The very definition of folk art is subject to endless debate. In a peculiar catch-22 situation those who consider themselves folk artists cannot, strictly speaking, qualify, for a conscious maintenance of the requisite traits is contrary to the spirit of the art . . . '

While knitted woollen cats and tables made of matchsticks fit neatly into the 'folk art' category, the work of so-called 'serious' artists challenges the book's boundaries. The work of painters like Tibbo and Dave O'Neill occupies a space between 'fine' and 'folk'. Their productions have a striking amount in common with the work of mainstream artists such as Tony Fomison, Nigel Brown and Michael

Illingworth. One drawback of a book like *All Our Own Work* is that it seems to be pulling the likes of Tibbo and O'Neill towards the other extreme, towards the 'craft' end of the spectrum.

Ultimately, it is impossible to fit artists into categories. How, for instance, do you classify art which has certain naïve characteristics but is also grounded in an awareness and understanding of Western art and modernism? I am thinking of practitioners like Peter Donovan, Hariata Ropata Tangahoe, Reginald Nicolas, Craig Collier and Brian Gregory, to name a few. These days, folk artists inevitably know about the tradition of Western art even while remaining aloof from it—witness O'Neill's enthusiasm for Goya, Turner and Degas. In this age of reproduction you don't need to have a university degree to know what a Picasso or a McCahon look like.

As I have suggested, McCahon isn't far removed from this vexed naïve-or-not question either. When McCahon's work was exhibited in Edinburgh in 1990, critic Tim Hilton tackled the matter in the *Guardian Weekly* of 13 May:

> Is Colin McCahon a primitive? For years we have been hearing rumours of this—apparently—isolated and eccentric New Zealand artist . . . McCahon wasn't a primitive in one elementary sense, for he was a keeper and deputy director of [the Auckland City Art Gallery]. He was an administrator as well as a professional artist, quite well aware of current worldwide trends . . .

Hilton summed up McCahon as a 'genuine, self-absorbed provincial'—a description which could well apply to the convincing naïve artists in Wolfe's book. There is an unashamed provincialism about their approach (and its sphere of reference); there is an element of self-absorption (as there is in all convincing art but even more so in art of a 'visionary' nature) and there is an element of honesty—of truth—which all genuine art must have at its core.

From beyond the confines of this book, figures like Illingworth—a highly trained artist whose mature work was produced in a deliberately naïve idiom—place even more stress on the folk art categorisation. If it's a question of whether or not an artist is self-taught, a figure like Jeffrey Harris could well enter this survey. A publication and/or exhibition of a different nature would be needed to traverse the space between 'conscious'/trained art and 'subconscious'/naïve art—a project that would productively bridge the gap between Tibbo and Michael Stevenson, Fergus Collinson and McCahon, Tangahoe and Rita Angus.

The current vogue in art circles for 'bad painting'—i.e. the work of Saskia Leek, Ronnie van Hout, Tony de Lautour and Peter Robinson—places some of the trappings of folk art closer to the centre of artistic discourse than, I suspect, they have ever been before. In a similar although less mischievous fashion, the folk art references that permeate the productions of Shane Cotton, Chris Heaphy and John Walsh reassert and develop the tradition of post-colonial Maori figurative painting dealt with in Roger Neich's important book *Painted Histories* (Auckland University Press, 1993). Prominent contemporary artists such as Harris, Dick Frizzell and Gavin Chilcott have all entered into a dialogue with the folk tradition, both in its localised permutations and with foreign productions such as the small marine paintings of Alfred Wallis. This traffic between genres makes it impossible to consider folk art as a ghetto—rather, it has to be seen as a part of the essential history.

There is a tendency in *All Our Own Work* to paint a rosy picture of the folk artist, belying the depression, anxiety and melancholy that often underlie this kind of art. Much supposed folk art, I would suggest, asks to be read as a non-conformist, subversive intervention into the national record rather than as the epitome of mainstream concerns. At times the art is tied up in kooky right-wing politics, neuroses, an intense (at times dysfunctional) sense of isolation and various forms of self-made or adapted spirituality or mysticism.

Despite the best efforts of James Mack, John Perry and a few other perceptive curators, folk art is still under-examined and under-exhibited in this country. Exhibitions of folk art are usually held in provincial centres, in places like the Sarjeant Gallery, Wanganui, and Lower Hutt's Dowse Art Museum. Committed dealerships are rare, perhaps the most notable being the Christopher Moore Gallery in Wellington, which has represented and actively promoted the work of O'Neill, Peter Donovan, Reginald Nicolas and Ivan Hill. Moore has also usefully produced a stream of small catalogue booklets to accompany these exhibitions, providing at least some documentation of this largely undocumented art.

2 *A ferment of faces: 'Colour and Light' at the Dowse Art Museum (1999)*

Is mental health to be equated with acceptance of prevailing opinions?
(Jean Dubuffet)

I can remember sitting on a step at the Dowse with blazing eyes with one hundred drawings on me. Must break into the Dowse Art Museum. Stick my paintings up. Yeah, that was what I was going to do.
(Steven Burrows)

Steven Burrows, *Portrait*, 1998, housepaint on board.

Engulfed by its blazing yellow background, Steven Burrows's *Portrait* could be a contemporary version of a Van Gogh self-portrait, only instead of the Dutchman's staccato brushstrokes, paint is applied in finger-like smears, and the sumptuous oil paint has been replaced with the flat, industrial surface of Dulux. The work is all light and colour but there's darkness and unease beneath the surface too. As we examine the portrait, the inscrutable face of Burrows's subject is, in turn, scrutinising us.

The painting was included in 'Colour and Light', curated by Damian Skinner for the Dowse Art Museum, alongside work by seventy-two other 'emerging' artists, all of them past sufferers of mental illness now involved with community-based arts centres in the greater Wellington area.

Psychiatric and post-psychiatric art hasn't received much serious attention in this country, although overseas its relationship to High Culture has been on the agenda for nearly a century. A landmark publication, Hans Prinzhorn's *Artistry of the Mentally Ill* (1922) reproduced many examples of work by psychiatric patients. Rather than using the works solely for diagnostic purposes (as many psychiatrists still do), Prinzhorn used them to highlight and illustrate the creative impulse as a basic tendency in all human beings. As part of his study, Prinzhorn pinpointed six basic artistic modes: (1) the expressive, (2) the playful or active, (3) the decorative or ornamental, (4) the ordered (using rhythm and rule), (5) that based on existing models and (6) art that responds to the innate human need for symbols. While a combination of these modes is at work in all the paintings in 'Colour and Light', the list is also an instructive one to run through the contents of any public gallery collection on display around the country.

In keeping with the ethics of his time, Prinzhorn masked the identity of the artists, using pseudonyms or numbers. While the works he examined were unlikely to be part of the road to recovery for their creators during what was to become a very dark period for the mentally ill in Europe, they certainly effected quite some change in twentieth-century art, being studied assiduously by artists including Paul Klee and the Surrealists. An exhibition at the Los Angeles County Museum of Arts in 1992, 'Parallel Visions', went some distance to acknowledging the influence of 'outsider artists' on the development of modern art.

Perhaps the key figure in the promotion of such artworks in the mainstream art world was Jean Dubuffet, who founded a museum of 'Art Brut' in Lausanne in 1975. As well as looking to non-Western cultures and children's art as a source of renewal in the visual arts, Dubuffet, from the 1940s, collected and studied psychiatric art. He wrote: 'These works created from solitude and from pure and authentic creative impulses . . . are, because of these very facts, more precious than the productions of professionals.' He believed that, after studying 'these flourishings of an exalted feverishness, lived so fully and so intensely by their authors, we cannot avoid the feeling that in relation to these works, cultural art in its entirety appears to be the game of a futile society, a fallacious parade'.

In the late 1990s, with the publication of John Maizels' *Raw Creation* and a raft of other 'outsider art' books and magazines, the genre (or fleet of genres, to be more precise) is having a renaissance. At the time of writing, England's Channel Four is broadcasting a new television series: *Journeys into the Outside with Jarvis Cocker*—yes, the lead singer of Blur taking us on a world tour of 'outsider art'.

*

Upon entering the Dowse exhibition space, the visitor was confronted by the charter of one of the art centres involved in the project. The exhibition signage highlighted the political nature of the project:

> When psychiatric survivors consent to open publication of their name with their work, it is because they genuinely and most generously seek to educate the public at large about consumer issues and mental illness, and as an act for truth and forthrightness amidst their constant struggle to survive.

While many of the works felt like expressions from the depth of crises, others seemed to inhabit the aftermath—you might almost call it an afterglow. These were paintings of recovery and a fiercely fought and tentatively won equilibrium—a fact which, doubtless, complicates the relationship between these works and Dubuffet's definition of 'Art Brut': i.e. if the artists are recovering from illness, does that mean that stylistically their work will relate more and more to

Reginald Nicolas, *The Three Crosses*, 1997, oil on canvasboard.

prevailing, mainstream cultural models? (Only a few pieces in 'Colour and Light' would support such a thesis, I believe.)

Beyond the confines of this show, a number of 'survivors' have made some headway in the mainstream art world, among them Reginald Nicolas, who has exhibited in recent years at the Christopher Moore Gallery, Wellington. Nicolas outlined his background in his exhibition notes of June 1996: 'At the age of nineteen I became mentally disturbed. This didn't affect my paintings, rather it eventually increased my personal visual insight. I have always painted—at ten I started in oils at Rotoiti and it remained mainly so except for a long spell later in hospital where I experimented in watercolours and other media . . . '

Nicolas first exhibited at the Barry Lett Gallery in 1980. His more recent shows have been devoted to religious subjects—these he paints while sitting on his bed in extremely cramped living/working circumstances. (These conditions lead to a characteristic thin coating of mattress- and room-dust in his oil pigment.) In Nicolas's religious scenes, the sinuous figures are merged in unsettling rhythmical compositions.

Institutional and market support for a practitioner like Nicolas isn't great. 'Visionary' artists tend not to attract anything more than a cult following while they are alive. The visionary statement tends to become a coherent—and, accordingly, marketable—narrative only after the protagonist's death. (The elevation of Tony Fomison from counter-culture rebel to primordial seer after his death is a case in point.)

Among the recurrent questions raised by the work of Reg Nicolas—and the artists in 'Colour and Light', for that matter—is: what part of the collective subconscious do naïve artists have access to that we don't? And how is it that the effectiveness of this art is so at odds with the difficult and limiting conditions of its making?

*

Many of New Zealand's central artists have grappled with mental illness or crisis, including such figures as Rita Angus and Patricia France. As well as being haunted by illness in its various permutations—physical, mental and spiritual—Tony Fomison landed himself in Banstead Hospital in England for three months after a presumably drug-induced psychological meltdown in the mid-1960s. The canon of this country's art includes work by schizophrenics and certainly an unsettling number of chronic depressives, alcoholics and sufferers of other psychological ailments. All of which points to the fact that the current exhibition is not as isolated from the mainstream as you might at first think.

'To paint is to start on a voyage of discovery,' wrote Patrick Hayman in 1959. 'The light, waxing and waning, colours one's thoughts.' The title of the Dowse exhibition—'Colour and Light'—highlights the base materials of all painting. It could just as easily be the title of an exhibition of Baroque masterpieces or, for that matter, paintings of the moon by astronauts.

'Colour and Light' was an act of habilitation, a placing of works by a disenfranchised sector of the community in a space that the community recognises and to which a certain cultural status is ascribed. There was no compromise on the part of the artists in such a placement—rather, it was the gallery visitors who were required to adjust their subjective positions and question a few preconceptions. Ultimately, all indications are that both parties were enriched by the experience.

McCahon back for opening

RETURN SHOW – Colin McCahon's painting Storm Warning,

By TOM CARDY, Arts reporter

A Colin McCahon painting sold by Victoria University amid controversy earlier this year is back on show in the new art gallery its sale helped fund.

The $2.2 million Adam Art Gallery on the university campus was to be officially opened today and be open to the public from tomorrow.

On display is McCahon's Storm Warning, which the university sold to an Auckland couple for between $1.2 million and $1.5 million in April.

It is being displayed above a piece by Maori protester Te Kaha, convicted of stealing a McCahon painting from the DOC centre at Lake Waikaremoana in 1997. It was recovered, damaged, 14 months later.

University Vice-Chancellor Professor Michael Irving yesterday again defended the sale of the painting. "We had a lot of controversy about selling that painting. Interest from money [from the sale] will be used to buy new [art] works."

Its owners allowed the painting to be displayed during the gallery opening.

Another university-owned McCahon, Gate III, was one of 10 artworks in the gallery's opening exhibition Manufacturing Meaning. It will be the only artwork to be housed permanently in the gallery.

Professor Jenny Harper, head of art history, said more than $2 million of the cost of the gallery had come from private donations, including $1 million from art patrons Denis and Verna Adam. About $150,000 came from the Wellington Community Trust.

The university has 240 artworks, most on display around the campus. Ms Harper said the gallery meant the public, students and staff could, for the first time, view a selection of its collection in one place. It would also be used as a teaching and research facility, with

Evening Post, Wellington, September 1999.

Somebody say something

Colin McCahon's Storm Warning, Wellington, 1999, a scrapbook

Can You Hear Me St Francis?

I'd like to preserve something
stand back a bit
make a kind of
invisible fence about
some form of life
so it could flourish
in its own way
unknowing not needing
to be grateful
the trouble is
none of the invisible fences
is strong enough
to keep out Man
(Peter Hooper)

'A few are riding, the rest have been run over.'
(Henri David Thoreau)

'I am painting what we have got now
and what we will never have again.'
(Colin McCahon, *Necessary Protection*)

On 19 April 1999, the day after Victoria University made public the 'intended' sale of Colin McCahon's *Storm Warning*, a painting the artist had gifted to the institution in 1981, I wandered into the Art History Department there. Like everyone I had encountered that morning at the university, I felt certain the proposed sale of the painting was a mistake which would, in due course, be rectified. The *Sunday Star Times* had reported the previous day that the work was being sold 'to plug an $80,000 shortfall in funds for the construction of a new on-campus gallery', with the additional funds being used to buy new artworks. Some bottom-lip biting went on when I cast around for comments from members of the department. Even at this stage there was palpable unease at the sale of the work for between 1.2 and 1.5 million dollars.

Just over a week later, the university announced the 'discovery' of a letter from Colin McCahon stating that the painting was 'a public work' and that he didn't want it to disappear into a private collection. By that time, a deluge of letters and e-mails objecting to the sale had descended on the Wellington daily newspapers as well as the vice-chancellor's office. It was subsequently announced that the painting had effectively been sold by the time the 'intended' sale was made public. Some members of the university staff were in tears over the sale. It is a rare painting that can have this effect.

Some disciplined mayhem

In June 1999, Sir Denis Mahon, an eighty-nine-year-old art collector, arranged for his collection of Italian Baroque art to be distributed among a number of British and European public art galleries. 'There was disciplined mayhem at the National Gallery in London,' reported the *Guardian Weekly* (27 June 1999). 'Saints, virgins, popes and angels were on the move to accommodate the premature arrival of 26 paintings conservatively valued at 17 million pounds.'

Sir Denis had decided to distribute the contents of his will while he was still alive. The *Guardian* continued: 'The treasures come with strings. They are loans that will become permanent after Sir Denis's death, on condition that none of the British galleries introduces admission charges, or sells anything from their collections. If they do, the National Art Collections Fund is charged with whipping the pictures off the walls immediately.'

In ailing health and painting only with great difficulty, Colin McCahon, by the early 1980s, was aware of his impending death. Like the admirable Sir Denis, he managed the preparation and execution of his will while he was still around to oversee it. He set to placing some of the important paintings still in his possession in public collections around the country, working out where they might be most effective. With neither Sir Denis's foresight nor his distrust, McCahon placed no written conditions on his gift to Victoria University (apart, that is, from writing informally that he did not want the artwork to disappear into a private collection).

McCahon believed passionately in the moral and spiritual dimensions of art. His innovations using language were principally to achieve such ends. He underlined the message-bearing capacity of art not only in the titles of his works (*Load-bearing structures*, *Teaching Aids*, *Necessary Protection*) but in just about every published statement he made: 'Painting can be a potent way of talking.' His stated reason for painting on loose canvas unencumbered by a frame (as is the case with *Storm Warning*) was because it gave the artwork 'more room to act'—his notion of the painting 'acting' went well beyond aesthetics to questioning and influencing how people went about their lives. He believed his paintings could act as 'environments', and written and spoken messages were an integral part of these environments.

In the early 1980s, Alexa Johnston, then Curator of Contemporary New Zealand Art at the Auckland Art Gallery, was involved in the purchase of a number of works from the artist. The gallery was also the recipient of a large number of gifted works. She recalls Colin McCahon 'clearly stating that he had specific destinations in mind for some of them—Wellington, Dunedin etc . . . gifts given with particular attention to what was being communicated and to whom'. So, in the last decade of his productive life, we find McCahon gifting the *Parihaka Triptych* to the people of Parihaka Pa, *The Wake* and *Song of the Shining Cuckoo* to the Hocken Library in Dunedin, *Storm Warning* to Victoria University and *The Lark's Song* to the Auckland Art Gallery.[1]

There is a purpose and a pattern to this gifting.

Just as McCahon grafted language and meaning onto the New Zealand landscape and night sky of his paintings, this time he was placing the paintings in the actual landscape. These markers or beacons were perhaps his last great statement as a painter, a final coming to terms with 'the terrifying present we live in' and a strategic placement of messages in places where they might be heeded.

What has been communicated

> Stroke and a stress that stars and storms deliver,
> That guilt is hushed by, hearts are flushed by and melt . . .

So chimes Gerard Manley Hopkins's suitably stormy 'Wreck of the Deutschland'. Hopkins was a bright light in McCahon's literary constellation. His 'Angel and Bed' paintings cite Hopkins's poem 'Felix Randal'. Another of McCahon's favourite poems, Hopkins's 'Pied Beauty', also serves as a manifesto for the artist:

> Glory be to God for dappled things—
> For skies of couple-colour as a brinded cow . . .
> Landscape plotted and pieced—fold, fallow, and plough;
> And all trades, their gear and tackle and trim . . .[2]

Words, for McCahon, were never inert or neutral—they functioned as catalysts and vehicles for meaning. They were links with the past, explorations of the present and messages for the future. As in Hopkins's poetry, the metaphor of the storm was a particularly poignant one in Colin McCahon's art. Storm, fog and encroaching darkness are three central visual metaphors of his late works.

In a series of painted scrolls exhibited at the Barry Lett Gallery in 1968, McCahon quoted his friend Peter Hooper (whom he had met at the Woollaston household in Greymouth during the 1950s). The seething cauldron of darkness and fire that is *Storm Warning* has an analogue in Hooper's 'Notes from the Margin', a poem which also locates itself in Wellington:

> Here is the weather forecast
> What was it for us?
> I missed it
> although who forecasts the
> storms that do
> the real damage?
> strong to gale
> southerlies in Cook Strait
> separate more
> than two islands

the roof falls
when
communication
is destroyed . . .

Certainly McCahon's intentions for his works are at odds with the manner in which much contemporary criticism deals with them. Postmodernism has, conveniently, made his work an easier pill to swallow, his 'messages' reduced to the status of quotations within quotations. The fashion may well be to treat a work like *Storm Warning* as primarily an example of semiotic sampling, an ambivalent re-rendering of lines from the New English Bible, headlined by the slogan: YOU MUST FACE THE FACT (which may well have been taken from a Christian religious tract). This kind of inability to 'read' the work in its intended manner, one can only assume, underlies the university's decision to sell it. Its religious and moral charge cast to the wind, *Storm Warning* becomes a signature 'McCahon' with all the prerequisite stylistic tics. A rare, if somewhat ungainly, bird.[3]

At the present time it would be a critical heresy to read *Storm Warning* as primarily a spiritual or social pronouncement. This despite McCahon's strategic use of virtually every visual device in the work to underline the literal meaning and urgency of his text. We are simultaneously given hellfire, a tempestuous Wellington evening and an all-encompassing night fog, partitioned off by McCahon's 'load-bearing structures', the bars and pillars that might once have supported bridges but are now frail and dissolving in the acid bath of McCahon's oncoming storm.

'The physical act of painting, its mechanics and its labour need not interest the viewer,' McCahon said. 'The work of art is done by the time the viewer views. What has been communicated is now of primary importance, indeed, this is the only importance a work of art has.'

Paradoxically, when in September 1998 the head of the Victoria University Art History Department was publicly criticised for hanging in her office a painting by Peter Robinson entitled *Pakeha Have Rights Too!*, featuring a swastika and not much else, she said the individuals critical of the work's placement were 'people unskilled in reading the visual'. Surely, such a dismissal could be just as aptly directed at those responsible for selling *Storm Warning*—one of McCahon's most clearly articulated statements.

More recently, the same academic has been dragged, rather unfairly it has to be said, into public discussions of whether or not McCahon could paint. In an *Assignment* documentary on Television One in June 1999 she was filmed nodding in agreement as self-professed man in the street Rob Harley droned on and on about McCahon's overinflated reputation. Her decision to cash in *Storm Warning* was upheld by Harley as that rare thing: a sane decision in the insane art world. Likewise, in the press, a number of correspondents, as well as *Sunday Star Times* columnist Frank Haden, endorsed the sale on the grounds she had palmed off a piece of junk for a cool million-plus.

Miserere

While I was studying at Auckland University in the early 1980s, one of my favourite items in the Elam library was the published version of Georges Rouault's series of 'Miserere' lithographs. This was before the time of computerised library withdrawals and borrowers had to write their names on yellow or red cards located in a pouch at the rear of the book. These cards provided a useful and endlessly fascinating

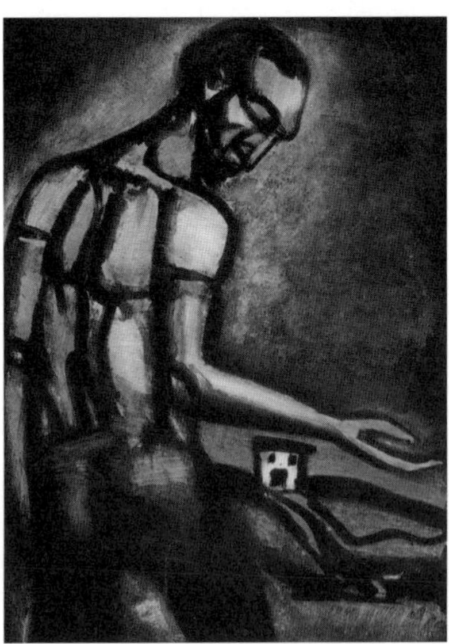

Page from *Miserere*, Georges Rouault, New York: Museum of Modern Art, 1952. 'In so many different ways, the noble vocation of sowing in hostile land.'

whakapapa of previous readers of any given book.[4] I recall being surprised that hardly anyone had withdrawn *Miserere* during the 1970s although—and there his handwriting was, in pencil—Colin McCahon had signed it out many times while teaching at Elam during the 60s.

So much for the temper of the times. While Rouault's crushing meditation on morality and the modern world was bypassed by students, the copies of *ARTFORUM* in the Elam library were so well read they were falling apart on the display shelves.

Like Rouault, McCahon was an artist concerned with moral and spiritual collapse. While a few commentators have married McCahon's paintings to the 'death of god', the works might more accurately be seen as explorations into the 'possibility of god'. (McCahon, as both painter and individual, didn't so much critique the idea of god as struggle towards some recognition or realisation.) McCahon's attachment to the work of the fervently Christian Rouault echoes through his word paintings with their moral imperatives.

> 'Tomorrow will be beautiful,' said the shipwrecked man
> Peace seems never to reign
> Over this anguished world
> Of shams and shadows.
>
> HOMO HOMINI LUPUS
> 'Man is a wolf to man'

These quotations are from Rouault's *Miserere*, although they could easily have been taken from McCahon's canvases. (Conveniently, the Auckland Art Gallery owns a number of Rouault's 'Miserere' lithographs which, no doubt, McCahon would have appreciated while he was employed there.) Like Rouault, McCahon was capable of the most abject despair. At other times, as in *Storm Warning*, he could also turn bull and charge.

> ROUAULT:
> 'Nous sommes fous'
> We are mad
>
> McCAHON:
> 'Men will love nothing
> but money and self . . .'

The McCahon Vacuum ('towards Auckland')

I imagine Colin McCahon—towards the end of his life—squirrelling some of his most potent works away in public collections to keep them away from the marketplace—a market he lampooned in the title and concept of his 1968 exhibition at the Barry Lett Gallery:

A few years ago, while working for the McCahon Trust, Gerald Barnett commented on how all the Colin McCahon paintings were heading for Auckland. It was as if a vacuum cleaner was positioned in the city and the paintings were being extracted from their collections and drawn inexorably northwards. More recently, Gerald observed, an even more powerful vacuum cleaner had begun shifting McCahons across the Tasman. And, in all likelihood, within the next decade an even more powerful vacuum will draw them further afield.

We witness the McCahons—apart from those secured in public collections—caught in this art-market whirlpool, a storm rather different from that in *Storm Warning*, although one into which the painting of that title has vanished.

*

According to the head of Victoria's Art History Department, 'the painting may have gone anyway . . . the issue of its value might have tipped the balance in the end'. A few years ago, our neighbours in McFarlane St, Mt Victoria were in a similar fix over a large painting which had been gifted to them. This work was on public display in the St Gerard's Monastery chapel, which opened directly onto Hawker Street. The door was left unlocked during daylight hours. Gagliardi's painting of St Gerard—after whom the monastery was named (see p140)—was gifted to the monastery at the turn of the century and, by 1992, was conservatively valued at just over one million dollars. So what was the church to do with it now the chapel was no longer in public use?

Far be it from me to endorse the fiscal policies of the Catholic Church in general, but in this instance the religious community ceremonially farewelled the painting, then shipped it back to the people of the Italian town of Mater Domini, whose forebears had gifted it to the Wellington parish a century earlier.

Nostalgia

In July 1998 I was talking with a successful young local painter at the New Gallery in Auckland, not far from a huge wall-mounted work, *Untitled* (1980) by the Greek artist Jannis Kounellis. The artwork comprised three industrial steel panels with beams bolted to them and pieces of clothing affixed between the beams and panels. When I remarked on what a powerful work it was, the artist replied that he couldn't bear the 'nostalgia' of it.

I queried this remark. The three panels obviously referred to the rather un-nostalgic business of the tripartite crucifixion on Golgotha. The aged articles of clothing evoked the forced emigrants and civilian prisoners of World War II and, more particularly, the persecution of Jews. 'Nostalgia' didn't feel like the right word.

Months later, amidst media images of the Kosovo crisis, Kounellis's artwork seemed to me to contain the essence of that catastrophe as well, the breaking of humanity on the the wheel of wanton power. (HOMO HOMINI LUPUS, Rouault might well have captioned the work.) I tried to think of who among contemporary New Zealand artists might plausibly create a work capable of articulating the

My brothers, not many of you should become teachers, for you may be certain that we who teach shall ourselves be judged with greater strictness. All of us often go wrong; the man who never says a wrong word is a perfect character, able to bridle his whole being. If we put bits into horses' mouths to make them obey our will, we can direct their whole body. Or think of ships: large they may be, yet even when driven by strong gales they can be directed by a tiny rudder on whatever course the helmsman chooses.

So with the tongue. It is a small member but it can make huge claims.

Left: Colin McCahon, *Untitled* (*'My brothers, not many of you'*), 1969, mixed media on wallpaper, McCahon Family Collection.

Right: Colin McCahon, *Untitled ('Parts of Speech', Peter Hooper)*, 1969, mixed media on wallpaper, McCahon Family Collection.

enormity and gravity of such public, social calamity. Which isn't to suggest this is the only area worth painting about (and, lord knows, public calamity has led to miles of rotten expressionist canvas), but who was there capable of painting with the necessary seriousness and self-excoriating honesty?

'Nostalgia', of course, is to do with events being lost in the past or being infused with a sentimental attitude to the past. Perhaps, on the terms of the young artist, McCahon's *Storm Warning* would also be a nostalgic work, especially if you packaged up its religious and, I guess, High Modernist references and consigned them to their historical niches. On the other hand, I would assert that a work that can reference and inhabit the past at the same time as it remains alive and relevant in the present cannot be exactly nostalgic. The work might appear unfashionable and untimely but surely that is something a sophisticated critical environment should explore rather than side-step or deride. Maybe the young artist's approach is akin to 'post-humanism'—a term that has crept into art parlance but which I've never found an explanation of, or justification for. Maybe 'post-humanism' suggests we have transcended art's ability to get inside the human situation? Such a state of affairs would have been anathema to McCahon.

The point at which the humanist or moral aspects of an artwork are deemed 'nostalgic' is, it could be argued, a point at which the work becomes eminently saleable. The artwork becomes a quotation rather than a statement, a semiotic hiccup rather than an outpouring—in the case of *Storm Warning*, a 'gift' in the material sense only. (And this would accord neatly with the parallel point in the history of Art History when the master-narrative of Western Art becomes a socio-economic narrative of the buying, commissioning and selling of chattels.) One can only assume that, at the point the *Storm Warning* sale was decided upon, the status of the item to be sold had been distorted and reduced accordingly. However, while the purpose and spirit of the work had obviously been decommissioned as far as those directly involved in selling the work were concerned, this was far from the case for the university community at large. The University Council's right to sell *Storm Warning* will always be contested, if not necessarily on legal grounds then certainly on moral and ethical ones. At the time of writing, with the Adam Art Gallery recently opened, the *Storm Warning* debacle lingers like a black cloud or busted Zeppelin over the Hunter Building, where the painting was once installed. The brilliantly conceived, Athfield-designed Adam Art Gallery deserved a better opening fanfare than the fallout from this piece of bureaucratic and art historical misadventure.

Get up, stand up

A parallel could be drawn between the case of the Peter Robinson painting with the swastika and the sale of the McCahon. In both instances, the ethical implications of the artwork were deliberately downplayed or anaesthetised—in one case to justify a work remaining on public display, and in the other to permanently remove a work. And what of the artists' intentions?

Certainly, in the case of the *Storm Warning* sale, you could be forgiven for thinking that the intentions of the artist don't count for much these days. A fortnight after the sale was announced I discussed the matter on National Radio's *Kim Hill* programme, having called up a number of people close to McCahon the previous night and asked what they thought the artist would have made of the sale. Without exception, they said he would have been appalled.

The artist is 'dead', so they say, just like the author. But if intentions don't matter, then, stripped of its irony, Peter Robinson's swastika in the office of the head of the Art History Department has the same status as Fascist propaganda (which was how it appeared to the Maori student who felt intimidated by its placement and lodged a complaint). On the other hand, if intentions do matter, then weren't McCahon's, in relation to *Storm Warning*, patently clear from the start—and underlined by the letter that surfaced later in the debacle?

'Someone has to stand up for what artists do,' the head of Art History stated in a 1998 *Listener* article. But what exactly is it that they do? If she will stick up for Peter Robinson's right to paint a swastika, why would she not stand up for McCahon's right to strategically place a work called *Storm Warning* on the hilltop above Wellington, overlooking the Beehive.

Impeded and unimpeded view

Colin McCahon's belief in art as a means of 'conquering spiritual death' must sound like mumbo-jumbo to the post-humanists and those sainted individuals bold enough to describe themselves as 'skilled in reading the visual'. How also would they cope with McCahon's stated objective 'to make a painting beat like, and with, a human heart'? Not that McCahon would have been particularly impressed by the theorists who, if forced to confront the ferocious religiosity of his work, would probably consign it to the same basket as, say, the folk art of Howard Finster—filed under Quaint, Eccentric Religious Visionary—or William Blake, a writer/painter whose anti-monetarist imperative was often cited by Toss Woollaston: 'Where any view of money exists, Art cannot be carried on.' A thought worth noting in the present circumstance.[5]

How do we—as viewers and commentators—cope with the confrontational aspect of *Storm Warning*? By retreating into formalism and seeing it as entirely self-referential and contained within a modernist tradition of art speaking only to itself? But wouldn't that mean fixing McCahon at the point he reached relatively early in his career with the infamous *Painting* (1958), in which he had dispensed

'I WILL NEED WORDS....

WORDS CAN BE TERRIBLE BUT A SOLUTION CAN BE GIVEN. IN SPITE OF A MESSAGE WHICH CAN BURN I INTEND A PAINTING IN NO WAY EXPRESSIONSTIC BUT WITH A SLOWLY EMERGING ORDER. ....)

(Heaven help us poor sinners.)

not only with imagery but with words. That painting was both a nadir and a watershed for the artist, a wall he hit hard, rebounding back into 'content' with the even more stridently voiced messages which would dominate his work for the next two decades.

Most likely, the answer is to bear in mind Octavio Paz's assertion that 'theory is grey, green the tree of life' and abandon all our discussions and speculations, and simply stand before a painting like *Storm Warning* in all its expressive, explosive vigour. As Julian Bell usefully points out: 'Who needs a theory of firework displays?'

Metamorphoses

While goodwill towards Victoria University certainly prompted the *Storm Warning* gift, other factors came into it.[6] According to Alexa Johnston, McCahon consciously placed the painting in a university that had an active religious studies department—and a continuing education programme involving the likes of Lloyd Geering, which provided a dynamic spiritual environment beyond, as well as within, the university proper. Geering's beliefs and non-conformist religious stance had greatly impressed McCahon over many years. A case could certainly be argued that the fate of *Storm Warning* should in fact have been placed in the hands of the Department of Religious Studies rather than the Art History Department—which, as a number of commentators have reminded us, didn't even exist at the time of the gift.

If McCahon had wanted to hand the painting over to an art history department (and a university with a well-organised collection) he might well have gifted the work to Auckland University. However, as it happened, Auckland in 1982 had no religious studies department and attempts around that time to found one had apparently been scuttled by an ardently secular university council. This state of affairs deeply troubled McCahon, Johnston recalls.[7] Despite the fact he taught at Auckland between 1964 and 1970, McCahon never, to my knowledge, gifted any of his own works to that university's collection.

The recent metamorphosis of *Storm Warning* into capital was certainly never a possibility McCahon would have entertained. To add to the absurdity of the whole business, it looked for a time as if the painting might well continue to metamorphose into even stranger forms. The *Evening Post* (24 June 1999) quoted some university staff members who thought some of the funds should go towards a McCahon Swimming Pool—a fittingly surreal conclusion to a course of events which tests the bounds of credibility anyway. [8]

The spirit of the age

If many contemporary artists like to think of Marcel Duchamp as the towering spirit of the age, I would argue it is in fact the spirit of Salvador Dali presiding over much contemporary art practice: witness the Dali-esque attraction to right-wing politics, banality and boyish/adolescent humour that now almost defines a movement in contemporary New Zealand art. One of my favourite stories about Salvador Dali concerns his falling out with the Society for the Prevention of Cruelty to Animals in the 1960s. In a proposed filmscript, Dali outlined a scene in which a number of swans, with gelignite attached to their backs, were to be released onto the flat surface of a lake. The camera would follow them slowly around the mirrored waters as, one by one, they were blown to pieces.

Such a mixture of bad boy-ism and showmanship certainly has its proponents here just as anywhere else in the world. A good deal of contemporary New Zealand art looks like a case of the rebellious grandsons and daughters of McCahon getting their own back on his solemn, deliberated art. Or are these artists simply drawing logical

Allan Kaprow, *Words*, Museum of Contemporary Art, Chicago, c. 1967.

conclusions from the cultural climate in which they live? Such a state of affairs Ernest Hemingway had figured in his 1960 poem 'The Age Demanded':

> The age demanded that we sing
> And cut away our tongue.
> The age demanded that we flow
> And hammered in the bung.
> The age demanded that we dance
> And jammed us into iron pants.
> And in the end the age was handed
> The sort of shit that it demanded.

Or, as that great punster Rrose Selavy would have said, 'Oh! Douche it again!' If, on the one hand, many contemporary artists dabble with 'transgressive' ideas/materials à la Salvador Dali, there is also a passivity to much contemporary practice which comes uncomfortably close to the complacency that George Orwell warned against: 'Seemingly there is nothing left but quietism—robbing reality of its terrors by simply submitting to it.'

While Peter Robinson's word- and number-based paintings have assimilated generous chunks of McCahon, the works' real affinity is with the 1960s word-productions of Allan Kaprow—a concrete poetry full of neutralised or ironised imperatives and large themes rendered playfully inert. Perhaps, if the art of Kaprow and Robinson is true to the fragmented reality of its time (and is, in the latter case, a by-product of the 'post-humanist' era), then McCahon is the anachronism?[9] More and more, then, McCahon reconfigures as a lone prophet, although in a different wilderness now.

In contrast to McCahon's impassioned 'way of talking', we find ourselves presented with a piece like Julian Dashper's *What I am reading at the moment* (1993)—an installation comprising a well-worn chair and a glass case full of back issues of—you guessed it—*ARTFORUM* magazine. Admittedly, Dashper's meditation coheres neatly with the narrative of reading and writing which runs through New Zealand painting since World War II; only now the artist's role has become that of a passenger, a wry consumer or commentator who has chanced little, rather than a citizen who, in Samuel Beckett's phrase, 'stakes his entire being'.

'McCahon's gift is still with us. We have just changed the nature of that gift.'

Given the obviousness of *Storm Warning*'s message, and the ease with which details surrounding the gift could have been gathered from people who were close to McCahon at the time, the fact that the head of the Art History Department went on national television and said she thought the sale was in the spirit of McCahon's gift underlines the implausibility and sheer outrageousness of this chain of events.

Within the university itself, opposition to the sale came, in particular, from the departments of English, Music and Religious Studies. Many staff members felt the painting didn't entirely belong to 'Art History'. The literary element in McCahon's painting certainly places it, at least partially, within the domain of the English Department. McCahon is unarguably an important presence in New Zealand literary history—his association with writers such as Caselberg, Hooper and Baxter has been explored in two recent exhibitions.[10] The artist wrote: 'I suppose writing is above painting. The beauty of words grab me. I love words—you get "told" by words.' I've already mentioned McCahon's relevance to the field of religious studies. His relevance to the music and dramatic arts of this country is unequalled by any other visual artist, with the possible exception of Ralph Hotere.

Maori members of staff had every reason to question the authenticity of the university's supposed biculturalism after the powers-that-be felt no compunction about secretly despatching a work of this nature—a gift from an individual to a Maori as well as a Pakeha community—without taking it through the appropriate Maori channels. It was even suggested, in at least one quarter, that *Storm Warning* might well inspire the kind of committed reclaiming that the *Urewera Mural* met with in 1997 (which would explain the decision to hang the work on hooks six metres high in the Adam Art Gallery, when it was returned temporarily to the university for the opening exhibition.)

And still the university simply refuses to admit the sale was a mistake. An official statement in the parish pump VicNews was jaw-dropping in its illogicality:

> Vice-Chancellor Professor Michael Irving said that the sale did not

> breach McCahon's wishes because the new owners had agreed that the painting will be made available for public exhibition from time to time.

Whether the institution admits it or not, the sale has led to a collapse in confidence on the part of donors and friends of the gallery and university. The Turnovsky Trust has written to the university concerning the 'gift' status of a number of grand pianos donated to the Music Department. A series of thirty-two photographs originally intended as a gift to the university has now been gifted to a specific department of the university on the condition it does not become part of the University Art Collection. It will take the university a long time to regain the goodwill and trust of countless artists, collectors and others. The whole business reads not only like a fulfilled prophecy (McCahon's pessimism confirmed) but also like some grim parable of the unstoppable, unmeasured opportunism of New Right economics.

Richard Killeen, discussing the sale recently, went on to draw the gloomy conclusion that, in the restructuring of welfare and education in particular, Pakeha New Zealand was showing its true colours. In short, the country had been colonised by a band of gold-diggers and the period of the welfare state was but a brief aberration before we returned to being who we really were all along: a nation of gold-diggers.

In the end, you could be forgiven for thinking that McCahon's *Storm Warning*—with its expressed sentiment—was exactly the kind of painting a university in the present monetarist era didn't want around.

*

'In this present time it is very difficult to paint for other people—to paint beyond your own ends and point directions as painters once did,' Colin McCahon wrote in 1972. 'Once the painter was making signs and symbols for people to live by: now he makes things to hang on walls at exhibitions.' This statement reads like an uncannily accurate description of *Storm Warning*'s progression from being a community-owned icon on permanent display to being an artwork temporarily on loan to a gallery from a private collection.

Gordon H. Brown, McCahon's biographer, said recently that more and more in his latter years the artist divided the people around him into two factions: the 'believers' and the 'betrayers'. The *Storm Warning* debacle was one occasion, Brown surmised, when the 'betrayers' had had their way.

Notes

1 McCahon, throughout his career, gifted works to his friends and family. Many of these have subsequently been sold on, for one reason or another. Maurice Shadbolt has said that sometime in the 1980s he had to sell a number of McCahons (works he had bought as well as been given) to enable him to continue writing full-time. He broached this matter with McCahon and his family, who approved of this course of action. These works were not, however, gifted in the manner of *Storm Warning* or the other public gifts.

2 McCahon selected these two poems by Gerard Manley Hopkins to be read out at the Auckland City Art Gallery in 1972 as part of a presentation, 'WORDS FOR PAINTING: poetry and writing influential in the work of Colin McCahon'.

3 Tellingly, at the 'Curating Now' conference in New Plymouth, September 1999, there was a discernible unease when a visiting American curator, Dana Friis-Hanson, said he believed artworks should not be shown in a way that the artist would not have approved of. Many of the curators in the audience, I presume, sensed a loss of power—or perhaps even a responsibility they did not want—in his statement, and responded quite aggressively.

4 Now that library withdrawal cards are a thing of the past, this traceable history is removed from the public gaze and lost—one presumes—somewhere in the inner brain of the institution. (Iain Sharp's *Landfall 156* review of Kendrick Smithyman is a paean to the virtues of this outmoded system.)

5 Woollaston, quoted from 'The origin of beauty and the function of appearance in art', *Art in New Zealand*, March 1938, pp165–6.

6 Peter McLeavey in the *Listener* (29 May 1999) pointed to the important friendships between McCahon and such Victoria University figures as Frederick and Evelyn Page, Douglas Lilburn and J. C. Beaglehole.

7 Conversation with the author, July 1999.

8 The much-vaunted justification for the sale was that, as well as meeting the $80,000 shortfall, it would enable the university to buy new artworks. In fact, the purchase of new works was always part of the project description at the time it was initially sanctioned by the University Council. Certainly, no mention was made of the possible selling-off of artworks to facilitate acquisitions in the fund-raising letter I received in my pigeonhole in the English Department in February 1998.

9 Paradoxically, Colin McCahon was himself aware of Allan Kaprow's work and had met Kaprow in the USA during his 1958 tour (their encounter is described in Gordon Brown's monograph). However, it is the differences between McCahon's and Kaprow's 'word environments' that are remarkable, rather than the similarities.

10 'A Candle in a Dark Room' (Colin McCahon and James K. Baxter), 1997, and 'Answering Hark' (McCahon and John Caselberg), both curated by Peter Simpson.

Opposite: Ralph Hotere, *Untitled (after 'Storm Warning')*, 1999, mixed media on paper.

A warning came
and then
the weather
Rain we took
as given
The wind proved
a volatile gift
blowing the painting
right out of
the picture

JENNY BORNHOLDT

RH
'99

The public interest
An annotated bibliography 1988–2001

The following list includes most of the essays, autobiographical pieces and longer reviews I have published between 1988 and 2001. Newspaper reviews are noted only when I have included extracts from them here. All the extracts were chosen because, in one way or another, it seemed to me they added to the ideas and themes touched on in the main essays.

An asterix denotes pieces that are included in this book. The following pieces are published here for the first time: 'An alphabet without edges—pages from a Janet Frame notebook', 'Widening horizons and worlds regained', 'An attempt at the first page of an autobiography', 'Wild horses', 'The exact size of the world (part two)', 'Radio Birdman', 'The shape of living children II', 'The man who wrote the book about the weather', 'Blue Monk, Black Light', '*These May Mornings* in October', 'I am a shepherd'.

***'After bathing at Baxter's'. Essay in *Sport 11* (Spring 1993).**

'All the juicy bits'. Book review of *The Firebox: Poetry in Britain and Ireland after 1945*, ed. Sean O'Brien, in *New Zealand Listener*, 24 April 1999.

'Ansel Adams: Classic Images'. Brochure essay for exhibition 'Classic Images', City Gallery, Wellington, 1998.

'Art in the Twentieth Century'. Introduction to catalogue for 'The Exhibition of the Century: Modern Masterpieces from the Stedelijk Museum' (Amsterdam), City Gallery, Wellington, 1998.

***'Aspects of his face'. Autobiographical story in *Meanjin*, Vol. 55, No.2 (1996).**

'Astonish Me—Edward Lucie-Smith in Wellington'. Interview with the English art critic in *Art New Zealand 67* (Winter 1993).

***'Back soon, Godot'. Autobiographical story in *North and South* (December 1997).**

***'Big Tree Transmission'. Brochure essay for exhibition 'McCahon: a view from Urewera' at City Gallery, Wellington, November 1999.**

***A blaze of colour: Gordon Tovey, Artist Educator*, Carol Henderson; *Dear Peggy: Letters to Margaret Garland from Her New Zealand Friends*, ed. Peter and Dianne Beatson; *Chemical Evolution: Drugs and Art Production 1970–80*, Martin Edmond; *Years Ago Today: Language and Performance 1969*, Alan Brunton. Untitled book review in *Landfall 196* (Spring 1998).**

Alan Brunton's wide-ranging cultural history, *Years Ago Today*, is a high-spirited and instructive guide to the non-conformist 1970s, encompassing all manner of 'period' behaviour, moving effortlessly from the poetry of Blaise Cendrars to composer Harry Partch to the chemical equivalents of these two ecstatic experimentalists . . . In a more enlightened society, thousands of copies of this book would be dropped from aeroplanes onto present-day student populations to wake them up to less market-driven realities.

Brunton's book—and Martin Edmond's similarly inclined production, *Chemical Evolution* —left me craving a television series. How about Brunton presenting—after the manner of James Belich in *The New Zealand Wars*—a series on the New Zealand cultural conflicts of the 1970s? We could have him standing, gesticulating on the Nambassa site or in the middle of the Grafton Gully motorway. Cut to Brunton with flailing madman arms, this time on a neatly cropped school lawn, intoning a litany of past heroes and villains: 'From Kings College, there was Jack Body, Ian Wedde and Rob Tongue, the son of a funeral director, whose eccentricity persisted long enough for him to take over his father's business . . .'

'Booked and Bound to It'. Review of Manawatu Art Gallery exhibition 'Opening up the book', in *Art New Zealand 70* (Autumn 1994).

As a storeroom of language, ideas or images, a repository of tradition, authority and wisdom, the bound book still conjures up ideas of permanence—although, these days, even that premise is under siege. Of the current epoch's obsession with the temporal and disposable, Chris Wallace-Crabbe has written that books represent 'a claim to continuity that we have been taught to despise . . . Permanence is bunk, like history. The isle is full of voices, electronic voices . . . ' A pessimistic note to strike and one that, if taken seriously, would mean that books are destined to be found only in museums and galleries.

The characteristics embodied in this exhibition, I would venture, are those that will keep the book alive and thriving—the materiality, the allure, the intimacy, versatility and a capability to move the viewer/

reader in ways unavailable to other media. Which isn't to privilege the 'literary' and the handmade at the expense of all else. Perhaps William Morris's belief in the possibility of a two-tier economy in which high-tech production develops alongside the handmade is a reasonable option . . .

***'Breaking open the luggage: Denis O'Connor and BIG AITCHE, LITTLE AITChE'. Book review in *Art New Zealand 97* (Summer 2000).**

'The Brother, the Author and "Your Man"'. Interview with Irish actor/ playwright Eamon Morrissey in *Landfall 191* (Autumn 1996).

'Cans, boots and poems'. Book review of Elizabeth Smither's *The Journal Box*, in *New Zealand Listener*, 25 May 1996.

Elizabeth Smither has written some of the best short lyrics ever produced in this country. In her new book, a collection of journals, she sums up the poet Denise Levertov in words that could well describe her own writing, pointing to the 'moments of great intensity' when 'the floor of the brain is being swept like a chicken yard or, a more elaborate image, one of those gravel gardens of the Japanese'.

'caught in this sensual music all—works by Janet Paul'. Catalogue essay for exhibition at Michael Hirschfeld Gallery, City Gallery, Wellington, April–May 2000.

A few years ago, while sitting with friends on the lawn behind the house of Rhondda Greig and Hugo Manson in the Wairarapa I watched Janet Paul drawing. What struck me on this occasion was the almost euphoric state she appeared to inhabit while making figure studies in one of her numerous sketchbooks. I also remember how the act of drawing did not in any way remove her from the assembled company—rather it became a way of *inhabiting* the group, of relating and remaining a co-equal part. That such refined artworks are also acts of irrepressible sociability and even communion is yet another remarkable characteristic of the woman and her art. While painting and the emotional life have their different conditions and structures, Janet Paul's best works are a painterly instance of Yeats's 'rhythmical animation', a musical merging and enlivening of art and the particulars of everyday life.

***'Changing the light—Noel McKenna in Taranaki'. Catalogue essay for exhibition at Niagara Galleries, Melbourne, July 1999.**

***'Chunk of landscape, chunk of memory: the paintings of Euan Macleod'. Essay, first published as 'Landscape, Deep Water, Memory' in *Art New Zealand 94* (Autumn 2000).**

'A Culbertbook'. Notebook first published in *Sport 19* (Spring 1997)

In 1988 I was living in an apartment across the corridor from where Bill and Pip Culbert were temporarily lodged. Knowing they did not have a washing machine or drier, I knocked on their door one afternoon and offered them the use of mine. They declined politely, saying that they never used a washing machine; their clothes they washed by hand. Later that night I observed articles of clothing hanging up to dry in their window, the light projecting through the fabric out into the night sky above Albert Park, Auckland . . .

Today at the City Gallery, Wellington, I find myself standing in front of a photograph of clothing strung on a line somewhere in southern France, and I am reminded of those articles of clothing, handwashed and wrung out.

And I am entertaining the possibility that perhaps light—as it is manifest in both art and life—isn't in a sense *complete* until it has passed through or touched upon those things that are close to us, those things that matter to us.

***'The dark plane leaves at evening—some notes on the history of aviation, the aerial perspective and turning 21 in Australia, 1982'. Notebook in *Sport 21* (Spring 1998).**

'Drinking tea because of you'. Notebook in *An Inward Sun: Celebrating the Life and Work of Janet Frame*, ed. Elizabeth Alley (Wellington: Daphne Brasell Associates Press 1994). Excerpts are included in *'An alphabet without edges'.

***The Drummer*, Ian Wedde. Untitled book review in *Landfall 186* (Summer 1993).**

Like the unplugged albums a plethora of rock stars were producing in the 1990s, this collection replays and reconstructs the sounds of old. After the theoretically inclined, often obfuscated work included in his 1988 collection, *Tendering*, Wedde has returned to picking homely, rootsy tunes on the acoustic guitar—lyrical, streamlined and accessible—and the *Earthly* stars are once again whizzing above the firmament.

Poetry, by its very nature, should be about possibility, not prescription. While *Tendering* might have had some readers worried that he had taken on board some prescriptive, purist agenda, *The Drummer* will blow that notion apart. It's a craggy, impressively realised hybrid, even if it is at times a little dazed by its multifarious lineage. The publicity for the latest Greg Osby CD release will do as a description of the latest Wedde: it's a 'multi-tracked, genre-switching, contemporary performance in which HipHop, jazz and street soul are Robochefed into a slammin' new mix'.

***'East born'. Essay in *Sport 15*, Spring 1995.**

***'Electricities'. Essay in *New Zealand Books*, November 1994. Supplementary material added for current version.**

'Engaging tour through the life of a cheerful artist'. Review of *Len Lye: A Biography*, Roger Horrocks, in *Evening Post*, 22 June 2001.

There are two kinds of biographers: swimmers and walkers. The first glide through the particulars of a life, freestyling a purposeful and narrow course. The second kind are perambulators, breathing the air of a life, picking up all the peripheral detail, tapping the collective living memory and available documentary sources.

Roger Horrocks is of the second variety. Rather than confine himself to one of the fast swimming lanes of theory or art history, in his authoritative biography of Len Lye, he is an engaging tour guide, taking us through the artist's life, from his birth in Christchurch in 1901 until his death in New York in 1980 . . .

The usual trajectory of a biography—in which the subject lives out their natural life—is the ascent to maturity, via childhood and youth, then the decline into either elder statespersonhood or neglect. It's an arc in which the notable activity is usually concentrated in the middle.

Len Lye is an exception to this rule. After a busy and productive youth, Lye kept on accelerating right up until the end. With hardly any decrease in creativity during his 60s and 70s, Lye's life ends on a high. The last chapters of this book recount the beginning of the Len Lye Foundation—the good crowd he fell in with at the Govett-Brewster Gallery in New Plymouth—and the ongoing realisation of his large sculptures, his youthful dreams, a dream of perpetual youth.

'Epic Appropriations'. Book review of *Ian Scott*, by Warwick Brown, in *Art New Zealand 88* (Spring 1998).

'For Victor Meertens'. Poem for Meertens's exhibition at the Sarjeant Gallery, Wanganui; published in *Sport 22* (Autumn 2000).

'Free Enterprise: New Zealand painting in the 1980s'. Catalogue essay for exhibition 'From the BNZ Collection', City Gallery, Wellington, 1998.

'Fresh Air'. Book review of Bob Orr's *Breeze*, in *Printout 2* (April 1992).

Breeze is imbued with the semi-tropical ambience of the largest Polynesian city in the world, Auckland, at the height of summer. Appositely, that season is mentioned seven times in the book while autumn is the only other season to appear, and then only once. The sun (including sunlight, suntan . . .) appears fourteen times, fifteen if you count blues singer Sonny Day.

Horizons, breezes and tides recur throughout, as do the dabs from Orr's characteristic colour box, blue and red being easily the most frequent colours—blue appears at least eighteen times, red eleven times—bringing to mind the poet's previous publication, which was titled *Red Trees* and wrapped in striking plain blue covers.

'Fresh Look—the art of William J. Reed and Gordon H. Brown'. Review in *New Zealand Listener*, 11 October 1997.

'The Great Pretender's Niece: Stephanie de Montalk's *Animals Indoors*'. Launch speech, Unity Books, 12 July 2000.

A year or so back I was involved in an obscenity trial. The case before the Censorship Appeals Board concerned the City Gallery's Keith Haring exhibition. Graham Capill, of the Christian Heritage Party, was seeking to repeal the censorship office's ruling that the exhibition catalogue be unrestricted. I recall being led into a bland meeting room at the front of which sat the ten eminently sensible-looking people who make up the Censorship Appeals Board. Among them was Stephanie Miller, aka de Montalk.

Those of you who know Stephanie might recognise a certain historical irony in her sitting on such a censorship board. Her famous great-uncle, the poet Count Potocki de Montalk, had been involved in similar court proceedings in 1932. He was in the dock facing charges of obscenity relating to the publication of a poem in England. The elder de Montalk managed to rally some heavyweight supporters including W. B. Yeats, T. S. Eliot, Edith Sitwell and Leonard and Virginia Woolf to his cause. Their support, however, arrived a little late in the day and, after a failed appeal, he served his time in jail.

The recent court hearing left me wondering what the famously eccentric Count Potocki would have made of his clear-minded and clear-sighted niece on the Censorship Board. And in relation to the present occasion what the self-professed genius and pretender to the throne of Poland would make of her collection of poems *Animals Indoors*?

Stephanie has no throne to claim, although she is happy in these poems to sit on any number of couches and chairs in the company of people, animals or things. To sit and observe and understand. Funnily, for someone who sits on a censorship board, the poet here does not make judgements—she is content to mull over the world and its objects then pass them along to the reader in an activated, atomised state. The poems are humane and funny, balancing the everyday and the mythical, the concrete and the ethereal, the outer and the inner life. As a real estate agent would say, they have excellent indoor/outdoor flow.

'Having good luck figured'. Catalogue essay for exhibition 'Black Frame: Nigel Brown, work 1964–87', Lopdell House, Titirangi, March 1988.

The country holds out its hands. Hands hold out their country. It would be good to think of.

*

Solzenitzyn, in one of Brown's collages, FREED AT LAST stamped on his forehead, a speech bubble from his mouth: 'Don't rush your work.'

*

Viewing the rewards of viewing.

*** 'High Cultural Life'. Untitled book review in *Landfall 193* (Autumn, 1997).**

'High Wind'. Book review of *Te Tangi a te Matuhi,* Leigh Davis et al., and *In Winter Vineyards*, Brian Gregory and Richard McWhannell, in *Art New Zealand 93* (Summer 1999).

***Hotere—out the black window: Ralph Hotere's work with New Zealand poets.* Text for book (Auckland: Godwit/City Gallery Wellington, 1997).**

'How to be somewhere'. Review of Ian Wedde's *How to be Nowhere: Essays and texts 1971–1994*, unpublished 1995.

The connection between art and commerce, 'the relationship between money and meaning', which Wedde makes much of in his introduction and elsewhere, is spelt out in the book's cover photo of greengrocer H. Quun's famously cluttered shopfront in Caversham, Dunedin. That image is also a deft pointer to a central concern of Wedde's: the brisk trade between words and images, writing and visual art. Like the successful fruit and vegetable seller, Wedde is capable of some fast talking and fancy footwork . . . Even if—as Wedde maintains—he, like the greengrocer, is first and foremost trying to *sell something*, to make a living. That said, a book this true to its brains and instincts must be a labour of not inconsiderable love . . .

***'Imagine the Imagination'. Book review of Margaret Mahy's *Dissolving Ghost*, first published as 'Branching Out' in *New Zealand Books*, August 2000.**

'Ink-Black, Gold & Grey Matter—a sculpture by Ralph Hotere and Mary McFarlane'. Article in *Art New Zealand 91* (Winter 1999).

(A version of this piece was written at Hotere's behest and distributed from the front desk of Te Puni Kokiri, in Lambton Quay, to perplexed passers-by who wandered in off the street to inquire what the creation on the footpath in front of the building was all about. See p15.)

'Inspired voice—"Beyond the Palisade" by James K. Baxter'. Article in *New Zealand Listener*, 13 March 1999.

***'A journey around Kendrick Smithyman's *Atua Wera*'. Review article in *Landfall 194* (Summer 1997).**

'Kendrick Smithyman'. Entry in *Encyclopedia of World Literature in the 20th Century* (New York: Hunter College, City University of New York 1999).

***Lands and Deeds: Profiles of Contemporary New Zealand Painters.* Text, with photographs by Robert Cross (Auckland: Godwit 1996).**

'Little Rotter—The Progress of a "Serious Artiste": Dick Frizzell Mid-Career'. Review of exhibition 'Portrait of the Serious Artiste', in *Art New Zealand 83* (Winter 1997).

There's a photograph of the Russian constructivist Kazimir Malevich lying in state in his Leningrad bedroom, taken shortly after his death in May 1935. Around his body hang pivotal works spanning his career: cylindrical renditions of Russian farmers, an almost realistic self-portrait, and at the head of his bed the painting *Black Square*. The mood of the photograph is one of repose, the canvas above the artist's head somehow the privileged work—you could easily think that the other images, with their busy referencing to the world, are what he has left behind and the black square, with its air of finality, is where he has now arrived.

It happens that Malevich's *Black Square* is the basis for one of Dick Frizzell's paintings in the current exhibition, 'Portrait of the Serious Artiste'. In Frizzell's painting, which is entitled *Little Rotter* (see p9), Malevich's blackness has been impregnated with a floating, cylindrical garden compost bin—the 'little rotter' of the title—which looks as though it has been lifted from an advertisement in a gardening magazine. As is the case with all of Frizzell's best paintings, the image is an uneasy, witty marriage of high and low art. Malevich's seriousness becomes Frizzell's playfulness, the Russian's single-mindedness becomes part of the Aucklander's broad repertoire of tricks.

Beyond its inherent mischief, *Little Rotter* is an oddly beautiful painting, rich in art historical echoes (did Frizzell intend the cylindrical composter to echo Malevich's cylindrical figures?) as well as being a whimsical glance at an overlooked corner of contemporary suburbia. While the painting is a corruption of a work which has been described as the *Mona Lisa* of abstract art, it is also a homage, a basking in the beauty and potential of the art historical inheritance. Frizzell himself sees *Little Rotter* as an allegory about the way art in general feeds upon itself—one set of ideas or style mushing down and composting into another. Accordingly, as well as regarding modernism as a straightforward, linear process, he would like us to think of it as a cyclic one—a process of growth, decay and renewal. His artistic project could also be said to share this cyclic nature, with its stops and starts, and frequent reconstitution of itself.

'The Living Spaces: "Hidden Lives", a photographic installation by Anne Noble'. Review in *Art New Zealand* 77 (Summer 1995–96).

***'A long sentence in Czech ending in English'. Autobiographical story in *First Fifteen*, ed. Bill Manhire and Damien Wilkins (Wellington: Pemmican Press 2000).**

'Looking for God between the lines'. Review of *The Oxford Book of Australian Religious Verse*, ed. Kevin Hart, in *Evening Post*, 2 December 1994.

The term 'religious' here contradicts its etymological root in the Latin *religare*—'to tie back'—rather, the definition seems to launch, indeed propel, the poets into, quite naturally, poetry. Instead of imposing order or restraint it suggests a busting apart of the supposed certainties of the material world . . . The book is broadly conceived enough to include John Shaw Neilson's 'Schoolgirls Hastening' (a religious epiphany based on a rather dodgy premise) but it doesn't stretch as far as the great Australian religion of greyhound racing, which found its voice in Ken Bolton's epic poem 'Bunny Melody'.

***'Lost and living children'. Autobiographical story in *Printout 11* (Winter 1996), first published as 'Come Sunday' in *Meanjin*, Vol. 55, No. 2 (1996).**

'Luna and Arthur'. Poem in memory of M. T. Woollaston (1910–98). First published in *New Zealand Listener*, 1998; reprinted in *Winter I Was* (Wellington: Victoria University Press, 1999).

The poem was accompanied by a note to the effect that a mountain in the Nelson area should be named after that region's greatest painter. To date no one seems to have taken note of that suggestion.

'Michael Illingworth's *Balloons over a landscape*'. Essay in exhibition catalogue, FHE Galleries, Auckland, 2000.

Thomas Merton wrote that 'the pessimistic outlook does nothing to change the future'. In Illingworth's paintings, as in some works by Rita Angus, we are confronted with a spirit of unabashed optimism—but without the blindness or foolishness which can often accompany it. Summoning the energies of 'art brut', children's art and lessons learnt in London and Paris during the heyday of Pop and Op Art, Illingworth delivers his imaginative truths to the world. Filled with the breath of the poet/artist, the balloons in *Balloons over a landscape* float across the eye and mind of the attentive viewer—a pristine image of being and well-being.

'Mike Nock talks to *Music in New Zealand*'. Interview in *Music in New Zealand* (Summer 1990–91).

'Misere Mitimiti, a meeting place'. Essay, first version published in *Hotere: Seminar Papers from 'Into the Black'* (Auckland Art Gallery, August 1998); second version published in *PNReview 126* (Manchester, England), Vol. 25. No. 4 (March–April 1999).

On the opening night of the exhibition 'Hotere—out the black window' at the Auckland Art Gallery, I was standing with Ralph Hotere in front of the freestanding, painted screen entitled *Aramoana Koputai*. One side of this work lists the names of places the artist could see from his now-demolished studio on Observation Point: Rangiriri, Mihiwaka, Teraweka, Mopanui . . . Hotere told me he had recently had the good fortune of being allowed to ride in the driver's compartment of the train which travels from Dunedin, via Port Chalmers, to Palmerston.

Hotere was sitting beside the train driver, staring straight ahead as the train hurtled through the landscape then vanished into the blackness of the first tunnel. Then, just as suddenly, they were catapulted back into blinding light. Then they hit another tunnel. As the artist described this journey he closed his hand when he mentioned the darkness of the tunnel then his fist sprang open when he mentioned daylight. He said the locations inscribed on the *Aramoana Koputai* screen flashed past as they rattled through the landscape.

This sporadic immersion in darkness is what makes the visible world come alive, what makes it vivid and even profound; just as the stretch of daylight is necessary for the darkness of the tunnel to work its inverse magic. The train trip exerted a certain hold over Hotere, I suspect, because it signalled something at the core of his art: this passage through an obscured and revealed landscape, this transaction between night and day, and the intensely *human* drama of these transitions. Like Ralph Hotere's hand opening and closing, the paintings have a similar sense of disclosure, releasing their meanings then withdrawing them again.

***Moments of Invention: Portraits of 21 New Zealand Writers*. Interview-based profiles, with photographs by Robert Cross (Auckland: Heinemann Reed 1988).**

***A Network of Dissolving Threads*, Richard von Sturmer. Untitled book review in *Landfall 183* (September 1992), also published in *Antithesis* (Melbourne), 1991.**

In keeping with Andrey Tarkovsky's notion that 'the work of art carries within it an integral aesthetic and philosophical unity; it is an organism, living and developing according to its own laws . . .' von Sturmer's writing is preoccupied with texture and construction, 'the imaginative bonding of images in an harmonic pattern', as Guy Davenport would put it.

***Nigel Brown*. Monograph (Auckland: Random House/Century Hutchinson, 1991).**

'No Place Fast, Some Place Slow'. Review of 'The World Over' exhibition at the City Gallery, Wellington, in *Art New Zealand 81* (Summer 1996–97).

***'No Road to Follow—Eric Lee-Johnson'. Untitled book review in *Landfall 188* (Spring 1994).**

***'North Piha bach with typewriter'. Autobiographical story in *New Zealand House and Building*, April–May 1998.**

'Notes on the Figure in Landscape in New Zealand Art'. Essay in *The Literary Criterion*, Vol. XXXIII (Mysore, India), 1998.

THE BEAUTY OF THE SOUNDS OF THEIR NAMES
At the time of writing, a series of my paintings is hanging at the Bowen Galleries, Wellington. One of the works (which is from a series relating to Taranaki) is painted around four sides of a cabinet and titled 'The beauty of the sounds of their names', referring to the vowel-laden place names of towns around the Taranaki coast, where my mother's family comes from.

OAKURA
OKATO
WAREA
PUNGAREHU
RAHOTU
OAONUI
TE NAMU

While considerable beauty resides in the sounds of these names, when we were children being driven from Auckland to the coastal settlement of Opunake for holidays, the beauty also lay in the fact that, as these names appeared by the side of the road, we knew we were nearing the end of our long journey. Our family's trips to Taranaki were the source of my long-standing preoccupation with the relationship between words and place (a preoccupation which has needless to say also figured, rather more grandly, in the annals of New Zealand art history). It was also as a child in Taranaki that I worked out the fundamental equation that a heightened sense of being somewhere is a heightened sense of being.

In the late 1980s I painted Mt Taranaki close-up, framed, for the most part, by gravestones. By way of contrast, the imagined views in the series I have just completed look to the mountain from far out at sea—which may well embody the distance I have travelled from the province since the earlier pictures. It is difficult, when reading through the history of Taranaki—be it the history since European settlement or, for that matter, further back—not to feel crushed by it. This residual harshness, I later came to realise, permeates even the beloved place names: Oeo, which means 'place of lice', Manaia 'bird-headed man', Warea 'to be absorbed or made unconscious'.

Amongst other things, the paintings in my current exhibition are my own private journey through, around and away from a sense of devastation. While it is true that one writes or paints to enter into or assert a relationship with place—an approach embodied by so much of this country's art by both Maori and Pakeha—it is also true that one might write or paint as a way of getting away, of gaining some kind of release from a place, for whatever reason—whether because it is too painful or too sad or even too beautiful.

'"Not by wind ravaged": some configurations of Parihaka in poetry, drama and song 1950–2000'. Essay in *Parihaka: the art of passive resistance*, ed. Te Miringa Hohaia, Gregory O'Brien and Lara Strongman (Wellington: City Gallery, Wellington/Victoria University Press/Parihaka Pa Trustees, 2001).

'Ode to Art History'. Poem published in on-line journal *Turbine* (October 2001). http://www.vuw.ac.nz/turbine/obrien.html

'On and around Creation: the hand-made books of Alan Loney'. Essay in *Art New Zealand* 57 (Summer 1990).

Loney sees himself as 'an artist working at a book, rather than simply a writer or printmaker'. He wants to 'make a book in which all the individual parts are of equal priority', believing that any part of the book's production—words, type, images, paper, binding—should be 'rewarding to pay attention to' . . .

Loney also makes collages out of handmade and painted paper. Like his books, they show a depth of concern, a reflectiveness. Sometimes using letters and optical effects, they achieve a subtle balance, the elements arranged so that 'the lovely harmony leans' (to use Loney's phrase from his poem 'dear Mondrian'). He shares Edgar Mansfield's belief: 'My philosophy listens to my creations, and reflects.'

***'Origin of a watercolour box—for Tony Fomison'. Poem in *Meanjin* (Melbourne), Vol. 54, No. 3 (1995). Included here in *'Electricities.**

'Out the black window—a conversation between Ross Stevens and Gregory O'Brien'. Transcript of Radio New Zealand programme, ed. Toby Manhire. Published in *Salient 16* (28 July) 1997.

'Outside the interior—Ken Bolton and Noel McKenna'. Essay in *Overland 146* (Melbourne) (Autumn, 1997).

I have an image of my brother Brendan and me sailing along in our little ship, crossing the calm, disinterested ocean. (In fact it is March 1982 and we are sharing a bedsitter in Challis Ave, Potts Point, Sydney.) To counter our boredom and to speed our vessel we decide to unload some belongings. The first thing to go overboard is the continent of Australia.

'Sink or swim!' our voices echo from the grumbling, matronly clouds. But the continent neither sinks nor swims, it rows off of its own accord, keeping pace with the spinning world.

My brother and I watch the Big Red Desert paddling across its blue ocean, one rowlock located at Adelaide, the other at Sydney—an arrangement which ensures the vessel will chart a purposeful yet indirect course wherever it is going. At one oar is the Sydney painter Noel McKenna, at the other the Adelaide poet and publisher Ken Bolton.

***'The outsider within'. Reviews of: (1) *All Our Own Work: New Zealand's Folk Art*, by Richard Wolfe, first published as 'Self-absorbed provincial' in *New Zealand Books*, Vol. 7, No. 5 (December 1997); (2) 'Colour and Light', exhibition at the Dowse Art Museum, first published as 'A Ferment of Faces' in *Art New Zealand 92* (Spring, 1999).**

'A Parable'. Autobiographical story in *Meanjin* (Melbourne), Vol. 55, No. 2 (1996).

'Pathway to the sea: fourteen lithographs by Ralph Hotere and Bill Culbert'. Essay in FHE Galleries catalogue, Auckland, 1999.

'Paul Dibble in Wellington'. Review in *Art New Zealand 80* (Spring 1996).

'Ploughing: Ralph Hotere's "Te Whiti" series'. Essay in *Parihaka: the art of passive resistance*, ed. Te Miringa Hohaia, Gregory O'Brien and Lara Strongman (Wellington: City Gallery, Wellington/Victoria University Press/Parihaka Pa Trustees, 2001).

'Poetry and the shape of things to come'. Essay in *New Zealand Listener*, 3 July 1999.

By the age of four, our eldest son had become a regular little factory of poem-like utterances. You only had to ask him a question:

'Could you tell me, Jack-Marcel, what is opera?'

And then the matter-of-fact reply:

'Opera, Greg, is people singing about their mothers.'

Or:

'Well, how was the world created then?'

A few moments to process this one.

'It was all just there.
Except for the sky.
Jesus and Mary did that.'

I spent years running around after him, collecting up these fragments in which wisdom and misunderstanding are one and the same.

According to Sigmund Freud, poets are grown-ups who continue to play the language games of childhood. Of course writing poetry isn't quite as simple as a return to a child-like state, but a sense of openness and wonder is a prerequisite. Children are constantly being surprised by the world and by words, reflecting an attentiveness to both that adults would do well to emulate.

Beyond notions of sense or nonsense, the object of poetry is to create a 'new sense' (and, on occasion—in the spirit of the Dada poets—a nuisance). If poetry can at times be obscure or remote, this befits an art form intent on discovering meaning rather than reiterating or broadcasting that which is already known.

'Points North—paintings by Nigel Brown'. Essay in catalogue for exhibition at Milford Galleries, Dunedin, June 2000.

At the beginning of the 1980s, Brown was painting images of the Springbok Tour protests: the humane, democratic spirit of the Left versus the oppressive arm of the Right. By the end of the decade, however, following the Lange Labour Government and a spate of free marketeering and national asset-stripping initiated by the supposed 'Left', the artist was left with nothing less than a state of public/political chaos which has yet to be satisfactorily resolved over a decade later. Brown's recent large-scale allegories are often shaped by this loss of national direction: a formal and iconographical chaos. So what exactly is the task these paintings set themselves?

Perhaps they represent what Phil Johnson describes as 'a final wail from a lost radical and humanitarian tradition. And as socialism gets increasingly hard to find in politics, its presence in art becomes all the more precious.'

'Proximities—found poems from the *Hotere—Black Light* catalogue index'. Limited-edition pamphlet (Wellington: Animated Figure, 2000).

1. recipe for a loft party, Manhattan, in the early 1960s

Add Reinhardt
After Dark

2. a bluebird in the hand

KING
KLEIN

3. fathers of us all

Jackson
Pollock
The Pope
Is Dead

'Ralph Hotere—*Aramoana 1984*'. Essay in exhibition catalogue *Home and Away*, ed. William McAloon (Auckland: David Bateman/Auckland Art Gallery, 1999).

'Ralph Hotere—*Port Chalmers Painting*'. Essay in *The Suter: One Hundred Years in Nelson*, ed. Susan Butterworth (Nelson: Nikau Press, 1999).

'Recognition—a conversation with William J. Reed'. Essay in *Art New Zealand 74* (Autumn 1995).

'Red Scarf'. Autobiographical notebook in *Landfall 176* (December 1990).

'Running Dog—the poetry of Ken Bolton'. Essay in *Sport 16* (Autumn 1996).

As both writer and occasional visual artist, Bolton has made it his business to examine and, for the most part, undermine the various complacencies or banal enthusiasms that masquerade as popular or national culture. On the subject of nationalism, Ken Bolton cheerfully and incessantly disavows the grand and the inflated, the heroic and the hieratic. Australia, for Bolton, is an image on a teatowel, the logo on a tin of Fosters or a trademark on an Eskie.

'The Second Ada'. Story in *Quote Unquote* (June 1994).

***Selected Poems*, Peter Bland. Untitled book review in *Landfall 198* (Spring 1999).**

In his 1954 essay 'Symbolism in New Zealand Poetry', James K. Baxter sums up the motif of the beach as, variously, historical locale, epiphanous zone, a 'no man's-land between conscious and unconscious'; then he chimes in with 'an arena for sexual adventure'. It's a surprisingly instructive résumé of the uses (and misuses) of the littoral in New Zealand verse, and it feels about right for Peter Bland, an explorer of all of the above, including—most refreshingly in the context of local poetry—the libidinous.

'Let's meet,' instructs one of Bland's poems, 'between Flora's Massage Parlour / and the Temple of Higher Thought'—a suitably Baxterian, although also quintessentially Blandian, set of co-ordinates. There's certainly a warm-blooded as well as warm-spirited quality to Bland's poetry, and a saltiness (à la Louis Johnson or 1950s Baxter) to his recurrent meditations on sexual matters—poems in which 'old tycoons wake up / as hushed lifts bring them nude Miss Worlds' and, elsewhere, 'small clay goddesses with ample breasts'. Similarly, the world outside is sexualised: witness 'Mt Egmont's frosty tit' in 'I.m. Ronald Hugh Morrieson'. For whatever reason, this anthropomorphic/erotic inclination is widespread among those creative souls caught somehow between England and the Antipodes: the painters Michael Illingworth, Patrick Hayman, and more recently Alexis Hunter, spring to mind. Perhaps in the poet/painter's scheme of things, Sex equates with the New World—'lust / is technicolour in a year of gloom', Bland writes in one poem. His early verse traces his passage beyond the smoky greys of council housing and rotten weather. From there, the poetry shuttles between north and south, colonial and post-colonial, past and present; with Baxter's symbolic beach never too far off.

> A chill February morning out of Glasgow;
> an immigrant ship, full of surplus flesh,
> limps in Cook's wake towards the Pacific.

***'Self-portrait'. Autobiographical story in *Landfall* 176 (December 1990).**

'A serious take on nature'. Review of *Lake, mountain, tree—an anthology of writing on New Zealand nature & landscape*, ed. Philip Temple, in *Evening Post*, 12 June 1998.

I'm puzzled as to why Temple has decided to use the book's introduction to put the boot into 'wannabe writers' on 'trendy creative writing courses'. My main memory of the only creative writing course I've ever enrolled in (at Auckland University in 1983) was spending two days knee-deep in mud, tramping through the Waitakere Ranges, led by C. K. Stead, in the throes of a midwinter storm. In the light of that experience, Temple's inference that universities are keeping real creative spirits from communion with nature strikes me as not only unfounded but bizarre.

***'The shape of living children'. Autobiographical story in *Meanjin* (Melbourne), Vol. 55, No. 2 (1996).**

'Silent Film—Anne Noble's "In the presence of angels"'. Exhibition review in *Illusions 17* (Spring 1991).

'The singular vision of Doris Lusk'. Book review of *Landmarks: The Landscape Paintings of Doris Lusk*, Lisa Beaven and Grant Banbury, in *Evening Post*, Wellington, 3 May 1996.

The fact that up until the 1980s you could walk into the Canterbury Public Library and take out on loan a major original painting like Doris Lusk's *Power House, Tuai* is indicative of the undervaluing of such supposedly 'regionalist' art. This publication is a timely reconsideration of the regionalist project and goes some distance to retrieving it from its marginal status.

. . . Now that the nationalism that supposedly replaced regionalism has itself been replaced by internationalism, perhaps we have almost come full circle and can now regard this kind of work sensibly if not uncritically.

'Skies of Canterbury, then Wellington'. A poem for Juliet Peter, published in *Outdoor People: A Tribute to Juliet Peter* (Wellington: Fernbank Studio in conjunction with City Gallery, Wellington, 2001).

***Slow Passes*, Alan Brunton. Untitled book review in *Landfall 182* (June 1999).**

Late in 1989 I saw Alan Brunton and Red Mole performing their play 'Comrade Savage' in a Wellington community hall. During the show, Brunton's collaborator, Sally Rodwell, flew across the performance space on a swing hung from the ceiling. At one extent of her transit, her pointed black shoe came within inches of my head and would have connected had I not manoeuvred in my seat—in fact I had to duck a number of times as she continued on her pendulous way, seemingly oblivious to my predicament. During the interval, others in the audience complimented me on my performance.

In *Slow Passes*, Alan Brunton as poet seems to be treating me, the reader, in a similar fashion. His work disorientates and throws off balance. He expects the reader to perform, demands a response that can be neither comfortable nor complacent. Brunton, as author and playwright, is concerned with changing relationships between writer/performer and reader.

'Some Paintings I Am Frequently Asked About—talking with Bill Manhire about Ralph Hotere'. Interview in *Landfall 194* (Autumn 1996), reprinted in *Doubtful Sounds: Essays and Interviews*, by Bill Manhire (Wellington: Victoria University Press, 2000).

***'Somebody say something—Colin McCahon's *Storm Warning*, Wellington 1999'. Essay in *Sport 23* (Spring 1999).**

***'Southern Woman: Collected poems of Ruth Dallas'. Book review in *Landfall 200* (October 2000).**

'Spring and all that Jazz'. Book review of Laurie Duggan's *Blue Notes*, in *Scripsi* (Melbourne), Vol. 6, No. 3 (November 1990).

In jazz a blue note is a particular note in a blues scale that has a 'cry' to it, a slightly off-key sound—it can be a flat third or fifth—that gives jazz music its 'voice'. Blue notes usually have a soulful, yearning quality, although when played by a trumpeter like Lester Bowie they can sound ironic, even funny. Laurie Duggan, in his poetry, is an adroit user of a similar effect. His attention is always on 'the detail', the right note at the right time. Particulars are played within the poem—like the blue note, they can be bent or manipulated, used harmonically or dissonantly.

Two musicians cited in Duggan's *Blue Notes*, Bud Powell and Thelonious Monk, both employed characteristically witty and enigmatic arrangements within their music. Pianist Monk said, 'There are no wrong notes.' And he was right, although the person playing the instrument has to know exactly what they're doing to handle that degree of freedom . . .

'Still Making His Own Rules'. Book review of *Piggy-back Moon*, Hone Tuwhare, in *New Zealand Herald*, 25 August 2001.

It can be interesting tracking a poet's progress towards old age or at the end of their life. With the exception of Allen Curnow, whose resolute gaze at and grasp of the world remain as tight as ever, poets tend to make various adjustments. Some start to burn and rage: one of James

K. Baxter's last published poems was the irreverent *Ode to Auckland*—a diatribe against the city and its citizens. Approaching death, Rainer Maria Rilke, who usually composed in German, took up French. Some poets stop writing.

Probably the closest model for what Hone Tuwhare is up to in his new book is the late poetry of Pablo Neruda. Near the end of his life, the Chilean wrote poems celebrating the physical surroundings and daily existence of his autumnal years on Isla Negra, in a village on his homeland's Pacific coast.

Staring back from the other side of the Pacific, Tuwhare, aged 79, sets himself a similar task in *Piggy-back Moon*. Locating himself firmly at Kaka Point, in South Otago, he contemplates time and nature, remembers friends who have died and converses with the sea-god Tangaroa, who is both provider and destroyer.

Like pages of a diary, the poems are relaxed and discursive rather than tightly formed. There's a playfulness, an unruliness and an immersion in the physical world with all its ripeness and rottenness, with all its textures, smells and particularly its sounds—the sighs, grunts and groans and the ever-present white noise of the sea.

***Stuck Up*, John Dolan; *First and Last Songs*, Alan Riach. Untitled book review in *Landfall* 190 (Spring 1995).**

During a recent tour of Scotland, comedian Billy Connolly was filmed visiting the hilltop at Scone, where the Scottish kings were once crowned. As the story goes, royal delegations would climb all the way up to the Stone of Scone with soil from their home districts inside their boots so that wherever they were standing they were on native turf. 'And after the ceremony,' Connolly added, 'they would empty their boots out; hence the hill we're standing on.'

Both Scotsman Alan Riach and North American John Dolan have arrived in this country their boots crammed with soil from their native lands . . . both books thrive on dislocation, the anxiety of distance and exile, but ultimately—and in spite of it all—they strike an overwhelmingly affirmative note. Dolan winds up his collection with an exclamation which recalls Ian Wedde in its glee:

And for a moment,
most unlike me, I love
and I admire all of it: Pope—
brave little man!
Brave bats!
Brave all of it,

that tries so hard!
Long live the mammals;
long live them all!
(from 'As I Leave')

Here we have a poetry of attachment to the gritty facts of place and identity. It is both a gathering and a celebration of its materials. Dirt in the shoes, rain on the head, the poet in between.

'The surface of the Walters'. Poem in memory of Gordon Walters, *Landfall 194* (Spring 1997).

THE SURFACE OF THE WALTERS

Seeking a more formal
resolution,
more or

less, the ocean
a canvas
across which

the blues and greys
are moved. A certain capacity,
resolve, among

other attributes,
an eye for rain
a day off. Now

it is evening, even more
or even less, and the remote yachts,
the astonished hand

will not scratch
the surface
of the waters.

***Swell*, Alan Loney. Untitled book review in *Landfall 175* (September 1990).**

Loney has consciously pushed his poetic product towards opposite ends of the market. In a recent number of the journal *Splash* his poems are xeroxed on cheap white paper and stapled together, while in the small-press production *Swell* they are hand-printed on damped Whatman mouldmade paper and sewn together. Whereas *Swell* invokes the tradition and longevity of finely crafted book making and binding, the *Splash* format is self-consciously new and disposable . . .

What *Splash* and *Swell* have in common (apart from their titles, which locate both in the New Zealand 'nautical' tradition of Curnow's *Not in Narrow Seas*, Glover's *Come High Water* and so on) is that both publications presume their audience is specialist and small, its concerns away from the mainstream of New Zealand writing and publication . . . Loney's writing itself also raises questions about poetry and its available avenues.

'Talking Toss Woollaston'. Interview in limited-edition photocopied booklet. (Wellington: *Animated Figure*, 1995).

GO'B: How did you come to meet Mary Ursula Bethell?

MTW: I went to Christchurch and my landlady was Mrs Coward. She went to St Nicholas's Church and Miss Bethell would come there sometimes. One day she was walking out in her blue clothes, her hands folded, meditating on divine matters, and my landlady interrupted and said, 'I want you to take an interest in this young man!' That's how I got introduced to her.

GO'B: You worked as her gardener?

MTW: She gave me gardening work and conversation. I met D'Arcy Cresswell there one day. He was a funny guy. He was coming for the day and she was all nervous and she arranged for me to be up there gardening so, if he wanted to, he could meet me and if he didn't he didn't have to.

GO'B: He had a literary reputation for a while but now no one much bothers with him.

MTW: He had a tremendous reputation with himself! I remember two things he said. We walked down the hill together having found we could tolerate each other during the day. We had had lunch and afternoon tea together. And he looked at the landscape as we were walking down and said: 'The colour of these hills reminds me of someone about to vomit.' And the other was: 'If you wish to pursue Art you should go to Sydney, the population of Sydney is equal to the whole of New Zealand and where there are more people there is more interest in Art.' He was a pompous ass. I didn't take his advice—I'd just seen [Robert Nettleton] Field's work and was on my way to Dunedin.

GO'B: When you were young, did the notion of being an artist suggest you might end up living overseas . . . in England?

MTW: I didn't think you needed to go to England to qualify. Everybody went to England but I couldn't afford it, neither did I want to go to

England. Everything that I wanted to paint seemed so interesting here.
GO'B: Did you talk with Ursula Bethell about art and poetry?
MTW: She endured my efforts at poetry, politely.
GO'B: What did she make of your efforts at painting?
MTW: Well it was very immature then—I hadn't met Flora Scales at that time. Miss Bethell thought I might be going to be a painter. We had a picnic in Hagley Park one day and I did a watercolour looking towards town. She said, that tells me you're going to paint pictures. She always spoke from a good height!

'Tenebrae—Transfigured Night—Ralph Hotere, a viable religious art and its traditions'. Essay in exhibition catalogue for *Hotere—Black Light* (Dunedin: Museum of New Zealand/Dunedin Public Art Gallery, 2000).

***The Time and How*. Collection of poems (Wellington: Animated Figure, 1996). Many of these poems appear in *'Electricities'.**

'Tokatoka—stones upon stones'. Essay in *Chris Booth: sculpture in Europe, Australia and New Zealand*. Text by Edward Lucie-Smith, Ken Scarlett and Gregory O'Brien (Auckland: Godwit, 2001).

'Towards Evening'. Essay in *The Source of the Song*, ed. Mark Williams (Wellington: Victoria University Press, 1995).

'Traditionally Speaking Screens'. Review in *Art New Zealand 46* (Autumn 1988).

'Tuwhare's world-size marae'. Book review of *Hone Tuwhare: A Biography*, by Janet Hunt, in *New Zealand Herald*, 1999.

Speaking at the Auckland Art Gallery during the recent 'Hotere—out the black window' exhibition, Hone Tuwhare recounted his first meeting with Ralph Hotere one evening in 1960 in a 'marae' behind Smith and Caughey's. He was, of course, referring to a hotel near the gallery where writers and artists used to drink.

It wasn't a wisecrack—Tuwhare was suggesting that, beyond traditional definitions, a marae is any social space where human value is acknowledged and experiences recounted and begot.

'Urgent Columns, Tall Rain—recent sculptures by Chris Booth'. Essay in *Art New Zealand 85* (Summer 1997–98).

***Viva la Vida—Frida Kahlo, Diego Rivera and Mexican Modernism*. Essays on Kahlo and Rivera, Mexican Surrealism, 'The Cactus and the Lily', Abstraction and Contemporary Mexican Art in catalogue for exhibition at City Gallery, Wellington, January 2000. 'Kahlo and Rivera'**

reprinted in *Frida Kahlo, Diego Rivera and Mexican Modernism* (Canberra: National Gallery of Australia, 2001).

'Bill Sutton's well-made paintings'. Book review of *W.A. Sutton, Painter*, Pat Unger, in *Evening Post*, 29 April 1994.

'It's at times like this you thank god for the South Island,' Vincent O'Sullivan commented during a session with Owen Marshall at the 1992 Writers and Readers Week. The work of Cantabrian painter W. A. (Bill) Sutton could well elicit a similar response . . .

Perhaps it is the conservatism of the South Island that makes it such a fertile ground for genuine originality and often radicalism, giving rise to painters like Colin McCahon, Rita Angus and Tony Fomison, and writers like Janet Frame and Marshall. One of the less overtly radical Southerners, Sutton has been an influential, albeit currently under-acknowledged figure in this country's art . . . His art is one of slow, carefully measured evolution, in contrast to that of, say, McCahon, whose work was in a permanent state of revolt with itself as well as with Sutton's beloved Tradition.

'Wide Open Interior'. Essay in *John Drawbridge—Wide Open Interior*, ed. Gregory O'Brien (Wellington: Mallinson Rendel/City Gallery Wellington, 2001).

'The Wide-Open Interior—Paintings and Drawings by John Drawbridge'. Catalogue essay for exhibition at Tinakori Gallery, Wellington, May 2001.

'Wild and cultivated iron—Jeff Thomson's recent sculpture'. Essay in *Art New Zealand 100* (Spring 2001).

'Words that are true'. Book review of Dennis McEldowney's *Then and There: a 1970s Diary*, in *New Zealand Listener*, 29 July 1995.

As well as being a notable critic and diarist, McEldowney is, as this book chronicles, a prodigious loser of wallets—I counted four misplaced between May 1974 and December 1977. Alongside the author's extraordinary attentiveness, there's an endearing absent-mindedness. On that account, he is surpassed only by art historian Eric McCormick who, McEldowney records, arrived at his office one day in a flap, having just left a 'priceless folio of [Captain] Cook engravings on the bus'.

Index

Artworks reproduced in the text are indicated by bold page numbers.

Aberhart, Laurence, 13
Ackroyd, Peter, 94
Alcock, Peter, 61
Allan, Rob, 30
Angus, Rita, 12, 13, 65, 128, 173, 201, 232, 237, 268, 282
Apollinaire, Guillaume, 140
Aristotle, 45n
Armstrong, Louis, 180
Arp, Jean, 134
Aubert, Mother Mary, 42, 45n
Auerbach, Frank, 223

Bacon, Francis, 98
Bambury, Stephen, 9
Barnett, Gerald, 246
Baudelaire, Charles, 200
Baudrillard, Jean, 167
Baxter, Glen, 42
Baxter, Jacquie, 61
Baxter, James K., 7, 17–45, 47, 88–9, 97, 132, 134, 141, 173, 203, 256, 258n, 275, 277–8
Beaglehole, J.C., 258n
Beatles, The, 158
Beauvoir, Simone de, 147
Beckett, Samuel, 124–5, 255
Belich, James, 261
Belitt, Ben, 164
Bell, Julian, 252
Berger, John, 58, 225
Bethell, Mary Ursula, 48, 168, 280–81
Bilbrough, Miro, 30
Binney, Judith, 71
Blake, William, 35, 93–4, 251
Bland, Peter, 275
Body, Jack, 13, 261
Bolton, Ken, 268, 272, 274–5
Borges, Jorges Luis, 122
Bornholdt, Jenny, 26, 27, 30, 45n, 158, 259
Botticelli, Sandro, 82
Bowie, Lester, 277
Boyd, Arthur, 223
Braithwaite, Joanna, 222
Brasch, Charles, 13, 47, 49, 51, 196
Brenstrum, Erick, 163–5
Bresson, Robert, 225–6
Britten, Benjamin, 123–4
Brooke, Rupert, 81
Brown, Gordon H., 207–8, 258
Brown, James, 201n, 212
Brown, Nigel, **18**, 19, **23**, **41**, 42, **44**, 214, 230, 266 273–4
Brubeck, Dave, 180
Brunton, Alan, 45n, 187, 191, 261 276–7
Burrows, Steven, 233–4, **233**

Caffin, Elizabeth, 98
Cage, John, 97, 132–3, 200
Cairncross, Sam, 176n
Capill, Graham, 265
Cardenal, Ernesto, 69
Carrà, Carlo, 225
Carrigan, John, 161
Carroll, Lewis, 64
Carson, Anne, 64–5, 212
Carson, Ciaran, 210
Caselberg, John, 256, 258n
Cendrars, Blaise, 130–31, 140, 143, 261
Chappell, James, 95
Chardin, Pierre Teilhard de, 130, 143
Charman, Janet, 29
Chilcott, Gavin, 232
Chills, The, 13
Chirico, Giorgio de, 225
Churchill, Winston, 105, 108
Clairmont, Philip, 19, 213–15, 219, 222
Clapp, Reg, 121
Cochrane, Geoff, 212
Cocker, Jarvis, 235
Collier, Craig, 231

Collinson, Fergus, 232
Coltrane, John, 146
Connell, Evan S., 69
Connolly, Billy, 278
Coppola, Francis Ford, 70
Cotton, Shane, 13, 207–8, 232
Cousins, John, 201n
Cresswell, Walter D'Arcy, 93, 280
Cross, Robert, 60, 62–3, **63**, **118**
Culbert, Bill, 186, 263
Culbert, Pip, 263
Curnow, Allen, 29, 40, 47, 80n, 140, 277, 280

Dadson, Phil, 13
Dali, Salvador, 253–4
Dallas, Ruth, 7, 46–51, 221
Dashper, Julian, 255
Davenport, Guy, 270
Davis, Leigh, 30, 39, 42
Day, Sonny, 265
Degas, 231
de Lautour, Tony, 232
Derain, André, 203
Dickinson, Emily, 49
Dobson, Rosemary, 199–200
Dolan, John, 278–9
Donovan, Peter, 231, 232
Dowland, John, 47
Drawbridge, John, 9, 135
Driver, Don, 201n
Dubuffet, Jean, 233–5
Duchamp, Marcel, 127, 253
Dudding, Robin, his chickens, 96
Duffy, Mary-Jane, 61
Duggan, Laurie, 69, 187–8, 277
Duggan, Maurice, 196
Durcan, Paul, 209–10
Durrell, Lawrence, 115, 119
Dylan, Bob, 121

Edmond, Lauris, 47
Edmond, Martin, 213–15, 261
Edmond, Murray, 30, 45n
Eggleton, David, 37, 39
Eisenhower, General Dwight D., 105, 108
Eliot, T. S., 265
Ellington, Duke, 180
Ellis, Robert, 134–5

Fahey, Jacqueline, 219
Fairburn, A. R. D., 47, 93, 195–6
Feldman, Morton, 132
Field, Robert Netterton, 170–71, 280
Finlayson, Roderick, 93
Finn, Neil, 123–4
Finn, Tim, 123–4
Finster, Howard, 251
Fitzgerald, F. Scott, 89–91
Fomison, Tony, 136, 144n, 175–6, 222, 230, 236–7, 282
Frame, Janet, 7, 10, 13, 37, 46, 50–51, 53–61, 62, 65, 223, 282
France, Patricia, 237
Freud, Sigmund, 273
Friedlander, Marti, **87**, **181**
Frizzell, Dick, 9, **9**, 232, 267–8
Fuchs, Rudi, 9
Funkadelic, 146
Fuseli, Henri, 25

Gagliardi, 139, 247
Gales, Larry, 187
Gascoigne, Ben, 200
Gascoigne, Rosalie, 8, 13, **198**, 199–201
Gee, Maurice, 95
Geering, Lloyd, 252
Genet, Jean, 81
Giacommetti, Alberto, 220
Gibson, Mel, 125
Gill, Eric, 23
Gill, Linda, 83
Glover, Denis, 47, 280
Goethe, Johann Wolfgang von, 35
Gopas, Rudi, 220, 222
Goya, 231
Grace, Patricia, 131
Greenberg, Clement, 28
Gregory, Brian, 231
Greig, Jason, 222
Greig, Rhondda, 262
Grünewald, 90

Haddow, Jack-Marcel, 273
Haden, Frank, 244
Haino, Keiji, 133, 143
Hall, Bernadette, 32–5
Hall, James, 11
Hammond, Bill, 13, 222

Hanzlik, Josef, 158
Hardy, Thomas, 59
Haring, Keith, 265
Harley, Rob, 244
Harlow, Michael, 30
Harris, Jeffrey, 220, 231
Harris, Ray, 189–90
Harrison, Michael, 13
Hart, Kevin, 268
Hawken, Dinah, 13, 30, 36, 39, 48
Hayman, Patrick, 126–8, **127**, **128**, 141–3, **143**, 173, 237, 275
Hazlitt, William, 98
Healey, Sue, 124–5, **124**
Healey, Teresa, 147
Heaney, Seamus, 210
Heaphy, Chris, 232
Hemmingway, Ernest, 254
Hendrix, Jimi, 42, 159–62
Hervey, J. R., 221, 223
Hickey, Sister Rita, 45n, **85**
Hill, Ivan, 232
Hill, Kim, 164, 250
Hilton, Tim, 231
Hitler, Adolf, 95
Hodgkins, Frances, 46, 65, 82
Holcroft, Monte, 47
Holmwood, John, 197
Hooper, Peter, 239, 242, 256
Hopkins Gerard Manley, 97, 206, 242, 258n
Horace, 8
Horrocks, Roger, 264
Horton, Michael, 97
Hotere, Ralph, 8–10, 13, **15**, 47, 80n, **87**, 91, 135, 144n, 179–94, **180**, **181**, **183**, **186**, 200, 201n, 256, **259**, 269, 274, 281
Hoxha, Enver, 148–50
Hughes, Ted, 214
Hulme, Keri, 30, 39
Hunt, Janet, 281
Hunt, Sam, 39, 57
Hunter, Alexis, 275
Hunter, Holly, 148–51
Hyde, Robin (Iris Wilkinson), 82–3

Illingworth, Michael, 231, 268, 275
Iti, Tame, 207

Jefferson Airplane, 17, 21–3, 40, 45n
Jenkinson, Megan, 13
Johnson, Louis, 80n, 93, 275
Johnson, Phil, 273
Johnson, Samuel, 55
Johnston, Alexa, 202, 241, 252
Johnston, Andrew, 26, 27
Jones, Frank and Pat, 145
Jones, Kevin, **136**, 137–8
Jones, Nicholas, 81, 145
Joplin, Janis, 42
Joseph of Copertino, Saint, 131, 143
Joyce, James, 7, 42, 71, 97, 121, 212

Kahukiwa, Robyn, 219
Kandinsky, Wassily, 133, 144n, 190
Kaprow, Allan, **254**, 255, 258n
Keats, John, 181
Keepnews, Peter, 182
Kelmsley, Viscount, 106
Kennedy, Anne, 30
Kiefer, Anselm, 219
Killeen, Richard, **12**, 13, 257
Kipling, Rudyard, 96
Klee, Paul, 137, 199, 228, 234
Kleinzahler, August, 183, 187–8
Klima, Ivan, 158
Knox, Chris, 45n
Kopf, Biba, 45n
Kounellis, Jannis, 247
Kruger, Barbara, 167

Laita, Lily, 219
Land, Janne, 214
Lawlor Bartlett, Margaret, **18**
Lawlor, Patrick, 18
Lawrence, Bruno, 215
Lawrence, D. H., 142
Lee-Johnson, Eric, 195–7
Leek, Saskia, 13, 232
Leggott, Michele, 30, 34, 48, 201n, 212
Leroy, Olivier, 130
Levertov, Denise, 200–201, 262
Lilburn, Douglas, 258n
Lille, Beatrice, 107
Lindsay, Graham, 31–2
Lone Ranger, The, 120
Loney, Alan, 42, 271, 279–80
Lorca, Federico Garcia, 163

Lusk, Doris, 46, 276
Luton Girls Choir, 105–10
Lye, Len, 75, 264
Lynn, Vera, 107
Lyotard, Jean-François, 207
Lysaght, Lauren, 201n

McCahon, Colin, 8, 10, 13, **38**, 90–91, 134, 137, 142–3, 173, 200, 202–8, **203**, **205**, 213, 227, 229, 231–2, **238**, 238–259, **248**, 282
McCaughey, Patrick, 135
McCormack, T. A., 197
McCormick, Eric, 81–3, 282
Macdonald, Vici, 201
McEldowney, Dennis, 7, 82–3, **87**, 85–98, 163, 282
McEldowney, Zoë, 92–3, 96
McFarlane, Mary, **15**, 186
McGonagall, William, 97
Mack, James, 232
McKay, Frank, 40
McKenna, Noel, **52**, **177**, 225–8, **226**, 272
Mackenzie, Edward, 201n
McLeavey, Peter, 125, 258n
Macleod, Euan, 218–24, **219**, **222**
MacPherson, Heather, 29, 39
McQueen, Cilla, 30, 46, 48
McQueen, Harvey, 47
McRae, Stuart, 83
McWhannell, Richard, 222
Madill, Kathryn, 46
Mahon, Sir Denis, 240–41
Mahon, Derek, 210
Mahy, Margaret, 62–5, **63**
Maizel, John, 235
Majella, Saint Gerard, 140
Malcolm, Greg, 201n
Malcolm, Janet, 214
Malevich, Kazimir, 8–10, 129–30, **129**, 138, 142, 267
Malley, Ern, 75
Mander, Jane, 70
Mané-Wheoki, Jonathan, 80n
Manhire, Bill, 25, 134–5, 144n, 184, 186, 201n, 212
Mann, Thomas, 88
Mansfield, Edgar, 271
Mansfield, Katherine, 65, 90
Manson, Hugo, 262
Maritain, Jacques, 32
Marshall, Owen, 282
Merton, Thomas, 19, 69, 147, 181, 268
Messiaen, Olivier, 133, 180
Millett, Bill, 24
Minogue, Kylie, 125
Mitchell, David, 39
Mondrian, Piet, 130
Monk, Thelonious, 179–194, **182, 186, 189**, 277
Montalk, Geoffrey (Potocki) de, 265
Montalk, Stephanie de, 265
Monteverdi, Claudio, 146
Montgomery, Field Marshal, 105
Moore, Christopher, 232
Morris, William, 262
Morrison, Jim, 42
Morrison, Robin, 26
Morrissey, Michael, 30
Moss, Stirling, 107
Motherwell, Robert, 221
Mrkusich, Milan, 71
Muldoon, Paul, 210

Nannestad, Elizabeth, 43
Neich, Roger, 80n, 232
Neilson, John Shaw, 268
Neruda, Pablo, 11, 31, 163–5, 278
Newman, Barnett, 135
Newton, John, 37
Nicolas, Reginald, 231–2, 236–7, **236**
Niedecker, Lorine, 34, 49
Noble, Anne, 13
Nolan, Sidney, 125, 135

O'Brien, Brendan, **99, 152–7,** 272
O'Brien, Flann, 212
O'Brien, George, 171–2
O'Brien, Gregory, **26, 80, 87, 169**
  poems:
  A century of marching, 174–5
  Composition, 170
  Directional, 173
  For G. O'Brien, painter, 172
  Man of Hay, 173
  Origin of a watercolour box, 176
  Painter with clouds, 173–4
  Proximities, 274

Recognition one, 170
Recognition two, 171
Solemn Islands 1941–45, 175
The surface of the Walters, 279
Titanium, 168
O'Brien, Justine, 115, 124, **124**
O'Connor, Denis, 8, 209–12, **211**
O'Leary, Michael, 30, 42
O'Neill, Dave, 230–31, 232
O'Reilly, Ron, 90
O'Sullivan, Fr Eugene, 24, 38–40
O'Sullivan, Vincent, 212, 282
Olds, Peter, 39, 42
Opo the Dolphin, 196
Orr, Bob, 187, 264–5
Osby, Greg, 263

Page, Frederick and Evelyn, 258n
Palestrina, Giovanni, 146
Palmer, Samuel, 225
Parekowhai, Michael, **216**, 217
Parmenter, Michael, 17n
Partch, Harry, 261
Patchen, Kenneth, 97
Paton, Justin, 166n
Paul, Janet, 176n, 262
Paul, Joanna Margaret, 32–5, 45n
Paul, Mary, 45n
Paz, Octavio, 228, 252
Peckinpah, Sam, 213
Peden, Margaret Sayers, 164
Pegler, Johanna, 13
Perry, John, 232
Peryer, Peter, 80n
Peter, Juliet, 176n
Phillipps, Martin, 13
Picasso, Pablo, 231
Piggott, Lester, 107
Plath, Sylvia, 214
Pliny the Elder, 122
Pollock, Jackson, 197, 199
Potiki, Roma, 29, 39
Pound, Ezra, 24, 50
Pound, Francis, 197, 206
Powell, Bud, 277
Preston, Margaret, 135
Prinzhorn, Hans, 234
Purvis, Neville (Arthur Baysting), 161

Quun, H., 266

Radio Birdman, 152–7
Read, Herbert, 77
Reed, William J., 174–5
Reid, Alistair, 165
Reinhardt, Ad, 135, 181, 184
Reynolds, John, 125n, 186
Riach, Alan, 20, 278
Riley, Ben, 187
Rilke, Rainer Maria, 278
Robinson, Peter, 232, 243, 250
Rodwell, Sally, 45n, 276
Rolling Stones, The, 120
Ross, James, 83
Rossini, 120
Rothenberg, Jerome, 42
Rothko, Mark, 135
Rouault, Georges, 24, 244–5, **244,** 247
Rouse, Charlie, 187, 192
Rua Kenana, 205–6
Rua Rukuna, 121–2
Rush, Geoffrey, 125

Sargeson, Frank, 80n, 93
Sartre, Jean-Paul, 147
Sayles, Jane, 166
Scales, Flora, 281
Scott, Dick, 86
Scott, Walter, 55
Shadbolt, Maurice, 93, 197, 258n
Sharp, Iain, 24, 25, 29, 45n, 258n
Sharrock, Sonny, 213
Shelley, Percy, 181
Simpson, Peter, 77–8, 258n
Sitwell, Edith, 97, 200–201, 265
Skinner, Damian, 234
Slick, Grace, 23
Smith, Allan, 210
Smithells, Philip, 95
Smither, Elizabeth, 32, 84, 262
Smither, Michael, 166, 195
Smiths, The, 228
Smithyman, Kendrick, 7, 66–80, 134, 258n
Solzenitzyn, Alexander, 266
Split Enz, 123
St Mary of the Angels choir, 13, 96
Stead, C. K., 30, 34, 39, 59, 98, 134, 276
Stein, Gertrude, 97, 142

Stevens, Ross, 91
Stevenson, Michael, 60, 232
Stewart, Helen, 176n
Strongman, Lara, 224n
Sullivan, Robert, 30, 37
Sutton, W. A., 282

Tangahoe, Hariata Ropata, 131, 231
Tarkovsky, Andrey, 137, 269
Taylor, Apirana, 29, 39
Te Kaha, Karaitiana, 207
Te Kooti, 205–6
Te Whiti o Rongomai, 90, 92, 227–8
Te Wiata, Inia, 107
Tek, Deniz, 153
Temple, Philip, 276
Texidor, Greville, 80n
Thomas, Dylan, 39, 70, 97, 147
Thompson, Pauline, 45n
Thomson, Jeff, 95–6
Thomson, John Mansfield, 189
Thoreau, Henri David, 239
Tibbo, Teuane, 230–32
Tito, General, 159
Tito, Mrs, of Te Namu, 159
Tohu Kakahi, 92
Tole, Charles, 176n, 197
Tongue, Rob, 261
Tucker, Albert, 223
Turner, J. M. W., 231
Tuwhare, Hone, 10, 39, 48, 277–8, 281

Van Gogh, Vincent, 215
van Hout, Ronnie, 232
Visconti, Luchino, 92
Vlaminck, Maurice de, 203
von Sturmer, Richard, 269–70

Wagner, Richard, 189
Walcott, Derek, 95
Wallace-Crabbe, Chris 261
Wallis, Alfred, 127, 232
Walsh, John ,13, 232
Walters, Gordon, 137, 279
Ward, John P., 92
Wearne, Alan, 147
Webb, Marilynn, 46
Wedde, Ian, 10, 12, 13, 30, 31, 39, 47, 98, 133, 175, 187, 201n, 261, 263, 266, 278
Weeks, John, 196–7
Wheelwright, John, 7, 10
Wilkins, Damien, 26, 47
Williams, Fred, 135, 137–8, 224
Williams, Jonathan, 199
Williams, Mark, 41
Williams, Robin, 136
Williams, William Carlos, 34
Wolfe, Richard, 229–32
Woolf, Leonard and Virginia, 265
Woollaston, Edith, 168
Woollaston, M. T. (Toss), 47, 168–70, **169,** 204, **205**, 206, 208n, 242, 251, 280–81

Yeats, Jack B., 223
Yeats W. B., 93–5, 262, 265
Younghusband, Adele, 176n

Zorn, John, 146
Zukofsky, Louis, 34, 133, 141, 147